ENTERPRISE
ONE TO ONE

Tools for Competing
in the Interactive Age

Don Peppers and
Martha Rogers, Ph.D.

CURRENCY

DOUBLEDAY

New York   London   Toronto   Sydney   Auckland

A CURRENCY BOOK
PUBLISHED BY DOUBLEDAY
a division of Random House, Inc.
1540 Broadway, New York, New York 10036

CURRENCY and DOUBLEDAY are trademarks of Doubleday, a division of
Random House, Inc.

Enterprise One to One was originally published in hardcover by Currency in 1997.

Book Design by Richard Oriolo

The Library of Congress has cataloged the hardcover edition of this book as follows:

Peppers, Don.
Enterprise one to one : tools for competing in the
interactive age / Don Peppers and Martha Rogers.
p.   cm.
Includes index.
1. Market segmentation. 2. Customer relations.
3. Relationship marketing. 4. Technological innovations.
I. Rogers, Martha, Ph.D.
II. Title.
HF5415.127.P465   1997
658.8—dc20   96-18618
CIP

ISBN 0-385-48755-X

First Edition: January 1997

First Currency Paperback Edition: February 1999

4   5   6   7   8   9   10

ENTERPRISE ONE TO ONE

Tools for Competing in the Interactive Age

To Bob
A great friend,
wonderful partner,
and terrific 1:1 mechanic

CONTENTS

The Basic Rules of Competition Rewritten for the Interactive Age

Information technology makes three important new capabilities available to businesses. The database allows you to tell your customers apart and remember them individually. Interactivity means the customer can now talk to you (rather than serve as the passive target for your messages). And mass customization technology enables businesses to customize products and services as a matter of routine. Combining these three capabilities creates a "customer feedback loop": I know you and remember you. You tell me what you want. Then I make it for you. While this feedback loop has the potential to make customers extremely loyal, to use it, the 1:1 enterprise must be able to *integrate* its actual production and service delivery processes with the feedback it receives from interacting with specific, individual customers.

Customers are different in two primary ways: They need different things from the enterprise, and they have different value to the enterprise. A customer's lifetime value (LTV) will depend largely on how long the customer remains loyal, and even small increases in the rate of customer retention add significantly to LTV. Knowing what different customers need involves much more than simply tallying what they've bought, because two customers might buy the same product for quite different reasons. Provided, however, that the enterprise knows what a customer's underlying need is, the firm can sell the customer more and increase the customer's value.

Depending on how differentiable a firm's customer base is in terms of (1) needs and (2) valuations, the natural competitive strategy of a firm might be mass marketing, niche or target marketing, frequency marketing, or something else. By mapping the customer base out according to how differentiable it is, the enterprise can begin to make plans for "migrating" toward doing business as a 1:1 enterprise. The enterprise must adapt itself to the potential of its customer base by managing two capabilities: (1) the flexibility of its production, logistics, and service delivery functions, and (2) the flexibility of its communications with customers.

MCI launched a customer retention program that failed because of organizational conflict and cultural resistance. The firm started by buying loyalty from some consumers, offering them staged rebates for continued patronage. Progressing to a customer tiering system, MCI identified three distinct groups of high-spending customers, each with an entirely different set of needs from long distance— needs that MCI tried to meet with different products and services to be offered to each group. Despite quantifiable progress in customer retention and value, the program was killed. Among other things, it conflicted with existing management incentives, which were based on customer acquisition rates but not retention.

While customers with the highest lifetime values (the "most valuable customers") are the ones you most want to keep, "second-tier customers"—customers who don't have as high an actual valuation—are likely to have the most potential for growth. Keeping a first-tier customer will usually involve different strategies from those needed for growing a second-tier customer. Most firms also have a bottom rung of customers who are, for all practical purposes, "below zero."

At its most basic, the 1:1 enterprise must be able to treat different customers differently. The enterprise must determine its actions toward an individual customer, not based on the products or services already produced, but on the needs of the particular customer. This requires the firm and the customer to *collaborate,* in order to determine jointly what the appropriate product or service is for that customer. The process has the effect of cementing the customer's loyalty to the firm. Whether we talk about customizing a product such as lighting systems, hamburgers, or brassieres, or a service such as consulting or grocery shopping, the principle is the same. The customer specifies some need, then you deliver a product or service that meets those specifications. The key is (1) to make it easy for the customer to specify his needs, and (2) to *remember* these specifications, so the customer never has to re-specify. That way, it will always be easier for him to reorder from you rather than go to the trouble of re-specifying with your competitor.

When you subscribe to a new magazine, the first year might cost $35.90 but the second year the price is $75.90. Why? Because presumably you like the magazine. Charging regular customers more is a natural consequence of trying to acquire new customers by using discounts, and virtually every business tries to do it. But by tailoring a product to a customer's individual specifications, and then constantly upgrading the product to match the customer's needs better and better, the enterprise can establish a Learning Relationship with the customer. Over time, the enterprise not only makes the customer more and more loyal, it increases its own value to *that* customer—as every interaction leads to a better tailored service or product.

8 EXPANDING THE "NEED SET"   195
How to Customize, Even if You're Selling a Commodity

Learning Relationships are attractive to customers (and therefore valuable to the enterprise) as long as one customer's needs are different from another's. The more differences that exist among customers in what they need from the enterprise, and the more difficult or complicated it is for a customer to specify those needs, the more benefit can be gained by customizing. If a company sells a product that appears commoditylike, it can expand the customer's set of needs in order to introduce more differentiation. In addition to the core product, which includes the features, characteristics, and attributes of the basic product or service itself, the enterprise might look at customizing its "product-service bundle"—how the product is invoiced, packaged and palletized, delivered, or promoted. Beyond the product-service bundle, the enterprise might even customize the "enhanced need set"—all the related products and services a customer might want. A customer who wants a new office building constructed, for instance, may also want office management services, relocation consulting, and telecommunications and computer systems installations. Many such products or services will be beyond a firm's core competency, but could be delivered through a strategic alliance with another firm.

Remembering a customer's individual needs and product specifications is a powerful mechanism for improving loyalty, but what if the customer conveniently retains this information himself, perhaps in his own PC? Then the customer can bid one supplier against another, and even though each is able to cater to the customer's specific interests, each has also been reduced to a commodity. However, if the enterprise's relationship with a customer is based not just on knowledge of that particular customer's interests but also on knowledge of how those interests compare to the interests of other, similar customers, then it may be able to *anticipate* what a customer *will* want—sometimes even before the customer himself realizes he wants it. This is a benefit the customer will be able to get only from the enterprise.

Individual customer feedback and dialogue are indispensable to the 1:1 enterprise. Interactivity with a customer raises two issues: the medium, or vehicle, through which the interaction occurs (e-mail, phone, fax), and the content, or purpose, of the interaction itself (billing, product specification, inquiry, complaint). The 1:1 enterprise will take a complete inventory of all the ways it interacts with customers and, in addition to tracking the media efficiency of its interactions (with measurements such as call abandonment rate), it will track the content effectiveness of the interactions themselves (measuring such things as the ratio of complaints handled on the first call).

The real role of any commercial medium, whether it's in broadcast, print, or outdoor, is to make matches between the medium's customers—advertisers—and *their* customers, the end users of products and services being advertised. As the supply of communications bandwidth increases, it will cost the enterprise less and less to access its customers, or be accessed by them. However, one resource much scarcer than bandwidth is customer time and attention, and purchasing this will require an escalating proportion of the 1:1 enterprise's communications budget. The interactive media company's success won't just be the result of owning the pipeline and content, but owning the database of individual customer preferences as well. Because of this, and because of the unique dynamics of interactivity compared to traditional media, the media company itself can consider a variety of different, sometimes unorthodox business models.

Most of the barriers that now prevent an enterprise from creating a better relationship with its customers individually can be found within a distribution system designed originally to sell commodity products to interchangeable customers rather than tailored products and services to individual customers. Under what circumstances should the enterprise risk "going around" its existing distributors? When does it make sense for the enterprise to treat the members of the distribution chain themselves as customers? What are the advantages and disadvantages of such a strategy? And if a firm is itself engaged in the distribution of products or services for other companies, then what strategy makes the most sense for dealing with these new technological trends, many of which are threatening to "cut out the middleman"?

13 MAKING IT 350
How to Get There from Here

Doing business as a 1:1 enterprise is not something that can simply be added to the management tool kit like one more technique for improving quality, reducing cost, or raising productivity. Rather, it represents a fundamental change in philosophy and strategy—a change in the *dimension* of competition. A true 1:1 marketing philosophy can't be implemented without integrating it into the entire organization. The firm must embrace significant change, affecting virtually every department, division, officer and employee, every product, and every function. Once there is commitment to the goal, however, there are basically four steps for making the journey, from here to there: visioning, organizing, measuring, and transitioning.

14 AN OPEN LETTER TO THE CEO 383

Because changing a business into a 1:1 enterprise will necessarily involve integrating the enterprise's activities across functions and among divisions, it is simply not possible to accomplish without the active participation and support of the CEO. The two principle concerns a CEO might have are: how to justify the investment in information technology that this strategy entails, and how to overcome the natural cultural resistance that any organization will have when faced with this kind of sweeping change.

ACKNOWLEDGMENTS

It would be impossible to mention everyone who contributed to the ideas found in this book. Since our last book, we've met and worked with people in a variety of businesses from around the world, and good ideas have come from many different sources. Some are consulting clients or former clients from whom we've learned much about how to crystallize the challenge and prove the benefits of implementing 1:1. We have shamelessly reappropriated many of these ideas and examples in *Enterprise One to One*, giving credit wherever possible. This book really "belongs" to all those friends, believers, enthusiasts, and supporters of the 1:1 idea.

Some who deserve special mention, however, include Tom Shimko at Westinghouse Corporation, Bruce Hamilton and Sandy Phernetton at 3M, Peter Boulter and Toni Hendrix at NCR Corporation, Steve Nichols at US West Direct, Tim Toben at Customer Management Services, Dick Kaverman at Owens-Corning, Srini Nageshwar at Iomega Europe, Mads Nipper at Lego Systems A/S, Anne Lockie at Royal Bank of Canada, Pehong Chen and Bob Runge at BroadVision, Rich Hebert of Sky Alland Marketing, Sam Ferrise and Bill Block at Bandag Incorporated, Jock Bickert of Looking Glass Inc., Sean Erickson at TCI Communications, Inc., Ray Kordupleski of AT&T, George Gendron at *Inc.* magazine, Renée Mezzanotte of Devon Direct, Paul

Scheufele at CS First Boston, Tim DeMello at Streamline, Lib Gibson at Bell Canada, Val Markos at BellSouth, George Harrop at Barista Brava, Mike Hilton of Bayer Corporation, Brian Weber at Cellular Linking, Michael Paolucci of inter-active imaginations, John Deighton at Harvard Business School, Steve Berger of Nationwide Communications Inc., Paul Palmer of IBM InfoMarket, Jeff Silverman of Measurably Pleasure (parent of The Custom Foot), Chris Davies of Group X Advertising in London, Chris Zane of Zane's Cycles, Dave Milenthal at HMS Partners, Judy Corson and Jeff Pope at Custom Research Incorporated, Richard Stone at Tribune Company, Eugenio Bernal and William Narchi of Corporación Medcom, Brenda French of French Rags, Mary Naylor at Capitol Concierge, Rich Karlgaard at *Forbes ASAP*, Ken Lang at Empirical Media Corp., Harry Schlagel of Datavision Technologies Corporation, Bob Jasper of Marketing Horizons, Wolf Schmitt at Rubbermaid Incorporated, Tony Levitan at Greet Street, Nick Grouf of Agents, Inc., Stephen Coulter of National Australia Bank, Fred Reichheld, Joe Pine, Jim Gilmore, Peter Sontag, Richard Cross and Janet Smith, Arthur Hughes, Stan Rapp, Don Schultz and Robert Lauterborn, Nicholas Noyes, Randy Goldrick, Seth Godin, Gayle Bock, Pat Norton, and George Gilder.

Harriet Rubin, the publisher and editor of Currency Doubleday, and Raphael Sagalyn, our agent, have been patient, tireless in their support, and wonderful to work with. A *very* special thanks to Jennifer Breheny at Currency Doubleday, whose painstaking editorial work contributed immensely to making the verbiage clearer and the arguments crisper. Everyone at *marketing 1:1, inc.* contributed to this book one way or another, including Ralph Caldwell, Andrea Levanti, Mary Cavello, Darlene Greene, Peter Seed, Felicia Bates, Beth Skoglund, and Colleen Bischoff.

Special thanks to Julia Lommatzsch Johnson, our research director at *marketing 1:1, inc.,* for her painstaking attention to all the nettlesome details of writing this book, including tracking down sources, calling companies to arrange phone interviews, and coordinating the back-and-forth madness of revision after revision after revision. Julia kept us organized and kept our lives a little more sane, all the time displaying a patient good humor that belied the pressure cooker we kept *her* in.

And thanks to Bob Dorf, our friend and partner, to whom this book is dedicated.

Most of all, thanks to our spouses, who have once again indulged the monomania: Pamela Devenney Peppers and Stuart Bertsch.

PREFACE

Anyone with a customer is an enterprise. We wrote *Enterprise One to One* for anyone with a customer.

As the Interactive Age arrives, every enterprise will have to learn how to treat different customers differently. That's what *Enterprise One to One* is all about.

Before you read *Enterprise One to One*, you might like to know a little about how this book got its start. In our first book, *The One to One Future: Building Relationships One Customer at a Time*, we proposed a radically different way of doing business, given the new reality of faster, more powerful computers and increasingly interactive media. To deal with this new reality, we proposed a new kind of competition—a customer-oriented competition we called one-to-one (1:1) marketing. Instead of selling one product at a time to as many customers as possible in a particular sales period, the 1:1 marketer uses customer databases and interactive communications to sell one customer at a time as many products and services as possible, over the entire lifetime of that customer's patronage. This is a strategy that requires a business to manage customers individually rather than just managing products, sales channels, and programs. While the traditional marketer gauges success in terms of market share growth, the 1:1 marketer also measures share of customer.

When we were writing it, we considered *The One to One*

Future a warning—a wake-up call for businesses and organizations of all kinds. We were writing to business managers who recognized the beginning of the end of the mass marketing era but had no other flag to rally around.

Our book caused a stir. Tom Peters read it and said we made his "close to the customer" axiom from *In Search of Excellence* "pale by comparison." What has pleased us most, however, is the variety of companies around the world that have enthusiastically embraced 1:1 strategies. It's obvious that 1:1 marketing has hit a major strategic nerve in the business community.

- Pitney Bowes reduced attrition at one end of its mailing systems business by 20 percent, growing its market share and shrinking its cost of sales in the bargain.

- Management attendees at BellSouth's internal Leadership Institute are now being trained in the principles of 1:1 marketing, to enable the company to survive and prosper when telecommunications regulatory protections are removed.

- NCR is launching a worldwide consulting practice in 1:1 marketing under the name Total Customer Management, designed to assist the firm's data warehouse customers to make full use of their information technology capabilities.

- BroadVision has launched new software for the World Wide Web which permits a Web site owner to practice 1:1 marketing by customizing Web pages dynamically, in real time, to the individual specifications and needs of individual users.

One result of all this activity has been that more questions have been raised by our own clients and others, and we have done a great deal more thinking about the topics we first raised in *The One to One Future*. In our consulting practice we have found that as straightforward as they might sound in principle, actually implementing some of the strategies we advocate is often not so easy.

The most common error most firms commit, when preparing to create one-to-one relationships with their customers, is underestimating the degree to which every facet of the enterprise needs to be involved in the process and integrated into the actual customer relationship. Probably the second most common error, however, is *overestimating* the amount of change required to begin an orderly transition from product-based aggregate-market competition to customer-driven competition. In most cases, the benefits of 1:1 marketing can be measured and proved without a wholesale restructuring of a firm's current sales and marketing system, although often the results of such testing will lead the enterprise to plan such a restructuring sooner rather than later.

It is not necessary for you to have read *The One to One Future* in order to get the full benefit of *Enterprise One to One*. We wrote the first book as a "why-to" book. *Enterprise One to One*, by way of contrast, is a how-to book—a tool kit chock-full of practical, experience-based advice. The tools in this particular kit will enable any enterprise to assess its own situation realistically, gauge the benefits of the kind of change that will be necessary, and then plan rationally how to make that change.

If our experience is any guide, *Enterprise One to One* can hardly represent the last word on 1:1 marketing. There will be many additional ideas and strategies generated by the businesses already engaged in this kind of competition, as well as by those just now figuring out how to make the transition. We expect this book to be distributed around the world, and we hope it is successful, but even as it is going to print, more tools are being invented, more examples are being documented, and more strategies are being hatched. One of the advantages of being at the center of this movement is that we often learn of new and interesting developments in a variety of different industries well before the mainstream business press writes about them. If you want to stay abreast of these developments, or if you'd like to find out about our own latest thinking on a particular topic, or if you have something of your own to share with us, please feel free to visit us at our Web site (http://www.marketing1to1.com).

The word "enterprise" can be defined as a daring project or undertaking, and this is, indeed, exactly what we are proposing in *Enterprise One to One*. Treating different customers differently is not a strategy that can be grafted simply onto any firm's existing systems and operations. Instead, it represents a completely unique, even daring, orientation for the enterprise, and requires an *integrative* approach, with a variety of enterprise functions all working together.

To implement the principles outlined here, you'll have to get the CEO actively involved sooner or later. Most business authors dream of writing a book that the CEO will read and then require everyone in the organization to buy. Our hope for *Enterprise* is to have a book that everyone in the organization will read, and then require the CEO to buy. For any enterprise to succeed with the strategies proposed in *Enterprise One to One*, the CEO will have to drive the change across divisional and functional boundaries throughout the organization. There is no other way.

Who should read this book? You, if you have a customer, or if you work for an organization that has customers. Read it if you want to survive and prosper—and keep your customer—in the Interactive Age.

—DON PEPPERS AND MARTHA ROGERS
http://www.marketing1to1.com

THE MUSICAL CONDOM

The Basic Rules of Competition Rewritten for the Interactive Age

A thousand years from now, speech-recognition technology will almost certainly be remembered as the defining innovation of the Information Revolution.

When our descendants look back on the twentieth century, they will note this as the century in which hunger and infectious disease were nearly eradicated in most Western countries, and life spans greatly increased as a result. They may note that it was during this century that brutal, totalitarian dictatorships menaced civilization, then crumpled under the weight of their own massive, centrally directed oppression. They will remember this as the century in which Einstein postulated relativity, and human beings walked on the moon for the first time.

And they will note that we were the last generation of

human beings to inhabit a deaf and dumb world—a world in which no matter what we said to the microwave oven, or the power saw, or the car, it didn't respond, and it didn't talk back.

Only now, at the end of the century, are things changing. Voice Powered Technology, a California-based company, makes a VCR you can operate with spoken instructions. Say "Record, 7, Sunday, 6 P.M. to 7:30 P.M.," and the VCR follows your spoken instructions. Car phones and PCs are available with the same capability. In less than a generation, nearly every appliance and tool in your home will incorporate some form of speech-recognition technology in the same way that most appliances today incorporate digital displays.

The impact these developments will have on business is almost unimaginable, but what ought to be clear to everyone is that *product* marketing will soon be nearly entirely supplanted by *relationship* marketing. After all, the first thing products with microchips will do is remember their purchasers' needs and specifications, and this is the primary requirement for sustaining an ongoing relationship with a customer.

Think what it will be like to get into your car in just a few years. The car will automatically recognize you by your weight and then adjust all the comfort items to your liking, such as seat height and angle, air-conditioning, mirrors, and radio settings. Because you're you, the car sets its shocks at a level that will return a real feel of the road, because that's how *you* like to drive. If another driver in your household prefers a smoother ride, he will get more cushioning. As you drive, the car notes and remembers how you start and stop, how you turn, accelerate, and brake. Fuel flow and timing are adjusted so the engine performs as economically and responsively as possible for your personal driving habits, in daylight or at night, on dry roads or wet, in the city or on the highway. If you want to change your comfort settings, you announce to the car, "This is the way I like it." Or, "Set my seat this way when I'm wearing heels."

The car will have a wireless data connection to the dealer as well as to your own personal computer ensemble. When the engine needs adjustment or a part is about to fail, the car connects to the dealer, coordinates with your calendar, and offers you three appointments to choose from. It will have a satellite tracking system that can give you directions to the nearest pizza place at any time, and it will plot which route will save the most time on the way to the airport based on where all the other satellite-tracked traffic is. You may be able to volunteer a microchip from your car to prove to your insurance company that you obey the speed laws.

Cars will be like this in less than a decade. Lincoln and Cadillac already advertise cars that automatically adjust the seat, radio, and comfort settings to the remembered tastes of different drivers. In ten U.S. cities Hertz already equips its full-size rental cars with Never Lost, its satellite tracking system for on-board navigation.

The appliances and machines around us will soon remember us individually and anticipate our needs.

Microchips continue to become smaller and more powerful even as they become cheaper. The actual cost-efficiency of information processing doubles every 12 to 18 months, a speed that is all but impossible to comprehend. In 1978 the Cray 1 supercomputer processed 160 million instructions per second. It was the fastest, most powerful computer in the world. But when Sony introduced its Play-Station video game platform in 1995, it processed 500 million instructions per second, making it three times as powerful as the Cray 1. The Cray 1 cost $20 million, while the PlayStation costs $299 at retail. Today's supercomputer is tomorrow's video game.

Because of its cost, very few Cray supercomputers were ever sold. In contrast, Sony sold 100,000 PlayStations the first weekend it was offered in the United States. If you were a potential customer for a Cray 1, you had to have a very specific idea of the things you were going to do with it before committing. But what risk are you taking by acquiring a $299 PlayStation?

Microchips continue to infiltrate everything around us. Vehicles that automatically dial 911 when the car or truck is in an accident are already being tested by New York motorists. The greeting card that plays a ten-second prerecorded greeting from your four-year-old nephew contains more processing power than existed in the entire world in 1950. Tiny microchips are injected painlessly under the skin of a pet to aid in tracking a missing poodle, and embedded in tire treads to signal pressure, balance, and tread wear. Philip Morris has filed for a patent on a microchip-controlled cigarette that senses the pressure exerted by a smoker's lips in order to send little puffs of smoke directly into his mouth and not into the air. Sandia Laboratories is developing a "smart gun"—one that can be fired only by its owner and cannot be operated by a minor. A U.S. engineer has patented a smart seat that automatically adjusts itself to people of widely different sizes, shapes, and weights, using microchip-controlled air bladders. The same technology could be used to create running shoes that automatically change their shape when the user goes from a walk to a jog to a run.

An Italian physicist claims to have invented a condom with a microchip that will play Beethoven if it leaks while in use.

The debate about whether it will be the television or the personal computer that actually evolves into the platform for in-home interactivity is just an ancillary skirmish, a side-show of short-term issues involving electronic protocols and formats. In the long run, the outcome of this debate is not in dispute. In the words of one technologist, "the computer industry is converging with the television industry in the same sense that the automobile converged with the horse." What is actually happening, of course, is that the computer is converging with *everything*, not just televisions and cars, but also telephones, wristwatches, refrigerators, credit cards, greeting cards, hair dryers, cigarettes, bathrooms, tires, frozen food packaging, athletic shoes, condoms, and the kitchen sink.

As it does, the environment we inhabit is becoming smarter and smarter. The possibilities multiply exponentially. Imagine:

■ A cigarette that can't be smoked by a minor

■ A car that can't be operated by anyone except its owner

■ Pills that issue reminders to be taken every day (or four times a day)

■ A winter coat that inflates its layer of insulation when the temperature drops

- Sunglasses that answer you when you call out to find where they are

- An alarm clock that reminds you to set it

- A microwave meal package that sets the microwave correctly all by itself

- Product packages that signal as they're being opened, automatically updating your shopping list

- Product packages that open themselves when you tell them to

Like the enchanted castle in the Walt Disney movie *Beauty and the Beast,* our home will soon be populated by dozens, maybe hundreds of talking utensils, tools, clocks, and appliances—cleaning, cooking, opening, closing, preparing, repairing. Some of them will get around on their own power, change their shape as needed, and wirelessly call for help or for updates on their human owner's constantly changing plans and intentions. Computer scientists are already studying the social etiquette of robots—how robotic machines will cooperate to accomplish a common goal more efficiently, teaching one another, and learning from their mistakes as they go along.

Objectives for You and Your Enterprise

This vast change in products and our relationship to them is just one aspect of an even more dramatic change in the relationships of *customers to companies*—and that is what this book explores.

Is there a company in business today that is not deeply concerned with the issue of customer attrition and margin erosion? Is there anyone out there who isn't worried about staying in *front* of this technological tidal wave? By the time you finish this book you will know how to harness the revolution in information technology and interactivity.

1. You'll be able to improve *customer retention,* not just incrementally, but dramatically—and you'll be able to increase your *share* of each customer's business, over time, despite the increasingly frantic nature of your competitors' customer acquisition campaigns.

2. You'll understand the strategies required to protect and increase your *unit margins* despite the "commoditization" that has begun to infect businesses in every conceivable product and service category today.

3. You'll have insights that will allow you to *create entirely new markets* for your enterprise—markets of *individual* customers with rich and diverse needs—enabling you to acquire not only new customers, but to sell a variety of new products and services to satisfy each customer's different and newly discovered needs.

4. You'll be able to plan a workable, businesslike *transition* to the Interactive Age—embracing utilizing, and even reveling in these new technologies rather than being threatened by them, and justifying the expense with clear return on investment (ROI) and cost-efficiency metrics.

These are the objectives we have for you and your enterprise. To achieve them, the first step is to understand how interactivity and information technology have rewritten the most basic rules of business competition.

Consider the intelligent automobile again. The wireless connection to a dealer means your car, as a product, is no longer a detached item, independent of the manufacturer. The company that made and sold you this product is now linked electronically to you, the customer. Like the microchip-controlled appliances in your home, this company will track how you use its product and, over time, the firm will do a better and better job of understanding and anticipating what you want, making it less necessary for you to waste time or brainpower on routine activities (such as readjusting your seat or re-selecting your favorite radio station)—not to mention adapting itself over time to the way you like to *drive.*

Say you've had this car for three years and decide to buy a new one. What would you choose to do—buy from another manufacturer and spend the first six months or so reteaching your new car's computer how to set all the dials, adjust to your driving, hug the road around turns, make phone calls, and schedule your service appointments? Or would you purchase a new car from the same company that made your current one, and then simply upload the computer's information?

Or consider a service as routine and mundane as grocery shopping. Suppose you could turn on your personal computer (or your interactive television set), call up a list of last week's grocery purchases, make a few changes to this list, then order them delivered to your door after five P.M., paying via credit card or direct debit. Time elapsed: seven minutes.

Is there *anyone* reading this book who doesn't find this scenario attractive? Interactive delivery services remarkably like this are already springing up around the country, catering especially to urban and suburban working couples. For many such customers the convenience of calling up their own regular weekly grocery list and getting the entire shopping necessity "out of the way," on-line, is irresistible.

But think about the additional conveniences such a service will be able to provide its customers as it relies more and more on the microchip. Say you've been a customer for six months—long enough for the firm to have compiled a good record of your regular weekly shopping, thereby learning from you the rate at which you consume various products. Now, as you place your order, the computer *reminds* you to remember potatoes, paper towels, and mouthwash, all three of which you are probably low on. Over time, it might be the computer that draws up the weekly list to begin with, and all you do is monitor the process and make additional suggestions.

As with the intelligent car and other intelligent products that learn from customers, *this firm is using computers to create an important barrier to competition, with respect to each of its individual customers.* Suppose a second computerized grocery delivery service were to open, offering the same services, with the same reliability and quality, at a similar price. Clearly, this new service would offer the same convenience to its customers—shopping lists based on previous lists, and a reminder service for overlooked items.

But for any single customer to realize the advantages of these services the customer would first have to spend another six months ordering groceries from the new service in order to teach it what the original firm has already learned! The competitive service may be on an equal footing with the original one in terms of getting more customers to begin with, but the original grocery delivery service is likely to have a *permanent and perhaps insurmountable competitive advantage* when it comes to retaining and increasing the business from the customers it already has.

Aggregate Markets vs. Individual Customers

Traditional competition among firms is based on exploiting aggregate or group markets of indistinguishable customers, but more and more the battleground is shifting to the individual, unique customer. The traditional business competitor succeeds by examining a representative sample of potential customers to obtain a scientific picture of their needs and preferences. Once products are developed and manufactured that deliver these benefits, they are promoted to attract potential customers.

This is aggregate-market competition. In business-to-business situations the promotion usually focuses on specific, identifiable product features, while in consumer-marketing situations it often focuses on the product's image-oriented, emotional attributes. Relying on increasing computer power to do the analysis ever more efficiently, companies have directed their marketing efforts toward smaller and smaller segments of customers. But in the final analysis, whether we talk about a mass market or a niche, the aggregate-market competitor is in business to sell a particular product to as many new customers as possible by treating all customers from any single market or segment the same way, and getting as accurate a fix as possible on their *average* needs.

Beyond improving the aggregate-market competitor's efficiency at finding niches, however, *the computer is now changing the actual character of the competitive model itself, supplanting it with a customer-driven model.* When we say "customer-driven," we are talking about a business that relies on delivering highly tailored, *individualized* products and services to *each* of its customers—whether these customers are consumers or other businesses—based on feedback from and interaction with these customers. The smart car and on-line grocery delivery service do not profit much from information about how the average customer drives or shops. Rather, the customer-driven model of competition is based on each firm's specific, individual customer interactions, *one customer at a time.*

New Competitive Rules

Customer-driven competition is what we call one-to-one marketing, a form of marketing that was prohibitively expensive, and therefore nearly inconceivable, to the traditional marketer just a few years ago. Today, as we enter the Interactive Age and microchip-controlled products, it has become a prerequisite for competitive success.

One-to-one marketing is made possible by three important capabilities that information technology now provides:

- **Customer tracking.** Computer databases can help businesses remember and keep track of numerous complex, individual interactions with their customers. A business can now focus on one single customer from among the millions in its database, examine his entire history of transactions with the firm, make an adjustment to the record (perhaps noting the resolution of his complaint), and then return the customer to the database—all in the few seconds it takes to answer a phone inquiry. And a company can do this with tens of thousands, or hundreds of thousands, of customers simultaneously, one customer at a time.

■ *Interactive dialogue.* The computer has also made an increasing array of interactive communications tools available. Now customers can talk to businesses. Businesses are no longer limited to talking to (or, more accurately, "at") their customers and prospective customers.

■ *Mass customization.* Applied to the assembly line and the logistical system, information technology now makes it possible for businesses to deliver "mass customized" products and services. Customization without computer technology is expensive and impractical, but with computers the production and distribution processes can be modularized, and many businesses today can *routinely* produce customized products or services tailored to the specific needs of an individual business or consumer rather than to the general needs of a "segment" of customers.

Taken together, these new capabilities not only make 1:1 marketing possible, but competitively essential. However, the capabilities *must be used together*! To compete as a

1:1 marketer, a business must become a 1:1 enterprise. The 1:1 enterprise creates a totally new dynamic of competition by *integrating* these three computer-enhanced capabilities—information management, interactive communication, and customized production:

Information: I know you and *remember* you individually. You're my customer, and you're different from my other customers.

Communication: You tell me what you want.

Production: Now I *make* it for you, to your own specifications. And I ask you, "Was this okay? All right, how about this?" With each transaction, I get better at giving *you* exactly what *you* want.

The One-to-One Enterprise

This new dynamic creates a "customer feedback loop" with each individual customer. The customer and the business together redefine what it means to participate in a commercial relationship.

> *I know you. You tell me what you want. I make it.*
> *I remember next time.*

What could be simpler?

Simple to understand, perhaps, but not to implement. Adopting the 1:1 model is not as straightforward as identifying an additional niche market, for now the marketing process itself can no longer be confined to the sales and marketing departments or the ad agency.

One-to-one marketing, because it requires an integrative approach to dealing with customers individually, can't simply be strapped onto a firm's other marketing efforts. In order to compete in a truly customer-driven manner, the 1:1 enterprise must integrate its entire range of business functions around satisfying the individual needs of each individual customer—not just marketing, customer service, and sales and channel management, but production, logistics, and financial measurement and metrics. To ensure the efficient integration of these functions around individual customers, the enterprise's organizational structure itself must also be altered.

But the reward for becoming a 1:1 enterprise is immense. Not only will the 1:1 enterprise be able to generate unprecedented levels of customer loyalty, it will be able to improve its overall unit margins as well, even in the face of parity-level product competition. In terms of continuing business, *the 1:1 enterprise can make itself practically invulnerable to competition from other firms—even from other 1:1 enterprises, offering not just the same products, but the same level of customization and relationship-building.*

The "Learning Relationship"

There is a strong link between an individual customer and a car that remembers its driver. It is similar to the link between an interactive grocery delivery service and the shopper it reminds to check her supply of paper towels, or between a television viewer and the interactive media firm that suggests programs this particular viewer might like, based on her previous viewing. Each is an example of a Learning Relationship.

A Learning Relationship between a customer and an enterprise gets smarter and smarter with every individual interaction, defining in ever more detail the customer's own individual needs and tastes. Every time a customer orders her groceries by calling up last week's list and updating it, for instance, she is in effect "teaching" the service more about the products she buys and the rate at which she consumes them. The shopping service will develop a knowledge of this particular customer that is virtually impossible for a competitive shopping service to duplicate, providing an impregnable lock on the customer's loyalty.

A Learning Relationship ensures that it is always in the customer's self-interest to remain with the firm that has developed the relationship to begin with. We aren't talking about emotional attachment here, nor do we suggest that a customer's loyalty to any firm will be derived from some sense of obligation or duty. Instead, by establishing a Learning Relationship, the 1:1 enterprise increases customer retention simply by making loyalty more convenient for the customer than nonloyalty. It works this way:

1. The customer tells the enterprise what he wants, with interaction and feedback.

2. The enterprise meets these specifications by customizing its product or service to the needs of that particular customer, and then it *remembers* these specifications.

3. With more interaction and feedback, the customer will have spent time and energy teaching the enterprise more and more about his own individual needs.

4. Now, to get an equivalent level of service from any other firm—even one offering the same exact level of customization and feedback—this customer will first have to *reteach* the competitor what he has already taught the original firm!

The Learning Relationship creates what is, essentially, a barrier that makes it more difficult for a customer to be promiscuous than to remain loyal. We will talk more about the nature of Learning Relationships throughout this book, particularly in Chapter 7. In Chapter 9 we'll see how a firm could leverage its Learning Relationships with current customers into an advantage in securing the loyalty of new ones as well, by employing "community knowledge." For now, however, it is sufficient to know that only a 1:1 enterprise can create a Learning Relationship, because it depends on integrating the business functions required not only to remember and interact with a customer, but to tailor particular products or services for the customer as well.

Products and Services as Tools in the Intelligent Environment.

Another way of looking at the competitive strength of the 1:1 enterprise is to think of the enterprise itself as a natural part of a customer's "intelligent environment." The interaction between such an enterprise and its customer is substantially the same as that between an intelligent product and its user. In each case, because of information technology, the *object* of the person's attention is capable of both *learning* from the person's past behavior and expressed preferences, and then *behaving* differently toward that particular person, based on this learning. In each instance, the manner in which the object (or the enterprise) interacts with the customer—that is, the products and services offered to this particular customer, individually—is chosen in the context of the customer's previous relationship.

Quantum Marketing

Consultants sometimes try to explain 1:1 marketing as a logical extension of niche marketing, in which the segment consists not of a target population, but of a single target—a segment of one. But in truth, once marketing is reduced to the level of *individual* customers, the rules change qualitatively.

> *The term "segment of one" is not only unhelpful but misleading.*

Segments are static, while individual customers are dynamic and interactive. Segments are the passive targets of marketing initiatives. They don't try things out, ask questions, negotiate price and terms, make adjustments, substitute spending for one item by sacrificing another, or complain and seek refunds. Niches and segments cannot communicate directly and interactively with marketers, but an individual customer or prospect can do all these things and more. Because the feedback-and-customization dynamics of customer-driven competition are so different from the survey-and-projection dynamics of the aggregate-market model, most firms find that traditional marketing strategies are simply not useful when applied to this kind of competition.

Explaining 1:1 marketing as a form of segmentation or niche marketing is no more useful than explaining the behavior of individual atoms by applying the rules of Newtonian physics. While we live in and experience the Newtonian world, in which objects are solid and dependable and space is empty, at the quantum level of the individual atom, Newtonian rules no longer apply. When physicists examine the quantum world, they know that matter is not a passive, dependable *thing*, but a probability wave, sometimes here and sometimes not. As intellectually baffling as this may sound, quantum theory's effects have been confirmed by thousands of real-world experiments. This very book, propounding a new theory of competition based on information technology, owes its existence to quantum theory. We wouldn't have written it except for the spreading influence of the computer, which was first made practical by the transistor, and it was quantum theory that led to the invention of the transistor.

Traditional aggregate-market competition as a discipline evolved in the "Newtonian" world of passive, target populations—markets that companies tried to influence by advertising standardized products the same way to everyone. But the feedback-and-customization dynamic of 1:1 marketing now makes it possible for a firm to navigate in a world of "quantum marketing"—a world in which individual customers interact with the firm, providing feedback and collaborative assistance so that the product can be individually tailored to the needs of each customer. In the 1:1 world most traditional marketing strategies and tactics are simply not useful, but, as with quantum theory, the *market* effects of 1:1 marketing are quite real and measurable.

Competing in the Customer Dimension

One useful method for contrasting the objectives and tactics of a 1:1 enterprise with traditional business strategies is to visualize competing for business in a different dimension. The aggregate-market competitor operates in the *product* dimension, while the customer-driven, 1:1 enterprise competes in the *customer* dimension. To be successful, any firm must accomplish two basic tasks:

1. It must satisfy some need.

2. It must find a customer who wants that need satisfied.

Satisfying customer needs is the quintessential definition of any business's ultimate reason for being. Everything else—production, engineering, logistics, accounting—everything other than satisfying a customer's need is just cost.

If we were to map these two tasks—satisfying needs and reaching customers—on a simple two-dimensional graph, the traditional firm would visualize its task this way:

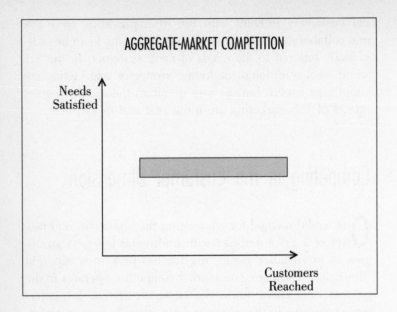

The firm driven by an aggregate-market approach focuses on one product or service at a time, satisfying one basic customer need. Then the firm plumbs the market to find as many customers as possible who want that need satisfied in the current selling period. Aggregate-market competition is inherently product-centered.

There is, however, an entirely different way to view the competitive task—a customer-driven approach. Instead of focusing on one need at a time and trying to find as many customers as possible who want that need satisfied, the customer-driven competitor—the 1:1 enterprise—focuses on one *customer* at a time, and tries to satisfy as many of that particular customer's needs as possible. To the 1:1 enterprise, the marketing battle is fought not in a product dimension, but in a customer dimension:

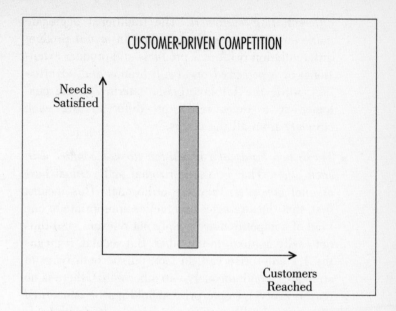

CUSTOMER-DRIVEN COMPETITION

A lot can be understood about the difference between traditional, market-driven competition and 1:1, customer-driven competition by comparing these two illustrations.

- The *direction of success* for an aggregate-market firm is to acquire more customers—that is, to widen the horizontal bar—while the direction of success for the customer-driven firm is to keep customers longer and grow them bigger. The width of the horizontal bar can be thought of as a firm's market share: The proportion of customers who have their need satisfied by the company. But the 1:1 enterprise focuses on *share of customer*, represented by the height of the vertical bar.

- The aggregate-market firm competes by differentiating products, while the 1:1 enterprise competes by *differentiating customers.* The traditional aggregate marketer tries to establish either an *actual* product differentiation (with new products and product extensions) or a *perceived* one (with brands and advertising), while the 1:1 enterprise, catering to one customer at a time, relies on differentiating each *customer* from all the others.

■ These *two kinds of competition do not conflict with each other.* That is, the horizontal and vertical bars are not *opposites*; they are orthogonal. This means, first, that the strategies and tactics appropriate to one kind of competition are simply not relevant, and thus not easily applied, to the other. But second, it means the 1:1 enterprise can, in fact, pursue both types of strategies simultaneously—in other words, there is no reason every 1:1 enterprise should not be concerned just as much with *getting* customers as it is with *keeping* them and *growing* them.

In the traditional aggregate-market business model, interaction with individual customers is not necessary, and feedback from particular customers is useful only insofar as it is *representative* of the market as a whole. An aggregate-market competitor produces and delivers the *same* product, meeting a single need, in basically the same way for everyone in any given market. But the 1:1 enterprise *must* interact with a customer, using the customer's feedback from this interaction to deliver a customized product or service. It is a time-dependent, evolutionary process. The product or service is increasingly tailored, and the customer is more and more precisely differentiated from other customers.

Five Principal Business Functions for the 1:1 Enterprise

To succeed in the feedback-and-customization realm of customer-driven competition, the 1:1 enterprise must integrate five principal business functions into its marketing strategy. Our book is meant to help you understand how these five principal functions must be put together to compete successfully in the Interactive Age.

1. *Financial Custodianship of the Customer Base* At most firms this function, if it exists at all, exists only sporadically. Costs are counted, physical assets are tallied, but usually no one takes an active interest in understanding the valuation of the customer base as an asset, or in evaluating the worth of individual customers within the base. The 1:1 enterprise treats the customer base as the *primary* asset of the firm, carefully managing the investment it makes in this asset. To compete successfully in an interactive world, when different customers can be treated differently, the 1:1 enterprise must understand how individual customers (1) add value to the business and (2) get value from the business. The firm must know how to allocate management time and effort to those customers who will yield the highest return to the firm—keeping the most valuable customers longer, and growing other customers bigger. What would it be worth to your business to increase the value of

your customer base by even five percent? How would you go about it?

In addition, the 1:1 enterprise must know which customers want to satisfy which needs. Even customers buying the same product or service might be doing so for quite different reasons. Understanding each individual customer's needs from the firm is a prerequisite for customizing the product or service that meets those needs.

The degree to which a firm's customers can be differentiated, either by their value to the firm or by what they need from the firm, will go a long way toward defining the actual strategy the enterprise must follow to cement loyalty and increase unit margins. A discussion of these issues, and a review of the appropriate strategies for businesses with a variety of customer base "configurations," begins in the next chapter, "Some Customers Are More Equal Than Others."

2. *Production, Logistics, and Service Delivery* Whether we talk about the actual product a firm manufactures, or the service it renders, or the services that surround a product, the 1:1 enterprise must be capable of customizing its actual offering to the needs and preferences of each individual customer. The feedback loop with an individual customer is useful only if the interaction from the customer can be incorporated into the way the enterprise actually *behaves* toward that customer. To receive a truly customized product or service, the customer first has to say what he wants and how it should be delivered.

This converts the customer from passive target to active participant in the selling process. The 1:1 enterprise and the customer collaborate—the customer specifies, and the 1:1 enterprise delivers. But this means the production and logistics functions themselves have to be integrated with the marketing function on the *micro* level of the individual customer rather than just on the *macro* level of the target market.

In Chapter 6, "The Asymmetrical Brassiere," we begin our discussion of how to treat different customers differently, how to collaborate either in the customization of a product or its surrounding services, and how to turn such collaboration into Learning Relationships that can make a firm nearly invulnerable to competition, one customer at a time.

3. *Marketing Communications, Customer Service, and Interaction* Dialogue and feedback from individual customers drive the 1:1 enterprise. Marketing communications and all forms of customer interaction must be combined in a single function to ensure that the dialogue with a customer today picks up where it left off yesterday with that particular customer. Without individual customer feedback, no collaboration or customization is possible, nor is it possible to specify a customer's needs in more detail. Creating dialogue opportunities with customers is a prerequisite for soliciting feedback. But the dialogue itself has to be integrated into the enterprise's existing knowledge of that customer and its need for additional information.

Strategies for cultivating more dialogue with customers, and making this dialogue more productive, are discussed in Chapter 10, "Surfing the Feedback Loop." In Chapter 11, "The Medium Is the Matchmaker," we take a good look at this dynamic from the point of view of the media company—the host system responsible for bringing companies together with their customers.

4. *Sales Distribution and Channel Management* One of the most difficult issues for the 1:1 enterprise is making a distribution system that was designed for disseminating standardized products at uniform prices work for customized products at customer-specific prices. Getting customer feedback is not easy at all if the firm must use intermediaries like retailers or value-added resellers. Often the only way for a 1:1 enterprise to achieve a genuinely integrative solution is to disintermediate the distribution network altogether, but planning for this is usually quite difficult. In some situations, the 1:1 enterprise can create collaborative Learning Relationships with its own distributors—managing inventory for a warehouse distributor, for example, or providing product support for a value-added reseller, or customizing the product packaging to meet the needs of an individual retail chain. In any case, however, the enterprise's channel management philosophy must be carefully integrated with its approach to individual customers.

We consider various implications of channel and distribution management throughout the book. Then, in Chapter 12, "The Busy Shoe Salesman," we systematically examine the benefits and drawbacks of various channel strategies as well as looking at them from the distributor's point of view.

5. *Organizational Management Strategy* Finally, in addition to customer base custodianship, production and logistics, customer interaction, and channel management, the 1:1 enterprise needs to organize itself internally in such a way that it can monitor progress and hold people accountable for competitive success or failure. This means placing managers in charge of customers and customer relationships rather than just products and programs. And the firm has to have a workable plan for making a transition from aggregate-market competition to customer-driven competition as smoothly as possible. Many obstacles block the path of any firm attempting to integrate itself enough to become a 1:1 enterprise.

You'll find a detailed case history highlighting one company's efforts to surmount many of these obstacles early on, in Chapter 4, "Infant Mortality at MCI." In Chapter 13, "Making It," we outline a four-step plan for making a successful transition from operating as an aggregate-market competitor to a customer-driven business model.

By the end of *Enterprise One to One* you will have a working knowledge of the nature of business competition in the information-intensive Interactive Age. You will have many ideas to apply to your own business, and you may discover a number of totally new business opportunities, either for your firm or for yourself.

FUNCTIONS OF THE 1:1 ENTERPRISE

Function	Contribution	Implemented by
Custodianship of the customer base	Differentiating customers by their needs from the enterprise and their value to it; allocating resources appropriately	Chief Executive Officer Chief Financial Officer Chief Information Officer Marketing Executives Sales Executives Vertical Market Managers Account Relationship Managers
Production, logistics, and service delivery	Mass customizing to build loyal customers at higher margins; creating Learning Relationships	Operations Executives Customer Service Executives Product Managers Area Vice Presidents
Customer communication	Providing dialogue feedback to specify (a) individual customer needs, and (b) share-of-customer opportunities	Marketing Executives Sales Executives Advertising Executives Information Systems Managers Customer Service Executives
Distribution and logistics	Defining the customer within the "distribution waterfall"; creating 1:1 relationships with distributors; distributing products/services more cost-efficiently	Sales Executives Marketing Executives Channel Managers
Organization and planning	Removing obstacles to implementation; integrating 1:1 strategies throughout the enterprise; transition planning and execution	Chief Executive Officer Marketing Executives Sales Executives Human Resource Executives Training Managers Vision Managers

Above all, however, you will reach a deeper understanding of what it will be like to inhabit a world that is no longer deaf and dumb—a world of talking appliances, smart products, and companies that *remember* you for who you are and what you want.

SOME CUSTOMERS ARE MORE EQUAL THAN OTHERS

2

How to Identify and Capitalize on Customer Differences

- Employees at Speedy Car Wash in Panama City, Florida, record the license plate numbers of cars that come in to be washed, using a simple PC-based file. The firm regularly generates a rank-ordered list of plate numbers showing the most to least frequent customers. Jimmy Branch, the firm's entrepreneurial CEO, provides a $10 cash award to the first employee every day who spots one of the firm's "top 50" customers—customers who are then singled out for special treatment.

- The National Australia Bank tiered its retail banking customers into five groups, rank-ordered by profitability, and over a six-year period it succeeded in increasing the top two tiers from under 20 percent of the base to more than 27 percent.

■ Farm Credit, a midwest lending company, performed a customer profiling study and found a series of 21 questions that can be asked of a customer or prospect to map him with 95 percent confidence into one of five attitudinal clusters. "Value shoppers," for instance, want to consider all the options on rates and make their own choices—as opposed to "reassurance seekers," who are threatened by the process and more likely to entrust the entire decision to the lending officer. Reassurance seekers are given a recommendation, take it, and get back to what they're really interested in—farming. Once customers are placed into a cluster, Farm Credit's selling process can be much more effective, because even though two customers may want the same exact kind of loan, their desire is often driven by dramatically different needs.

These examples illustrate the two most useful differences among customers—*needs* and *valuations.*

Customers have different **needs from** *a firm, and they represent different* **valuations to** *a firm.*

All other types of customer description—demographics, psychographics, firmographics, business category, satisfaction level, transaction history, business culture—are just proxies for discovering the customer's *needs* and *value.*

To compete in the Interactive Age we have to be able to treat different customers differently, and that means understanding customer differences. The value of a customer determines how much time and investment should be allocated to that customer, and a customer's needs represent the key to keeping and growing that customer.

Customer Valuation

The traditional aggregate-market competitor treats all customers the same. They all receive the same product benefits, they are charged the same price, and they aren't engaged in individualized interactions. But if we acknowledge that each customer is unique, then we can take full advantage of the fact that some customers are simply more valuable than others.

To think about customer valuation the right way we need to use two concepts: the customer's *actual* current valuation, and the customer's *strategic*, or potential, valuation. For the purposes of this chapter, we're going to limit our discussion to actual customer valuations. In Chapter 5, we'll analyze what it means to think about a customer's strategic valuation.

The ideal expression of actual valuation is customer lifetime value (LTV), the stream of expected future profits, net of costs, on a customer's transactions, discounted at some appropriate rate back to its current net present value. Remember, however, that the profit on a customer's relationship with a firm is not necessarily derived just from future purchases the customer makes. Customers also give a firm other benefits, such as referrals of other customers, knowledge of other customers' tastes and preferences (as well as their own), and help in designing new products or services.

From this stream of profits we must then deduct expenses. Maintaining any sort of relationship will require communicating individually (via phone, fax, e-mail, personal sales call, and so forth), as well as setting up information systems necessary to track and remember interactions. These costs must not only be calculated but, whenever possible, allocated to the specific customers to whom they apply. Those who call in to customer service the most will cost the firm more money to serve.

While it's important to keep LTV in mind, it isn't really a quantity that *can* be precisely calculated for any particular customer. No matter how sophisticated our modeling methods become, we will never be able to factor in *all* the variables, including nonquantifiable ones, such as the help we might get in designing a product. LTV is essentially a forecast based on probabilities. While certain groups of customers might yield a fairly accurate *average* LTV, we will never know precisely what a particular customer will do in the future, even if we knew exactly how to value it. But that's okay for this discussion. The purpose here is to *compare* customers, and we'll be able to compare them more and more accurately as information technology makes increasingly sophisticated modeling possible.

A subscription business with frequent repeat purchase provides an ideal venue for this kind of modeling. Suppose you were the circulation director at a weekly magazine. Your standard new customer offer is a one-year subscription at less than half the regular price, or $35.90. Let's say that 40 percent of your first-year customers drop out, while 60 percent resubscribe in year two at the higher, regular rate of $75.90. Then, 65 percent of those who are still left resubscribe the next year, 70 percent the next year, and so forth. Let's assume variable costs—mailing, soliciting resubscriptions, and printing, net of ad revenues—total $30 per year.

You can easily use a spreadsheet to model this scenario. You have all the statistics, and your goal is simply to gain an understanding of the "average" customer's actual, long-term value to you. How much profit can you reasonably expect from, say, a thousand typical customers recruited in year one, given the costs and attrition rates you predict?

The table on the following page shows that after acquiring a thousand customers in year one, you can expect a total stream of profits of nearly $100,000 over a ten-year period, the net present value of which, when discounted at a rate of 15 percent, is a meager $67,000, or $67 per customer. By the time you reach year ten, only 65 of the original thousand customers you started with will still be your customers. Furthermore, if it costs, say, $50 to recruit a new subscriber, then your actual NPV profit, over and above acquisition costs is only about $17 per customer.*

For a magazine with several years' history on hundreds of thousands of subscriptions, modeling customer LTV is fairly straightforward. Using this model, if we were to increase the renewal rate by just 2 percent, from 60 percent to 62 percent in the first year, 67 percent in the second, and so forth, on up to a "terminal" renewal rate of 82 percent, instead of the 80 percent shown on the table above, then the average new customer's LTV would increase by 7.5 percent. If the marketing costs of obtaining these customers remains at $50 each, then the leverage is truly phenome-

---

* We could have extended our business model out to 15 or 20 years, or even more, but for simplicity's sake we tabulated figures for only the first ten years of a customer's relationship with us. As a practical matter, because of the combination of net-present-value discounting and customer attrition, the difference in NPV profit between a ten-year model and a twenty-year model is very small, at least for this particular set of assumptions.

YEAR	TOTAL SUBSCR.	RENEWAL RATE	SUBSCR. REVENUE	VARIABLE COSTS	NET PROFIT	NPV at 15%
1	1000	60%	$35,900	$30,000	$ 5,900	$ 5,900
2	600	65%	$45,540	$18,000	$27,540	$23,948
3	390	70%	$29,601	$11,700	$17,901	$13,536
4	273	75%	$20,721	$ 8,190	$12,531	$ 8,239
5	205	78%	$15,541	$ 6,143	$ 9,398	$ 5,373
6	160	79%	$12,122	$ 4,791	$ 7,330	$ 3,645
7	126	80%	$ 9,576	$ 3,785	$ 5,791	$ 2,504
8	101	80%	$ 7,661	$ 3,028	$ 4,633	$ 1,742
9	81	80%	$ 6,129	$ 2,422	$ 3,706	$ 1,212
10	65	80%	$ 4,903	$ 1,938	$ 2,965	$ 843
				Total:	$97,695	$66,940
					LTV	$ 66.94

nal. A mere 2 percent increase in retention would raise the actual value of each new customer, net of acquisition costs, by more than 25 percent—from $17 to $22. [We have put this table of figures and other more comprehensive retention-attrition spreadsheet models on our Web site (http://www.marketing1to1.com). Feel free to sign on and try out a few scenarios for yourself.]

With this kind of leverage, we have to ask ourselves why it is that so many firms concentrate so heavily on trying to figure out which new prospects to turn into customers, when they could so easily turn such a high profit by keeping the customers they have for a longer period.

Our magazine example might be simple to visualize, but the actual LTV calculation for most companies is more complex, sometimes too complex even to model very precisely. Among other complications, the nonmonetary components are sometimes much more significant. At Harley-Davidson, for instance, even if the number of dollars two bikers spend is identical, the one who is out there riding every day is a billboard for Harley, but the one who rides only a few days a year is not so valuable.

The benefits of modeling LTV are not just understanding the *average* customer's valuation and the leverage that different variables, like customer retention, might have on the company's overall value. We also use LTV to create a reliable rank-ordering system, allowing a firm to *differentiate* its customers by their individual valuations and to allocate more marketing time and effort to retaining the most valuable customers. While LTV is the rank-ordering system of choice, if it can be defined and measured, most companies settle for some sort of "proxy variable" instead. A mail order firm might use what is known as an RFM model to rank-order its customers based on the *recency, frequency,* and *m*onetary value of each customer's purchases. Airlines count miles flown. Car washes may just tally license plates.

One thing should be immediately clear, however: The 1:1 enterprise, because it treats its customers as individually as possible, will try to understand the *relative* valuation of each of them. Customers are individually different, and have individually different values to a company, and the most accurate picture of a customer's value is LTV.

Some customers are simply worth more than others.

But wait a second here. Didn't we just make the explicit assumption that a magazine's customers are all the same? Didn't we just compile a table of renewal rates over a ten-year period, and the result was an *average* LTV? Yes and no. Most magazines will have enough *other* data about their customers, including the kind of neighborhoods they live in, their response to related offers, and their promptness in paying, to be able to break their customers out into different groups, with different renewal patterns and different expected LTVs.

However, even if the only thing you know about your own magazine's customers is how long they've been subscribing, you can still separate them into different LTVs. The more times a subscriber renews, at least over the first few years, the more likely he is to renew again, and therefore the higher his LTV is. He's the same customer, but as he stays with the magazine, his loyalty—and therefore his LTV—increases. With the original assumptions we made for renewal rates, a brand-new subscriber is worth around $67, but once he agrees to renew the subscription at the end of the first year, he's worth $118, and after his fifth resubscription he's worth $147. (See table on following page.)

YEAR	TOTAL SUBSCR.	RENEWAL RATE	SUBSCR. REVENUE	VARIABLE COSTS	NET PROFIT	NPV at 15%	TEN-YEAR LTV
1	1000	60%	$ 35,900	$ 30,000	$ 5,900	$ 5,900	$ 66.94
2	600	65%	$ 45,540	$ 18,000	$ 27,540	$ 23,948	$ 118.12
3	390	70%	$ 29,601	$ 11,700	$ 17,901	$ 13,536	$ 129.15
4	273	75%	$ 20,721	$ 8,190	$ 12,531	$ 8,239	$ 138.35
5	205	78%	$ 15,541	$ 6,143	$ 9,398	$ 5,373	$ 143.45
6	160	79%	$ 12,122	$ 4,791	$ 7,330	$ 3,645	$ 145.55
7	126	80%	$ 9,576	$ 3,785	$ 5,791	$ 2,504	$ 146.81
8	101	80%	$ 7,661	$ 3,028	$ 4,633	$ 1,742	$ 146.81
9	81	80%	$ 6,129	$ 2,422	$ 3,706	$ 1,212	$ 146.81
10	65	80%	$ 4,903	$ 1,938	$ 2,965	$ 843	$ 146.81
11	52	80%	$ 3,922	$ 1,550	$ 2,372	$ 586	
12	41	80%	$ 3,138	$ 1,240	$ 1,898	$ 408	
13	33	80%	$ 2,510	$ 992	$ 1,518	$ 284	
14	26	80%	$ 2,008	$ 794	$ 1,214	$ 197	
15	21	80%	$ 1,607	$ 635	$ 972	$ 137	
16	17	80%	$ 1,285	$ 508	$ 777	$ 96	
17	14	80%	$ 1,028	$ 406	$ 622	$ 66	
18	11	80%	$ 823	$ 325	$ 497	$ 46	
19	9	80%	$ 658	$ 260	$ 398	$ 32	
20	7	80%	$ 526	$ 208	$ 318	$ 22	

Now imagine you were to calculate your customers' values individually and then rank-order them into just five equal groups, or quintiles, somewhat as National Australia Bank did.* Each quintile of customers should represent 20 percent of your customers. If you were to produce a bar chart to display the actual valuation of the customers in each of these quintiles, it might look like this:

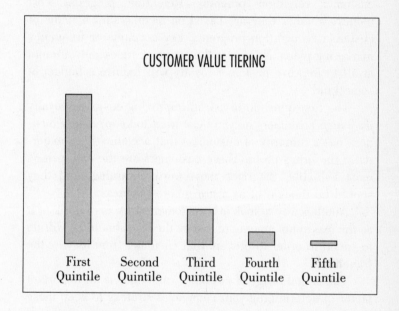

CUSTOMER VALUE TIERING

First Quintile   Second Quintile   Third Quintile   Fourth Quintile   Fifth Quintile

Every company's quintile chart will look different, but it is not uncommon for each quintile to be two or even three

---

* While National Australia bank used five value-based tiers, labeled A through E, they were not actually quintiles because the tiers were composed of different numbers of customers. The bank simply located a few logical "break points" in valuation, and divided its customers into groups accordingly. Then, by concentrating its efforts on providing additional services and benefits to the top two groups, it was able to grow the size of these more profitable groups.

times the size of the next biggest quintile. Clearly, the bulk of this particular firm's business is delivered by the top 20 percent of its customers.

Of course, instead of quintiles we could tier our customers by value into four quartiles, or ten deciles, or a hundred percentiles. Having an idea of a customer's actual valuation is essential if, for instance, a company wants to launch a customer retention program. Retention programs cost money, whether they are based on membership benefits or customer recognition programs, key accounts or frequency marketing plans. No matter the venue of attack, any attempt at all to improve customer loyalty will require a budget of some kind.

The first question to ask in improving customer loyalty is: *Which* customers do you most want to keep? Every business has a minority of customers that accounts for a majority of the firm's profit. These customers are the enterprise's most valuable, the ones most worth retaining, and they should be thought of as a firm's core business.

Another way to look at a customer's LTV is to think of it as the maximum amount of money the firm should be willing to spend in order to prevent that customer from leaving the franchise.

The actual *range* of customer valuations is an important factor in determining your company's strategy to keep these customers. Some businesses have a steeper "skew" of values than others, so in order to develop the right strategy, we need to know how flat or steep the skew is. An airline or car rental firm is likely to have a *very* steep skew, with a small percentage of travelers accounting for a very large proportion of revenues and profits. Pharmacies, brokerage houses, and computer manufacturers would also be likely to have steep value skews, as would a commercial construction contractor with two or three key clients who do as much business as its 50 other clients put together, or a toy manufacturer that sells 40 percent or more of its products to just three retail chains.

Other businesses have customers with less diverse valuations. A hamburger chain, a bookstore, or perhaps a janitorial service is likely to have a flatter skew:

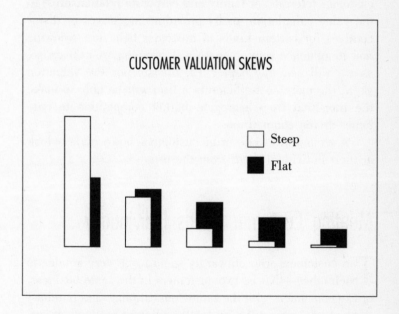

CUSTOMER VALUATION SKEWS

☐ Steep
■ Flat

If a business has a relatively steep customer valuation skew, it will be naturally attracted to marketing initiatives that emphasize the importance of its best customers—initiatives such as key account sales programs or frequency marketing plans. A business that has a customer base with little skew will have less reason to allocate its marketing budget disproportionately to one set of customers, at least based on customer valuation.

Each firm has a customer base with a "natural" skew that can be pictured by calculating individual customer values and then arranging them in rank order. A company can influence this skew somewhat by tracking customers more precisely, by explicitly including additional variables (like customer referrals, or family and corporate relationships) in the value calculation, or by providing incentives or disincentives for certain kinds of customer behavior. Knowing how to influence your company's skew is important because, as we will see in Chapter 13, the steeper the valuation skew, the more cost-efficiently a firm will be able to make the transition from aggregate-market competition to customer-driven competition.

A second way to describe customers, however, is to look at their individual *needs from* the firm.

Meeting Customer Needs Individually

Two customers who outwardly seem to be very similar to each other—that is, two customers in the same business, or two consumers with the same demographics and purchasing history—may still want totally different products or services from the enterprise. Even a standardized product manufactured the same way every time with the same product features is often used differently by different customers.

Some businesses are characterized by customers with a very diverse set of needs, while others are characterized by customers with fairly uniform needs. Clothing marketers, entertainment companies, and manufacturers of complex, made-to-order business equipment, for instance, are likely to have a base of customers with highly differentiated needs. No two people are likely to have the same exact pants size, nor to enjoy the same exact mix of classic rock and Verdi. On the other hand, a farm operator who grows corn or wheat is likely to find that his customers all have the same basic use for his product. Similarly, a gas station is unlikely to have many customers who need gas for any purpose other than to propel their vehicles.

Just because a product is a commodity doesn't mean that customers can't be diverse in their needs and uses of that product. A retail lending operation deals in the commodity of money, in a largely price-driven and highly efficient market. As a result, many of these companies treat their customers as commoditylike and interchangeable. Other lenders—like Farm Credit—know that two different borrowers requesting the same loan, with the same exact terms and conditions, could be doing so for two quite different reasons.

Differentiating your customers by their needs and then addressing those individual needs individually is a simple, commonsense selling technique. It is also one of the most powerful steps you can take toward increasing customer loyalty and unit margin.

US West Direct publishes Yellow Pages directories. Against a background of escalating sales costs and threatened competition from other Yellow Pages providers, the firm recently began tailoring its selling effort to each individual business customer rather than continuing to segment the effort by territory, directory title, and advertising product.

US West's research found that businesses choose

whether and *how* to advertise in the Yellow Pages in order to satisfy one of five principal kinds of needs. One customer, for instance, might want to grow his businesses faster than his competitors, while another might need to reach a small niche of the market more efficiently. A growth-oriented customer will almost certainly want highly noticeable ads, and each ad might show a different phone number, allowing the company to track the effectiveness of different ads and to measure the overall effectiveness of the Yellow Pages compared to other media. A niche marketer, on the other hand, will be more concerned about ensuring that potential customers can find the firm easily, no matter what category they might turn to. He may want a one-line listing in several different books and under a variety of different headings in each.

In the process of researching its customers' different needs, US West was also careful to identify a few very specific questions that a sales rep could use to map a particular customer into the right group. For example, "How do you see your business in five years?" After categorizing the customer, the sales rep can turn the discussion toward the key points most likely to persuade *this* customer to buy more advertising from the company. The rep also records the customer's categorization in the firm's marketing database, so all future marketing initiatives with respect to that customer will start with the customer's own particular needs.

US West has always had the ability to give different customers what they wanted—whether it was a splashy ad with a unique phone number or a dozen one-line listings in different product categories. The company's standard "Six-Step Selling Process" enumerated each of these potential benefits and discussed how each could be of benefit to a business. But *every* customer was exposed to *every* benefit, and had to choose for itself, from among all the options available, which type of strategy would be most useful.

The Yellow Pages ad campaign is easily customized to fit the individual advertiser's requirements. But even an apparently noncustomizable, commoditylike product—one that appears to have a simple, straightforward purpose—will often be purchased by customers who have dramatically different needs for it. By understanding the individual needs behind a customer's purchase, an enterprise can sell additional products and services to this customer, creating a more profitable, long-term relationship.

Consider Iomega, for instance—or any other maker of tape and disk backup products. Iomega's biggest product hits, so far, have been the Zip Drive, a 100-megabyte disk-drive backup system, and the Jaz, a similar system that provides a gigabyte of storage space. The firm makes and sells both the drive mechanisms themselves and the media for them, the tapes and disks that get inserted into the drives.

Each of these products connects conveniently to a PC and, on the surface, each serves a simple purpose: backing up data. But how might Iomega analyze the particular *needs* its customers are meeting with this set of products? Trans-actional records (if the firm maintains them on individual end-user customers) will show that some customers buy the mechanisms, some buy the media, and some buy both. If a customer is a repeat buyer of backup media, then we might be tempted to visualize this customer as someone who is storing large amounts of data off-line.

But the truth is, individual customers might buy any of Iomega's products for at least four independent reasons:

1. *Reliability* A customer may want to back up his data every week, or every night, to make sure he doesn't suffer much damage if his system crashes.

2. *Security or privacy* Another customer may want to remove his data periodically, keeping it out of the system so as to protect commercial secrets or to ensure privacy.

3. *Mobility* Or, a customer might have one PC at his office, another at home, and another at a different office. Rather than shipping massive amounts of data over the phone lines, he transfers the data from place to place on a Zip or Jaz disk.

4. *Capability* Still another customer may have an old PC with a smaller hard drive. If he wants more memory capacity without having to purchase a new PC, he can supplement his system with an Iomega product.

If Iomega only knew *why* a customer was considering its product, then at a minimum it could customize its sales pitch to that customer. Eventually, it could even customize its product, or the services surrounding it.

If a customer purchases a Jaz disk from Iomega in order to ensure his computer's reliability, then why not incorporate a periodic reminder screen into the Jaz's own software? Every twenty-four hours or so, the software could flash a warning screen to the computer user suggesting that it's time to back everything up again. For a customer who purchases the same product, to transport data from PC to PC, Iomega could create automatic disk comparisons to avoid duplication, with a manual "flag" on the Jaz disk to indicate whether it is going or coming.

Even if a firm already organizes its marketing efforts by market segment rather than relying on a straight product-management approach, in most cases these markets will be defined either demographically or by industry rather than by customer.

The Lego Group uses a market management system to ensure that its many products are positioned, promoted, and sold correctly to the various markets for whom they are intended. There is a manager in charge of younger boys ages five to eight, one in charge of somewhat older boys, another in charge of mothers of young boys, etc. These markets correspond roughly to the types of toys Lego produces, although every toy also has a product manager responsible for it elsewhere in the company. By defining its markets in strictly demographic terms, Lego's advertising is more efficient.

A more useful way for Lego to define its customers, however, would be by the particular *needs* they have. Three seven-year-old boys, for instance, might use the same Lego toys for at least three different reasons:

1. *Role playing* One boy enjoys pretending that he is the captain of the spaceship he's just built with the blocks.

2. *Constructing* Another enjoys using the diagrams that come with the blocks to figure out how to put things together.

3. *Creativity* Still another uses the blocks simply to create interesting and novel things, avoiding diagrams altogether.

If Lego knows that a seven-year-old boy is a "constructor," it could offer more diagrams, even a separate catalogue of diagrams. A "role player" could be sold videotapes and storybooks to accompany the Lego sets he owns. These *needs* could be crossed with each boy's *interests*—play preferences such as medieval castles, pirates, rescue squads, or space travel.

Any marketer can overlay third-party demographics onto a list of current or prospective customers, but information about an *individual's* needs and preferences can come only from talking with that customer.

There are many barriers that inhibit companies like Lego or Iomega from addressing their end-users' individual needs. Many of these barriers exist in the company's own distribution system, which is set up to move products through trade channels rather than to relate to end-user customers individually.

Using Dialogue to Learn a Customer's Needs

The most obvious problem, of course, is that Lego and Iomega don't have direct sales forces as US West does, nor do they have a branch lending system as Farm Credit does. Instead, these firms sell most of their products not to end users but to intermediaries in the distribution chain. They have no mechanism for conducting a dialogue with their end users, except for the small minority of customers who call the firm's customer service number.

Using standard market research, either firm could discover what needs customers with different demographic or psychographic characteristics are *most likely* to want to satisfy with its products. But that still doesn't allow the firm to customize its sales message, its product features, or its delivery mechanism to fit the individual requirements of a specific customer. If either firm is to turn itself into a 1:1 enterprise—if either one hopes to create Learning Relationships with its customers individually in order to lock them in as loyal customers and improve its unit margins over the long run, it must first create some sort of feedback link to end users.

Determining how a particular seven-year-old child in, say, Nebraska, uses his Lego set may sound like a difficult proposition for a large plastic-products manufacturer headquartered in a small town in Denmark. Lego is separated from this customer by a U.S. subsidiary and a network of wholesale distributors and retail chains. However, even seven-year-olds get on the World Wide Web these days. If Lego were simply to invite dialogue from its customers by printing the address of its Web site on its packaging and the included written material, it might find out some things about individual customers.

Officials at Lego have already counted more than thirty Internet news groups and Web sites for Lego toy enthusiasts all around the world, set up by the enthusiasts themselves. Lego could attract the enthusiasts to a company-sponsored Web site even without competing with the other sites by offering customers the chance to do interesting things, like swapping stories, or downloading complicated diagrams of different Lego toy structures. Lego could make it easy to get highly specialized pieces, or customize sets of replacement parts based on what a customer wants to build next, and make all this easier with on-line inventory control. Then, as the PC penetrates more and more homes, and as the various interactive tools available to consumers continue to increase in utility, Lego could probably expect to hear from a larger proportion of its most enthusiastic, and most valuable, end users.

At first glance, it might seem that Iomega will have a more difficult problem generating any meaningful dialogue with its customers, who have no reason to go on-line to swap stories or ideas. On the other hand, since the company is in the technology business, it can assume a very large proportion of its customers have modems.

For those who call in to the company's customer service line, an Iomega rep could ask one or two questions about how the product will be used and map the customer into a needs-based category. To implement this, the firm would have to do a bit of research to create the right needs-based groupings, and arm its phone sales reps with scripts. Then Iomega could put in place a customer database to capture the information, so that when a customer calls in again, the firm already knows his history from previous interactions.

For many of Iomega's end users, the most obvious way to get this kind of feedback is to include a written survey with the warranty card. If it's useful to learn from a warranty card such facts as how a buyer first heard about the product, or where the product was bought, then it's certainly useful to learn what the customer plans to *do* with the product. The firm needs to place questions in the survey that when asked of an end user will reveal the true reasons behind that particular customer's use of the product.

But if Iomega is like most such firms, the number of end users who actually return warranty cards is probably in the range of 20 percent or less. Therefore, the firm must take some steps to ensure that a greater proportion of end users fill it out and return it. One way to do this would be to create an electronic registration form that could be sent in by modem, or printed out and mailed in a postage-paid envelope.

The most obvious way to get registrations returned would be simply to *remove the barriers* that prevent customers from sending them in. As we will see in Chapter 12, removing the barriers that stand between your customer and you is a simple, direct way to increase the amount of business you obtain. It is a principle that should be applied whenever you are trying to get the customer to do anything at all. A firm in Iomega's situation might consider several steps to increase response rates.

- Put the warranty card on the outside of the packing material, so it is the first thing a customer sees after opening the box.

- Put the model and serial number for the equipment on the warranty card in advance, so the customer doesn't have to look anything up.

- Assure the customer that registering the product will not result in any additional mail or solicitations, or allow the customer to "opt out" of such additional communications simply by checking a box.

- Allow a customer to register the product using a variety of media—mail, e-mail, fax, or by calling a toll-free number.

There may also be ways to generate a greater return of warranty cards by performing some service for an end user that is actually connected to the user's need for the product in the first place. The "reminder screen" prompting a user to back up his data could double as a prompt urging him to register his product, for example.

Even after making it more convenient, it may still be necessary to provide some sort of incentive to the customer—perhaps a discount on a future upgrade, a complimentary magazine subscription, or a free gift of some sort. There is a technique to collecting information when the enterprise plans to use it, not to create summary research, but to develop a better understanding of each individual customer's needs. Every communication, every response from a customer, has the potential to tell a 1:1 enterprise more about exactly what that particular customer wants.

*If a firm is not in direct touch with its customers,
then every single interaction is a priceless opportunity
to learn more.*

Almost all new car purchasers' identities are known to a manufacturer, because the car itself is sold with such specific sets of warranties and guarantees. But few auto companies are very proficient at tracking those names over time. Dealers don't necessarily like the idea of "their" customers dealing directly with the manufacturer anyway, and cars get sold to other drivers after a few years. So the most common mechanism most auto companies have for obtaining a current list of the people who own their cars is to buy that list from a company like R. L. Polk, which gets its information mostly by buying it from various state motor vehicle departments.

To establish and maintain contact directly with its owners—even people who bought their cars used—one car company was preparing to launch an owner-management program involving roadside assistance, a newsletter of touring information, driving tips, and other features. To encourage owners to sign up for the program to begin with, the firm concluded it would need to provide an incentive, in the form of a free gift, for which they were prepared to budget about $10. Enlist in their program, send in your name and address and a little information about your family, and the car company would provide . . . what? The first idea was to give out a free pair of racing gloves. But not everyone would find racing gloves attractive. So the firm considered other gifts with different kinds of appeal, such as a discount on an oil change or a collapsible umbrella.

Finally, this car company hit on the very commonsense idea of allowing a customer to *choose* an incentive from among a small selection. But the selection was designed to be eclectic enough that the gift a particular car owner chose would tell the firm a great deal about that customer's future needs. The items the customer could choose from included a pair of racing gloves, a collapsible umbrella, a road atlas, and a package of three children's videotapes.

No matter what an enterprise sells—from cars to car washing, from bank loans to disk-drive backup systems—its various customers will (1) buy to satisfy different needs, and (2) return different values to the enterprise. It has always been this way, but only recently, as information technology has improved, has it actually become possible for an enterprise to identify and act on these customer differences in a cost-efficient way.

By tracking customers individually, interacting with them, and then treating different customers differently, the 1:1 enterprise can change the nature of competition entirely, generating increased customer loyalty as well as higher unit margins. In the next few chapters, as we examine the differences among a firm's customers in more detail, we will propose a variety of strategies to deal with different types and levels of customer differentiation in the Interactive Age. We'll provide specific examples of companies that have tried to capitalize on the differences they have identified among their customers. Some have succeeded, and some have not. Then, beginning with Chapter 6, we'll show how to create impregnable relationships with individual customers not only by interacting with them, but by treating different customers differently, right down to the level of the individual.

MAPPING THE STRATEGY

3

How to Use Your Customer Base to Map Out Your 1:1 Strategy

T hink for a minute about the differences between airlines and bookstores, in terms of each one's base of customers. An airline's customers are characterized by a very steep value skew, with a small proportion of high-value customers accounting for the vast majority of the airline's profit. Once an airline customer is on board the aircraft, however, there is very little different about the service needed. What the passenger wants is what every other passenger wants—to get safely and comfortably from point A to point B, on time. The bookstore's customer base, on the other hand, doesn't have nearly as steep a value skew as the airline, even though clearly some customers will consume more in any given year than others. But everyone who goes in to a bookstore will want a *different* book, and there may literally be a hundred thousand or more to choose from.

Every enterprise's customer base can be characterized in these ways—by customers who have a diverse set of values (as in the airline's case) or a diverse set of needs (as in the bookstore's). Of course, a customer base could also be highly differentiated on both counts, or on neither. The nature of customer differentiation at a firm can point the way to an appropriate marketing strategy, and that's what we're going to discuss in this chapter. Depending on how differentiable your firm's customer base is in terms of these two characteristics, your "natural" competitive strategy might be mass marketing, niche or target marketing, key account selling, or something else.

In the following pages we're going to show you a tool for thinking about your customer base, and then we'll show you a similar tool for dealing with the enterprise capabilities you need to pursue an appropriate strategy. By comparing your enterprise's capabilities with the type of customer base you serve, you can actually map out a *new* strategy, aimed at improving those capabilities most needed to turn your business into more of a 1:1 enterprise.

We should warn you that this chapter introduces a number of new concepts. It may seem like a lot to absorb all at once, but to make it easier we've included some diagrams we hope you'll find helpful, and we tried to illustrate most of our points with real-world examples. When you get to the end you'll probably be drawing the diagrams yourself.

If your business has customers who possess widely varying tastes and preferences, like the bookstore, or a clothing manufacturer, or an entertainment company, then it makes sense for you to differentiate your customers first on their *needs*. Naturally, the more customers differ from one another in things like tastes and sizes, the more benefit can be gained from offering a variety of products, and even customizing—treating different customers differently right down to the individual level. On the other hand, while the airline industry has customers who are highly differentiated in terms of their value to the firm, these same customers are much more uniform in their needs and preferences, so customization is less compelling, while a more appropriate strategy would be to secure the continued loyalty of those most valuable customers—even purchasing their loyalty, if necessary, by rewarding them for their continued patronage.

In the Customer Differentiation Matrix below, we have divided the range of potential business situations into four basic quadrants, depending on how diverse the enterprise's customers are, in both needs and valuations:

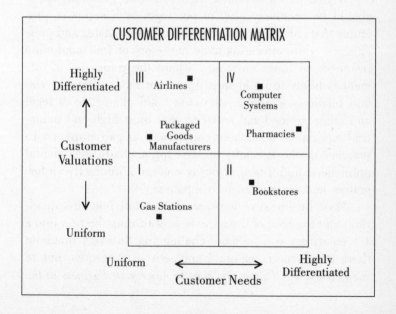

True 1:1 marketing is easier to implement and more beneficial to the firm in Quadrant IV, at the upper right of this matrix, where a business is characterized by customers who are clearly diverse both in needs and valuations. One example of a Quadrant IV business is the computer systems manufacturer who sells direct to consumers and other businesses. Think of Dell, for instance, and all the different ways a customer might need to have his computer system configured. Dell offers more than 10,000 different combinations and permutations of system configurations, and it recommends a particular configuration based on what its telephone representative learns during his or her discussion with the customer. Dell's customers also come in a wide range of sizes, from the $1,000 single-purchase consumer to the $500,000 multisystem enterprise that buys repeatedly.

If your firm's customer base falls into Quadrant IV, it should be relatively easy to put together a series of programs that cater to customers with different tastes and preferences, while allocating more and more of your marketing resources to those customers where the return on investment is likely to be highest. Quadrant IV is where we can find businesses such as the best hotel chains, most legal and other professional services, and most high-end industrial equipment manufacturers, as well as gardening, cooking, and similar specialty lifestyle firms, pharmacies, digital publishers, and a host of newly emerging interactive information and entertainment companies.

Most businesses, however, do not fall into this quadrant, and for each of them the task of turning the firm into a 1:1 enterprise can be more challenging. In every quadrant there are certain "natural" competitive strategies, but *in each case we will show you how to move your business in the direction of Quadrant IV*, where you'll earn more customer loyalty and higher unit margins by creating interactive 1:1 relationships with individual customers.

Quadrant III businesses, in the upper left of our diagram, are those characterized by commoditylike services or products but diverse customer valuations. That is, even though the customers of a Quadrant III business have fairly uniform needs from the firm, they will have wide variations in their value to the firm. In Quadrant III we might find businesses such as airlines, car washes, and packaged goods firms, or other businesses that sell primarily to warehouse distributors and similar commodity intermediaries.

Airlines fall into Quadrant III because, while a small minority of business customers account for the vast majority of all air travel, the customers all get the same commoditylike service from the airline. Routes and schedules are different, of course, but prices are matched instantaneously by all competitors and, within any given category of air carrier, the service is totally generic. Once onboard the aircraft, there is no mad scramble among passengers for a particular seat or any other kind of special service.

A similar situation applies to a packaged goods manufacturer as well as to many other firms that sell to intermediate warehouse/distributors, or to large retail chains. Each of these firms' business customers is likely to want the same basic mix of products and services from the manufacturer, because the stores being supplied all need to carry virtually the same set of products for consumers. On the other hand, some of these distributors or retailers are likely to do vastly greater volume than others, and to have correspondingly more value as customers to the firm.

The natural strategy for a business that finds itself in

Quadrant III is to secure the continued loyalty of those most valuable customers who mean the most to the business. For the airline, this strategy translates to a frequent flyer program, while for the packaged goods firm it will mean the development of a "key account" sales management structure.

If this is the nature of your own business, you should do two things: First, since your customers have widely varying valuations, be sure you can actually identify them by value, individually. If you don't track customer transactions now, you'll need to figure out how to do so very soon. Once your competitor figures it out, he'll take your customers away from you, starting first with the most valuable ones. So focus on best-customer loyalty. You might even want to *purchase* the loyalty of your most valuable customers, as the airlines purchase theirs with frequent flyer miles. Airlines know that without these very few high-value customers their entire business would be threatened. Or, if you have a direct sales force, you might allocate extra resources to your key accounts—those high-value customers without which you just wouldn't have a tenable business.

Second, however, a firm in Quadrant III should also be searching for new services, ancillary benefits, and added, customizable product features, to try to move the business to the right, toward Quadrant IV. By offering additional products and services you might be able to ignite additional, more diverse sets of needs among your customers.

We'll talk a good deal more in Chapter 8 about how to "replot" the customer base by adding services and ancillary products to expand the customer's set of needs, but let's consider a couple of examples now. A packaged goods manufacturer, for instance, could consider packaging or palletizing his products differently for different retail chains and distributors, or making an electronic connection with a customer's own inventory control system and automatically replenishing the customer's inventory. Airlines, on the other hand, might simply record and remember your regular onboard drink. Particularly if you travel first class, the flight attendant should be able to ask if you want your "usual" beverage when you sit down.

In Quadrant II, at the lower right of the Customer Differentiation Matrix, we find a business characterized by customers who have more diverse needs but relatively uniform valuations. In this case, the diversity in customer tastes and preferences presents an opportunity to cultivate long-lasting 1:1 relationships, but the lack of variation in customer valuations can make it difficult for a firm to prioritize its efforts. Quadrant II would include most businesses that sell apparel and fashion items to consumers, either in their own stores or directly; bookstores, music stores, and retail sellers of other information and entertainment products; automotive retailers; and many low-end consumer and business services such as tax-return preparation firms, florists, or janitorial services.

The natural strategy for a Quadrant II firm is to create different products and services for customers with different needs. An aggregate-market competitor will turn to segmented and niche marketing, increasing the variety of products and services it offers to accommodate each additional market niche. Segmented marketing offers different products to different customers if the business has little or no way of interacting with customers individually, or if the postal mail (which is still the dominant form of individually addressable media) is simply too costly for the particular products or services being sold. To operate efficiently, the niche marketer must have niche media—advertising vehicles that are specifically aimed at different target segments.

As computer power has enabled companies to analyze their customers in more and more detail, the result has been an expanding panoply of product choice for customers. But even though different segments of a market might be valued differently by a niche marketer, the individual customers within any given segment will all be valued the same. The niche marketer is still actually a mass marketer, only the masses are smaller.

One example of a needs-differentiation tactic is the Avid Reader Club offered by Smithbooks, a Canadian bookshop chain. The program, similar to Waldenbooks' Preferred Reader program in the United States, now has over 120,000 members. When a shopper joins the Avid Reader Club, some general demographic information is collected: age, income, children, hobbies, and so forth. But, most important, every purchase is tracked and linked to the individual member. Often compared to an airline frequent flyer plan, the Avid Reader frequent-buyer program is designed not so much to stratify customers by value (which is the main purpose of a frequent flyer program) as to differentiate them by *needs*.

While the program does reward repeat book buyers for their loyalty, gauging its success just in those terms would be wrong. Instead, by using a discount to entice customers to show their membership cards when they buy books, the firm is able to track different readers' interests in different subject matters and authors. This means, for instance, that any Avid Reader member who purchases an income tax preparation book might later receive a promotional flyer on financial planning books. Or when a new golf book is published, Smithbooks might dig into its customer database and mail an offer to each customer who has bought a golf book previously.

In order to move from Quadrant II toward Quadrant IV, the 1:1 enterprise must complete the feedback loop between an individual customer's specifications and how the firm behaves toward that customer. In other words, the enterprise must be capable of (1) *remembering* individual customer needs, and (2) *interacting* with individual customers in a cost-efficient manner. The major problem with today's "frequent buyer" programs, especially when they are applied to products and services with relatively small purchase prices like books (as opposed to air travel or computers), is that interacting with customers using the postal mail is just too costly and inefficient to make any sense.

It's worth pointing out here that the Customer Differentiation Matrix defines a natural strategy for a firm not based on the *product* it sells, but on the nature of the *customer base* it serves. Thus, even though retail bookstores clearly fall into Quadrant II, because everyone who enters a bookstore wants a different book, the book publishers themselves fall into Quadrant III. Publishers and bookstores sell the same physical products, but they sell them to completely different customer bases. The publisher doesn't sell to book readers, but to bookstores, and almost all bookstores want to have a similar, wide variety of books available for their own customers. On the other hand, while few if any consumers would buy hundreds of books in a year, some large bookstore chains may do hundreds of times more volume with a publisher than a smaller, independent book retailer does. In other words, while the *store's* customers are less diverse in value but more differentiable in what they need from the store, the *publisher's* customers have considerably different values to the publisher, but what various customers need *from* the publisher is very similar:

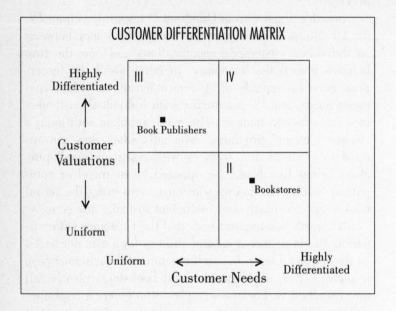

CUSTOMER DIFFERENTIATION MATRIX

Highly Differentiated

III

IV

■ Book Publishers

Customer Valuations

I

II

■ Bookstores

Uniform

Uniform ⟷ Highly Differentiated

Customer Needs

If customers are uniform in both their needs and their valuations, as they would be if your business is in Quadrant I, then the *natural* strategy is to treat them uniformly and continue with a traditional mass-marketing approach.

To move into Quadrant II, these firms must look for ways to "expand the customer need set" by attaching ancillary services and benefits to their products—services that can be more tailored than the commoditylike core product. Even the customers of a commodity grain dealer probably prefer to be invoiced at different times, for instance, or to have their individual delivery requirements and specifications remembered. Or, to go up in the matrix to Quadrant III, a Quadrant I business should make more efficient use of interactive technologies so that it can identify and connect with individual customers. It should also look for ways to track its customers' values more accurately and even to aggregate its customers into larger units, in order to create a more diverse set of valuations. A gas station owner, for instance, could track license plates to get a better idea of the different values of various customers. And if a customer comes from a two-car family, then the gas station obviously wants to fill both cars' tanks.

The following diagram shows the natural strategies for each of these quadrants, along with the "migration" strategies needed to move more toward doing business as a 1:1 enterprise:

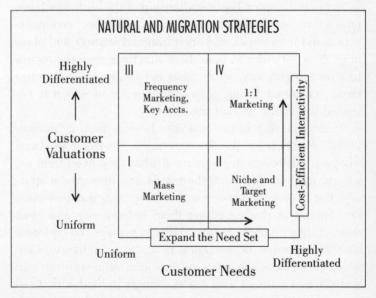

NATURAL AND MIGRATION STRATEGIES

Integrating the 1:1 Enterprise

A business can be mapped onto the Customer Differentiation Matrix simply by describing the diversity of its customer base. Depending on its position, the business will in fact tend to gravitate to certain natural competitive strategies.

In our description of how this matrix works for different businesses, we have also been *prescribing* a set of migration strategies for the firm—strategies designed to help the firm evolve itself toward the 1:1 enterprise business model. To implement any of these strategies will require the enterprise to adjust various mixes of the five corporate functions referred to in Chapter 1—custodianship of the customer base, production and logistics, distribution, customer communication and interaction, and organizational strategy and planning. Now, in order to map these functions onto the matrix in a meaningful way, we're going to collapse them into two basic "customer facing" capabilities, each of which is essential to moving around the matrix.

Custodianship of the customer base is, first, a "navigational" function for the 1:1 enterprise. Provided we *know* what our customers are worth and what they need from us, we can map our firm onto the matrix and prescribe a strategy. But in order to know what our customers want, we must be capable of distinguishing them individually and even *interacting* with them. So our ability to manage the customer base (as opposed to managing products or delivery channels, for instance) depends on how cost-efficiently we can address and interact with our customers individually. Custodianship of the customer base and communications with customers are clearly linked. We'll call this overall capability "communications flexibility," and in order to move *up* on the Customer Differentiation Matrix, an enterprise must be able to increase its communications flexibility. High communications flexibility exists if a firm can cost-efficiently interact with individual customers, while low communications flexibility limits the firm to sending out a uniform, one-way message to everyone.

The second enterprise function—production, logistics, and service delivery—determines how the enterprise "behaves" with respect to its customers. The more differentiable our customers are in terms of what they need from us, the more important it is for us to be flexible in our behavior toward them, delivering different products and services to different customers, even to the point of customizing individual products for individual customers if we can. Managing the sales channel and distribution function is necessary to facilitate the production and service delivery function, while the organization and planning function facilitates everything. This second overall enterprise capability we will label "production and logistics flexibility," and in order to move to the *right* on the Customer Differentiation Matrix, a firm must be able to increase its production and logistics flexibility. The most flexible production would involve customizing and delivering individual products made to order for individual customers. The least flexible would be mass producing a standard product or service for a large, aggregate market.

Simply put, there are two principal capabilities a firm must *improve* in order to move up or to the right on the Customer Differentiation Matrix. It must improve its flexibility in communications by figuring out how to increase the addressability and interactivity of the customer base, and it must improve its production flexibility by increasingly tailoring products and services to particular customer needs. This means our *descriptive* Customer Matrix can now become a *prescriptive* Capabilities Matrix:

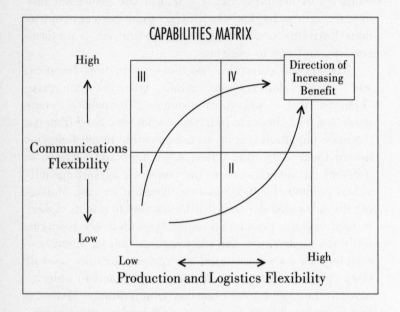

CAPABILITIES MATRIX

One implication of denominating our matrix with these new enterprise capabilities is that a firm may in fact plot its customer base into one part of the matrix, while the enterprise's current capabilities map it into another place altogether. In most cases, this is because the firm is not yet taking full advantage of the computing power now available to it, or is not as interactively connected to its customers as it could be. If a firm has customers with highly diverse valuations, but it hasn't yet taken steps to address its customers in a more individualized fashion, for instance, then it will be incapable of even prioritizing its marketing effort by customer. So while its customer base will map it into Quadrants III or IV of the Customer Matrix (highly differentiated valuations), its enterprise capabilities will map it into Quadrants I or II of the Capabilities Matrix (low communications flexibility).

The laser-printer business unit at Hewlett-Packard does not know most of its end users individually, because those users buy from intermediaries like retailers and value-added resellers (VARs). Hewlett-Packard must rely instead on identifying the small proportion of its customers who send in their registration cards. So, even though Hewlett-Packard's end-user customers would map into Quadrant IV, the company itself would probably map into Quadrant II—it produces a wide range of different products to meet a variety of customer needs, but it is not capable of individually addressing and interacting with more than a small proportion of its customer base. To succeed as a 1:1 enterprise, the firm must figure out how to establish interactive contact with a greater proportion of its customers. Alternatively, instead of focusing on end-user customers, Hewlett-Packard could choose to treat its distributors and resellers as customers, and with respect to *this* customer base its current capabilities would be a better match—both probably in Quadrant III (see Chapter 12).

Even if an enterprise does have direct contact with its customers and their needs are diverse, the firm may still find itself incapable of interacting with individual customers in a truly cost-efficient manner. Personal sales calls, mail, and toll-free help lines are cost-efficient in the computer peripherals business, but not in businesses with much lower unit margins. To make the case for this argument, let's return to a business with much lower unit prices—the bookstore.

Consider Amazon.com, Inc., the on-line, interactive bookstore. Amazon's position on the World Wide Web allows it not only to track customer interests and purchases, but also to interact with them very cost-efficiently. It is the interaction process itself that now drives the business. When a reader expresses an interest in a particular book title, Amazon will automatically suggest other, related titles. If you want to know when a book is released in paperback, Amazon will e-mail you. Ask them to keep you posted on new books in a particular area, and Amazon will feed a constant stream of useful information to you.

Not surprisingly, with this kind of business model Amazon is ideally positioned to generate sales from repeat customers. And when customers post messages and book reviews for other customers at Amazon's site, the result is often a whirlwind of additional "referral" sales. One obscure title, *Sponging: A Guide to Living Off Those You Love,* generated such a chorus of reader raves that it became an Amazon best seller.

With over a million titles available, Amazon offers five times as many books as the largest retail superstore. And because most of Amazon's books are not even ordered from distributors until a reader requests them, the firm's actual physical inventory consists of just a few best sellers—and turns over 150 times a year, compared with the four turns that most bookstores expect.

But while the economics of Amazon's business are unhampered by a costly interaction process, delivering physical products to customers who are not physically present in a store does pose a significant barrier. The company discounts most of its books 10 to 30 percent, but charges $3 per order and 95 cents per book for delivery in the United States. While this is a reasonably good deal in the U.S., Amazon's customer base is drawn from more than sixty countries, and delivery outside the U.S. can often be prohibitively expensive. It probably won't be long before a substantial number of authors begin offering their works electronically, through on-line stores like Amazon.

Realizing the Potential of the Customer Base

The more diverse the customer base is, the greater potential exists for creating individualized, profitable relationships. The first step is simply to ensure that the enterprise's own capabilities live up to this potential. By laying the Customer Matrix over the Capabilities Matrix, we'll see a strategy for developing a firm's capabilities to match the potential represented by its customer base. The result is an Enterprise 1:1 Strategy Map.

The Enterprise 1:1 Strategy Map is, fundamentally, a useful way to visualize how to transform your firm into a 1:1 enterprise. By comparing the characteristics of a firm's customer base to the capabilities the firm has for both allocating its investment in customers and flexibly producing and delivering its products and services, you can map out a strategy to become a more effective 1:1 enterprise. You can navigate more easily from where you are to where you want to be. For Hewlett-Packard's laser printer division, the Strategy Map would look like this:

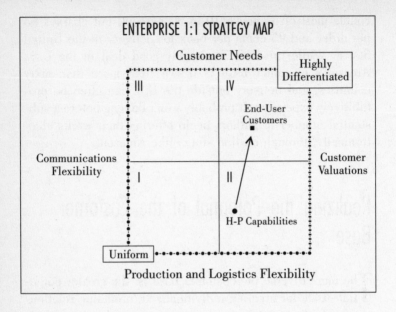

HP's most important task is to identify and make interactive contact with a larger proportion of its individual end users. The most obvious requirement is to generate a higher return rate for warranty cards, but a more effective tactic in the long term would be to offer some on-line help or service attractive enough to entice users to interact electronically. Regardless of the specific program or tactic employed, the more customers Hewlett-Packard identifies individually, and the more efficiently it can *interact* with those customers, the faster it will become a 1:1 enterprise.

In addition, even though HP's laser printing business already produces a wide range of products, there is clearly room for even more flexibility of production and delivery. New products and services could in fact be designed to help it establish and maintain interactive contact with its end users. For example, the firm might develop a "toner warning" for its print-manager software. When the toner cartridge is within a week or so of running low (based on the individual customer's rate of usage, as tracked by the software) a warning could flash onto the user's computer screen to install a new toner cartridge in a few days, accompanied by an invitation to place an order for another toner cartridge immediately for UPS delivery. The order could go by modem, fax, or through a toll-free number shown on the warning screen. To make this into a viable business proposition, Hewlett-Packard has to be willing either to sell cartridges directly to end users, or to relay orders from its end users to a distributor—perhaps to the same VAR who sold the original printer to this particular end user.

Another strategy for a firm such as Hewlett-Packard would be to focus not on the end user as a customer but on the distribution channel—the VAR, the system integrator, or even the retail chain. This is not strategically desirable in the long term for several reasons, including the simple fact that the actual end user of any product or service is at the very top of the "demand chain," and any other member of the chain is always under threat of being disintermediated by some new technology (we'll talk more about this issue in Chapter 12). But the short-term advantages of dealing with distributors as customers include the fact that a firm will already know their individual identities, and it is easier to establish a cost-efficient mechanism for interacting with them.

In addition to conforming the enterprise's current capabilities to the nature of its customer base, the Strategy Map also provides a prescription for making any business even more customer-driven by introducing programs and tactics designed to change the character of the customer base itself.

To continue with the computer industry, let's consider Dell. Dell's customers map the firm into Quadrant IV of the matrix, and the company's own capabilities map it into the same quadrant. Dell knows which of its end-user customers are worth the most because it is in direct contact with them, and it has a database of customer transactions, linked over time and integrated by individual customer. Therefore, Dell's capabilities are well suited to 1:1 marketing activities, and creating loyal, highly profitable customer relationships. The Dell customer base is certainly just as diverse as HP's in terms of needs and valuations—perhaps a bit more so, because Dell sells such a wide range of products, configured in thousands of different individual ways. But Dell itself is also capable of conforming its system configuration and its customer investment pretty closely to the potential of its customer base. Whether the firm actually does what it is capable of doing is another question, for a different book. For our purposes, let's agree that it comes close.

In this situation, if Dell is to make itself into more of a 1:1 enterprise, it should be working to replot its customer base by making its customers even more diverse. The principal way to do this would be by introducing ancillary products and services, perhaps delivered through strategic alliances with other firms—even Hewlett-Packard. By introducing products or services in related fields, Dell could in fact create a customer base that is more differentiated, both in what the customers individually need and in their valuations. The turn-key, flat-fee computer maintenance agreement it now offers to its midrange and larger corporate customers is one example of such an enhancement. A systems integration consulting service for high-end "enterprise" customers would be another. At the low end, a used-computer secondary market would create a more diverse set of customer needs. More strategies for expanding the customer need set like this will be discussed in Chapter 8.

So the Enterprise 1:1 Strategy Map for Dell involves not only moving the firm's capabilities, but actually moving the position of its customer base as well:

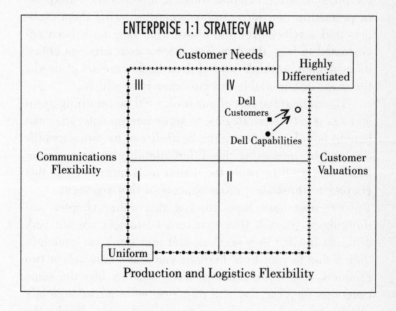

What's really going on here, as we plot both the customer base and the enterprise's capabilities, is that there are two ways for a business to migrate from lower left toward upper right. An enterprise can improve the flexibility of its own capabilities, *or* it can increase the differentiability of its customer base. Improving the enterprise's capabilities requires *better integration* of the production and service delivery work processes into the firm's knowledge of its customers and their needs. It requires finding more cost-efficient ways to identify customers and interact with them individually. Increasing the enterprise's capabilities is hard work, but for the most part it is internal work focused on gaining more from the enterprise's own work processes.

Increasing the differentiability of the customer base, on the other hand, is external work. It involves the enterprise in promoting new ideas to customers, showing them products and services over and above what they have been accustomed to from the firm. The more a company can entice its customers to think beyond their basic core set of needs, the more differentiable the customer base will be.

Throughout the rest of our book we'll be returning again and again to these strategies, to argue how an enterprise can benefit both by improving the flexibility of its own capabilities and by increasing the differentiability of its customer base. And we'll be using the matrix tools introduced in this chapter to illustrate various aspects of this argument.

You may have been reading this entire chapter and thinking to yourself that your own customers are not very different in what they need, or that they don't vary much in their value to your firm. Perhaps you make only one or two products, and these products have more or less the same functions for everyone. Or your firm sells an infrequently purchased product, with few repeat customers. Maybe the purpose of your business really is to be the lowest-cost producer of a product or service that sells as a near commodity, to nearly indistinguishable, interchangeable customers.

But *every* company can, in fact, take steps now either to improve the flexibility of its own capabilities or to replot the customer base itself. If your firm's current capabilities are already matched with the relative uniformity of your customer base, or if you think there is little chance to differentiate customers in your category, then you probably face a much greater opportunity than you could have imagined. When the business category you inhabit is characterized by companies who see their customers as uniform and undifferentiated, then becoming a 1:1 enterprise can prove to be a brilliant competitive strategy. The alternative is that you won't see this opportunity, but your competitor will.

After all, every one of your customers is entering the Interactive Age with you. As are your competitors.

At the very beginning of the book we said our objectives included showing you how to improve customer retention and protect unit margins. To do this, we first had to set the stage by analyzing how individual customers are individually different. From the examples we've used so far it should be clear that treating different customers differently will yield important benefits for the enterprise.

But the truth is, most managers don't simply wake up one day and decide they want to turn their firms into 1:1 enterprises. They don't start with the idea of creating 1:1 relationships and treating different customers differently. Instead, they wrestle first with some other issue or problem, and one of the most threatening issues any enterprise can face—an issue on the minds of a great many managers in an era of declining margins and volatile competition—is the problem of customer retention.

How does a firm go about the task of increasing the likelihood that customers will remain in the franchise, often in the face of dramatic and hard-to-resist promotions by competitors? Sooner or later, most businesses that tackle this problem come to the conclusion that the only reliable way to protect their customers from competitive predation is to create relationships with them.

Declining customer retention is exactly the problem MCI first faced just a few years ago. Before we go any further in our analysis of what it means to differentiate and interact with customers individually, we want to devote the entire next chapter to a detailed and revealing account of this one company's effort. No matter what your business is, this story will resonate with familiar-sounding issues for your own enterprise.

INFANT MORTALITY
AT MCI

4

How to Fix the "Leaky Bucket" of Customer Attrition—and How Not To

One of the most common problems any business faces today is how to increase customer retention—how to keep customers for a longer period and even grow them into bigger customers, in the face of increasingly strident competition. In this chapter we're going to treat you to an inside look at how one company conceived and executed a customer retention program. We'll first see how this program improved the firm's overall profitability, increasing both the loyalty and long-term profitability of a select group of customers, and then we'll watch as it dies, overcome by internal conflicts in the firm's organization, and by a corporate culture that didn't measure long-term profit, but instead focused itself exclusively on immediate, tactical customer-acquisition opportunities.

You may read this story thinking about all the ways your business is not like MCI's. But the lessons of this failure will still be relevant, because the organizational and cultural obstacles that defeated MCI's program will defeat yours, too, unless you are prepared to integrate a customer-driven competitive strategy throughout your entire enterprise. No matter what your business is, the scenarios you encounter in this chapter will have a familiar look to them.

The Background

MCI's long distance business was organized into two divisions, serving businesses and consumers. On the consumer side, the Marketing Department acquired new customers, using advertising, direct mail, and outbound telemarketing, and sold additional products to existing customers, using the same media vehicles. The Sales and Service Operations Department ran the company's six call centers, handling mostly inbound inquiries from the company's ten million current customers.

In 1992, MCI, AT&T, and Sprint were locked in a no-holds-barred competition for new customers. If you live in the United States and have a household income over $30,000, then you've almost certainly received a check from one long distance company or another for $25, $75, or even more, with instructions that simply depositing the check would automatically switch your long distance carrier. No further action required on your part. Just deposit the check. Putting checks out in the mail is a powerful customer acquisition weapon, no matter which company wields it, and since all of them were doing the same thing, the result was ferocious customer churn.

In the middle of this chaos the president of MCI's consumer business asked his newly appointed head of Sales and Service Operations to take on the task of improving customer loyalty. As one executive put it, the firm seemed to be "losing more customers out of the bottom of the bucket than we are pouring in at the top." The Marketing Department was pouring large numbers of new customers into the bucket, and Sales and Service was asked to fix the leaks— to keep these customers in the franchise.

MCI did have two groups of customers who were particularly loyal, despite being subjected to the same competitive entreaties as everyone else, and one of the first initiatives the firm took was to try to expand both these groups. The first consisted of customers who participated in MCI's Friends & Family program, a famously successful retention vehicle launched in 1991. When a customer goes to the trouble of recruiting a circle of friends and relatives for a discount from MCI, all the customers in the calling circle are then subject to their own mutual peer pressure not to disconnect. Second were the partner-recruited customers, mostly airline frequent flyers and credit card holders now earning rewards not just by flying more miles or charging more purchases, but also by using MCI's long distance services. The loyalty of these customers was related to their allegiance to the partner, whether it was Northwest Airlines or Citibank Visa.

Outside these two groups, however, MCI's customers were churning at an alarming rate, and the firm attacked the problem with short-term tactics as well as a more comprehensive long-term strategy.

The "Infant Mortality" Problem

The immediate tactical problem was that the propensity for any given customer to leave was highest in the first few months of the customer's tenure. Only about 70 percent of newly acquired customers remained for more than three or four months! Early customer attrition, inelegantly dubbed "infant mortality" by some of the company's staff, is common in most businesses. Magazines, TV cable companies, and credit card firms all find that renewal rates increase in proportion to the number of years a customer has remained with the company. But the extremely early attrition MCI was experiencing seemed almost perverse.

Research showed that by far the greatest proportion of early defectors came from those customers acquired via the most aggressive marketing offers, including the notorious check-in-the-mail program, the very promotions that had, until then, been considered the most "successful." The data showed unmistakably that the higher the conversion rate for any given promotion, the higher the infant mortality rate was among those conversions. Another way to state it, a way that would never have occurred to an aggregate-market competitor focused on getting more customers, is that for many of MCI's promotions, *the customer acquisition rate was apparently too high*!

Some people were switching back and forth, back and forth, in a kind of customer acquisition "squirrel cage," earning a nice return by maintaining their status as *prospective* customers to a firm's competitors. This is not an uncommon dynamic in any highly competitive business. Because aggregate-market competitors measure their success primarily on the basis of customers obtained, each firm's *prospective* customers are actually *more valuable to it than its current customers*! Savvier customers know how to convert that value differential for their own benefit, and no one should blame them.

In any case, based on this learning, MCI began to rethink its aggressive customer acquisition efforts. It soon launched a series of offers that required new customers to remain for some time before collecting. Instead of sending out a check for $50 in immediate cash, for instance, the firm tried offering a certificate good for $50 at the end of the customer's first three months with the company. It tested an offer of three free months of service to a new customer—not the *first* three months, but the third, ninth, and thirteenth months. And it tested the "savings bond"—a rebate certificate that grew dramatically in value over a customer's first eighteen months or so with the firm.

The first step any firm takes to staunch the immediate flow of defectors is usually just this straightforward: It attempts to "buy" the loyalty of its newest customers, as MCI did. While purchasing loyalty is often a good first tactic, it has its drawbacks when held up to the metrics that govern marketing success at most firms.

Naturally, none of MCI's "staged rebate" offers generated as large a conversion rate among prospects as did the check-in-the-mail promotion, and often the results were dramatically lower. But every one of the new offers was more successful at preventing infant mortality. In most cases, the customers who signed up in response to these restructured offers could be shown, over a period of just a few months, to be adding substantially more value to the customer base, even after allowing for their fewer numbers initially. In other words, one way to avoid having so many customers leaking out of the bottom of the bucket was to pour *fewer* in at the top, and make sure the ones being poured in were the right ones to begin with.

On the assumption that it was only a matter of time before their competitors also figured out that offering staged rebates rather than cash up front was a more cost-efficient way to acquire *and retain* customers, MCI then began wrestling with the issue of customer retention for the longer term. The company knew that just as they had been buying new customers with the check-in-the-mail offer, they were essentially just buying loyalty with the staged rebate. The long-term question was what else—besides bribery—could ensure customer loyalty?

Keeping Customers for the Long Haul

The first strategy in keeping customers longer is to figure out *which* customers? Obviously, the customers most worth keeping are those with the highest actual value to the firm, just like the customers most worth acquiring are the ones who are likely to spend the most. To identify its most attractive prospects, MCI relied on income projections and demographic comparisons from outside data sources, but to identify its most valuable current customers, the firm planned to use its own records of customer spending and behavior to rank-order its customers by their value.

MCI first tried to agree on a criterion for valuing customers individually, based on its detailed database of individual customer information and transactions. The problem they encountered, however, was that there simply was no such database. Instead, customer information came from a variety of unrelated databases within the firm, including the invoicing engine, call center files, and interconnect records. Altogether, these sources contained a year's worth of calling records, billing and payment information, and customer service transactions. More data, from earlier records, could be accessed by tapping into archived computer tapes.

But there was no reliable customer identifier that could be used to link the files of a single customer across multiple phone numbers, or from location to location. A customer who moved showed up as both a "lost" customer and a "new" one. A customer with more than one phone line in his home was usually not identified as one customer but two. And even though a customer might have called in to ask about a bill, or to request some other type of information, these interactions were not recorded unless some service action was taken, such as a new calling plan started or an old one terminated.

Similar issues are faced by many companies attempting to turn their operations into more customer-centered businesses.* The computer's power has grown so fast, and its use has become so ubiquitous, that in most firms there isn't just one database, but many. A firm might find that the same basic customer will show up in different databases for invoicing, customer service, and warranty claims. The firm may dub these databases "silos" or "chimneys," because each is a self-contained universe of information, gathered and maintained for a single purpose within the enterprise. Integrating these data silos around individual customer information—often the single most common element of information among all the silos—is one of the first steps in becoming a 1:1 enterprise.

---

* AT&T and Sprint, in fact, had customer tracking and database problems nearly identical to MCI's.

With basic interactions and facts missing, MCI found that while it could easily calculate the profitability of a particular product or program, it could not calculate the profitability of a customer. This is, in fact, the first problem encountered by most aggregate-market competitors, and one of the side benefits of trying to differentiate customers at all is that in order to do so a firm is forced to "clean up" its databases and record-keeping systems.

In the end, MCI created an algorithm to rank-order its customers by their valuation, determined mostly by previous long distance calling volume and a credit risk score from the company's finance department. The firm discovered that *the top 5 percent or so of its customers accounted for nearly 40 percent of revenues.* Unit margins are more difficult to calculate in such a business, but it was a good bet that this small sliver of customers accounted for an even higher proportion of the firm's profits. In general, each of these 500,000 high-value customers, representing the core of the long distance company's consumer business, tended to yield $75 per month or more to MCI.

Sales and Service launched a direct-mail and telemarketing program called Customer First, a best-customer recognition program designed to improve loyalty among this top 5 percent of the customer base. Customer First members were given a welcome "thank you" call, a newsletter, membership card, and a series of staged discount certificates. They were also given a special toll-free number to call for any type of assistance. The number routed their calls into a particular calling center, and made it possible for the firm to keep better track of how these customers were being handled.

Differentiating by Needs

MCI's next task was to understand *why* these high-value customers were spending so much on long distance. Having first tiered its customers by their value, MCI now needed to differentiate its most valuable customers by their needs to gain a better understanding of how to make its most valuable customers happy. By examining its transactional records, MCI found its best customers tended to fall into one of three groups:

- *Frequent travelers* call home often, likely to be heavy users of long distance credit card services.

- *Overseas callers* call a particular foreign country, perhaps to reach family, business associates, or fax machines.

- *Work-at-homes* call from their own residences during weekday business hours.

While these three types of customers could be quickly identified based solely on calling patterns, there were still some important things that could be learned about these customers only by conducting dialogues with them individually. For instance, even though an out-of-country caller was easy to identify, there was no way to tell from the transactional records whether the caller spoke English or not. Nor was it possible to tell from transactional records alone whether a work-at-home customer was self-employed or working as an outside sales rep or telecommuter.

Fencing Off the Best Customers

Once the needs of their high-value customers were identified, the next step was to launch some needs-specific programs to keep them loyal. So within Sales and Service, three customer managers were to be appointed to oversee three different portfolios of high-value customers. Under the Customer First umbrella, MCI had already set up a "picket fence" around these customers, preventing the company's own product and program managers from soliciting them for any of the various special calling plans and other programs usually marketed in to the entire customer base. Instead, the Sales and Service executive in charge of Customer First was responsible for all addressable communications to and from this group. Over time, increasing levels of responsibility would be given the customer managers.

Now the Sales and Service executive running Customer First would be contracting out for his own direct mail campaign and creating his own outbound telemarketing effort to welcome an increasing number of existing customers into the program. Part of the program's goal was to gain interaction and feedback from those who enrolled in it, so even though membership cost nothing and returned significant benefits, a customer still was required to respond by phone or mail in order to enlist. This was a critical part of the program, ensuring that everyone in it was aware of its benefits and its reason for being, and allowing MCI to gain a bit of insight into the individual customer's needs.

Outside the picket fence, among the other 95 percent of

the firm's retail customers, marketing-as-usual reigned, with a wide variety of products promoted in mailings and phone calls. But the customer manager's job was to ensure that any program offered to the customers in his or her own portfolio were appropriate and attractive, based on these customers' better understood needs.

Each portfolio manager was to be evaluated on how the company's database algorithm showed she increased the value of the customers within her own portfolio. Since most of the algorithm was based on monthly toll, the customer manager's principal job was to find ways for the customers in her own portfolio to make long distance calls more often. As a result, frequent travelers were the first to be solicited for "personal 800" numbers, an MCI innovation, while to satisfy the needs of ethnic callers the Customer First manager persuaded management to increase the in-language capabilities in operator assistance and in-bound telemarketing.

It is possible, of course, that MCI would have discovered things like the need for more in-language capability without having placed someone specifically in charge of these groups of customers. But the discoveries would have been by chance, uncovered in sample-and-projection consumer research. Until the customer portfolios were set up, no one's job depended on figuring this kind of thing out.

As a part of its overall effort, Sales and Service also reevaluated the metrics MCI used to evaluate its calling centers. In the past, the only real metrics employed had been the call abandonment rate and the time it took to answer the phone. The reps were evaluated generally on their "productivity" which, besides the sale of products and calling plans, was determined by the number of calls handled per day. Reps knew that to handle more calls, each call needed to be dispensed with as quickly as possible. So while there was a fair amount of quality spot-checking (i.e., supervisors listening in on a random sample of calls as they were being handled), most reps worried more about finishing a call than about taking the time necessary to satisfy a customer.

This is a common affliction among aggregate-market competitors. Focused on moving products out the door rather than raising customer profitability over the long term, such firms tend to measure customer-interaction activities from the standpoint of cost-efficiency rather than effectiveness. But time-to-answer measurements don't necessarily correlate to customer satisfaction. Their principal advantage is they're easy to report; the disadvantage is they're the wrong metrics. We'll return to this topic in Chapter 10, when we discuss the management of customer interaction. MCI found that as long as a call was answered within sixty seconds, the important measurement was whether the caller's issue was handled courteously and resolved the first time. So the calling centers began tracking second calls from customers, evaluating individual reps on the percentage of complaints and inquiries successfully handled the first time.

Analyzing MCI's Customer Differentiation Strategy

One way to visualize MCI's plan to improve customer retention would be to plot it on an Enterprise 1:1 Strategy Map. When MCI began its quest to improve retention, the firm was not flexible at all in its delivery of products and services to customers. It had no mechanism set up to match particular products and services to the different long distance needs of individual customers. Instead, all customers were treated the same. Even though the firm had to know that some customers were much more valuable than others, aside from credit-risk analysis by the finance people it had done little to understand what individual customer data was already available. As a result, MCI was not capable of addressing and interacting with its most valuable customers any differently than with its least valuable ones.

Moreover, the various calling plan products and service enhancements that MCI periodically created for its customers were all offered the same way to more or less every customer. Friends & Family, Friends Around the World, the MCI Card, account coding, messaging, the personal 800 number—all these product innovations and ancillary services were promoted the same way to nearly every segment of the MCI retail customer base. These promotions were managed by product managers, and every product manager wanted to "fish the whole pond." So even if MCI's executives knew their customers had different needs, as an enterprise they were not prepared to treat customers individually.

However, while the firm's own capabilities placed it squarely into Quadrant I, a brief amount of research had quickly revealed that the value and needs of MCI's individual customers varied substantially. So MCI's customer base was clearly in Quadrant IV.

The Strategy Map would have looked something like this:

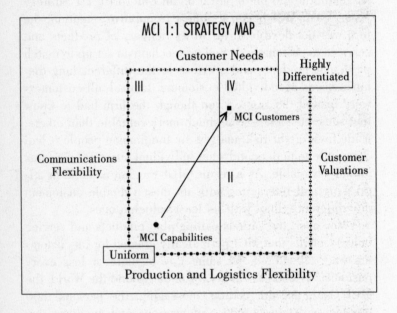

Adding services designed specifically for frequent travelers, ethnic callers, or work-at-homes is an enterprise strategy that relies on knowing individual customers and treating each one differently. This strategy required the management of customers and customer relationships to take priority over the management of products and marketing promotions. For these highly valued customers, MCI needed to tailor both its marketing communications and its products. The program would require MCI to coordinate and integrate several different functions at the firm, crossing well-defined departmental lines of authority.

And Now for a Dose of Reality

It would be nice to conclude by reviewing the beneficial effects of Customer First on retention and overall profitability in the years since its launch. Unfortunately, however, despite its demonstrable early success, Customer First was killed, and the longer-term results that might have been achieved will never be known.

In implementing this strategy, MCI encountered its most severe obstacles not from AT&T or its other competitors, but from the politics of its own organizational structure. The conflict between Marketing's acquisition-oriented objectives and the retention objectives at Sales and Service proved extremely difficult to resolve. Marketing recruited new customers and sold products to existing customers. The psychology within the department equated every sale to a "conquest," and nearly every manager was on a bonus plan that rewarded acquisition and product sales, but not customer retention.

Only the Customer First managers had a compensation plan that rewarded them for improving the loyalty and profitability of the customer base, but these managers were located in Sales and Service, not Marketing. So, even though executives in Marketing were vicariously pleased that the company was making progress in retention, thus steadily adding more value to the customer base, the company's falling acquisition rate was money out of their own pockets.

Similarly, the product managers in charge of moving more packages out the door and bringing revenue in from the firm's existing customer base were upset that the most valuable 5 percent of MCI's customers were suddenly off limits. Instead of simply rolling out offers and selling programs, feeding everyone into MCI's highly effective telemarketing operation—instead of fishing the whole pond—they now had to get permission from the Customer First managers.

To add to the interdepartmental conflict, Sales and Service was now running its own outbound communications program, signing customers up for Customer First which, to all outward appearances, looked suspiciously like any other marketing program—it involved mailings and solicitations, premiums and benefits. Sales and Service had its own direct mail contractor, and crafted its own messages. But direct mail and outbound telemarketing were media vehicles that were "owned" by Marketing, which soon objected to Sales and Service's use of such media to send out messages that hadn't been cleared against Marketing's own creative standards.

Nevertheless, the company tried its best to cope with these conflicts, at first on an ad hoc basis. A joint team of managers was set up to oversee Customer First's communication plan and make sure it remained effective while not interfering with other outbound marketing activities. This effort soon succumbed to middle-management rivalries, however.

So the Customer First program was finally transferred completely to Marketing. Sales and Service agreed to stop doing "marketing stuff"—like sending out mail and making calls—while Marketing agreed to focus more on retaining high-value customers. Because the firm had not changed the basic metrics by which it judged the performance of its various departments and managers, however, simply placing Customer First under the Marketing umbrella was a doomed idea. The program was soon subjected to an altogether different success criterion, a criterion based on acquisition rather than on retention and growth.

Marketing replaced Customer First with a program called Personal Thanks—a rewards-based frequency marketing program now known as Friends & Family Rewards. Even though this was the only real loyalty program implemented by Marketing, its qualification criteria were steadily lowered, and its reward structure diluted, in order to make it attractive to a greater proportion of customers. The effect, as the rewards gradually diminished, was to make the program less and less effective at promoting loyalty among the company's higher-value customers. But Marketing did this to prove the success of the program. The problem was they gauged its success not by the increased loyalty of the most valuable customers, but by the overall number of customers recruited into the program.

MCI's corporate culture also worked against long-term customer retention. Impatient in the extreme, the company's fast-moving entrepreneurial management knew how to count the customers they *acquired* on a daily basis. Measuring an improvement in how many of those customers were *retained* requires a good deal more time. Without question, better customer retention creates a long-term improvement in profit, but it requires long-term metrics and a patient, deliberate approach. MCI's senior management just didn't have the attention span. One popular maxim at MCI was that the only marketing program really worth pursuing was one that had network television potential. Friends & Family clearly had it. Network MCI had it. Customer First didn't.

Nor did management ever take the time to restructure Marketing's incentive structure, which means there are still no penalties for attrition, while the pot of gold lies in beating last year's acquisition numbers. Every spare moment is spent trying to bring additional prospects into the franchise or move additional product solicitations out the door. And Marketing does this because, as Willie Sutton said about robbing banks, "That's where the money is."

Growing the "Best of the Best"— a Postscript

Despite all the conflicts that led to its failure, one element of the Customer First program did survive, and flourishes as of this writing, yielding a continuing benefit to MCI. Having fenced off the top 5 percent of its customers with the Customer First program, MCI looked within this group to find an even more select group of high spenders. It turned out that about 3 percent of this top tier regularly incurred more than $500 per month each in residential long distance charges. These 15,000 customers—only a little more than one-tenth of one percent of MCI's total U.S. retail customer base—accounted for more than 7 percent of the company's revenue!

Taking Customer First to a higher level, MCI introduced some truly red-carpet, first-class treatment for these very elite customers. They built an even more impermeable wall

around them than had already been built around Customer
First. A cadre of forty of the best customer service representatives was set up as an entirely different kind of customer
service organization in a special area at one of the call
centers. They operated in small teams and worked on their
own management plan. They didn't have formal supervisors,
and instead were subject to "360" personnel reviews by
their superiors as well as their peers and subordinates.

Each rep was given a pager, which he or she was to
keep close at hand at all times, and a set of business cards.
Each was assigned responsibility for a specific group of
elite customers, who received a phone call or letter from the
rep advising them of the program, and offering to resolve
any future issues and solve any problems. MCI found that
these customers never called their reps on the pager numbers, but simply having the pagers improved the reps' sense
of service and their attitude toward "their" customers.

As one former MCI executive put it, the company would
love to have had the resources to treat everyone to such
coddling. But in a resource-limited world, priorities had to
be set. Clearly, these were the customers MCI wanted to
keep loyal above all others, and that's what the firm is doing
now.

While Customer First was defeated by MCI's own internal conflicts, it's important to note that even had it succeeded, it would barely have scratched the surface of the
customer retention strategies we'll be outlining later. A telecommunications firm—like MCI, or Ameritech, or Cable &
Wireless—is actually in an *ideal* position to create highly
customized, collaborative services for individual customers.
These services can become a platform for creating Learning
Relationships with the firm's customers, not only increasing
their loyalty to the enterprise but guaranteeing a higher unit

margin as well. We'll begin our discussion of the mechanics behind this kind of retention effort in Chapter 7, and in Chapter 8 we'll come back to the telecommunications industry for some more specific ideas.

First, however, we want to return to the issue of how customers are different, in order to understand not just which customers are the most appropriate to keep, but which ones are the easiest to grow. They often aren't the same customers, and the strategies an enterprise uses to keep its customers longer are not always the same as those it would use to grow its customers bigger.

GROWING YOUR CUSTOMER BASE

5

*How to Increase Your Share
of Customer and Improve Your
Bottom Line*

MCI used its own database of customer transactions to rank-order its customers by their value, and then it differentiated the top tier of customers by their needs, grouping them into three categories. Because the firm was aiming specifically to *retain* its customers longer, the only real variable it considered in its customers valuation model was a customer's *actual* value—its current LTV. If, however, MCI had launched a program designed more to *grow* its customers larger, it would not only have applied different strategies, but the strategies would have been aimed at different customers—the ones with the highest *strategic,* or potential, value to MCI.

In this chapter we'll look more carefully at the issue of strategic value, and we'll see how it affects the choice be-

tween keeping and growing customers. Along the way we're
going to develop a "taxonomy" of customer valuations, and
we'll catalogue a number of different types of customer retention and growth strategies.

Finding Your Customers' Strategic Value

Strategic value is the total profit a firm *could* realize from
a customer if it were to develop a strategy, or take some
marketing initiative, with that particular customer. Strategic
value represents the *potential* business a customer could do
with us, much of which may in fact never be realized.

To gain a better understanding of the difference between *actual* and *strategic* value, imagine you run a retail
bank. Think of a banking customer who has a checking
account, savings account, and car loan with you. This customer provides a certain regular profit to your bank every
month, generated by her transaction fees and the investment spread between what your borrowing and lending rates
are and the rates your customer pays you. Like the hypothetical magazine publisher whose customers were modeled
in Chapter 2, you have modeled your customers, and you
expect this one to remain with your bank for a number of
years, giving you a continuing income stream more or less
similar to your current earnings. The net present value of
this continuing income stream represents her LTV—the
lifetime value loss you would suffer if she were to defect to
another bank.

In addition to the accounts she has at your bank, suppose your customer also has a home mortgage at a competitive bank. To your competitor, the profit on her home loan

represents her actual value, but to you it is only an unrealized potential. The home loan is his to lose and yours to gain. The expected profit from that loan would represent one aspect of this customer's *strategic* value to *you*.

Similarly, if the customer owned a computer and modem but didn't participate in your bank's home banking services, or if she were a medical student with few current assets but a promise of high future earnings, then each of these factors would also represent different aspects of her strategic value to you. In each case the customer could return more profit to your firm if only you could entice her to do so.

With this analogy we have illustrated three separate aspects of a customer's strategic value to an enterprise:

1. *Competitive business* This is business your customer does with a competitor that could be yours if you could entice the customer to give it to you. Stealing business directly from your competitors is a time-honored competitive tactic, whether it is a bank taking a home loan from a rival, or a systems integrator winning an IT (information technology) consulting contract away from a computer manufacturer.

2. *Behavior change* In many situations you could earn a higher profit if you could only get the customer to behave differently. You might get the customer to do some additional task, or participate in some added service, or manage its own business a little differently. For the retail bank it might mean getting a customer to do more banking from home by using a modem, or beginning a regular savings investment.

3. *Customer growth* A customer's strategic value also encompasses the potential a customer has when it becomes bigger on its own. The retail bank catering to medical students is only one example. A US West Direct growth-oriented customer might in fact buy more and bigger Yellow Pages ads as it becomes a larger business.

While in each of these cases the result of a successful strategic initiative should be a larger, more profitable customer, there is an important difference between the first method—stealing from a competitor a greater share of your customer's business—and the other two. If you share a customer with a competitor, then you should consider yourself in a race to actualize that customer's strategic value. After all, what if your competitor beats you to the punch and gets your customer to say how much business she's doing—with *you*?

While the customers most worth keeping are the ones with the highest actual value, or LTV, the customers more likely to *grow* are those with the highest unrealized potential—that is, the biggest difference between strategic (potential) value and actual (realized) value. Sometimes these are the same customers, but more often they are not. Moreover, the initiatives and tactics required to grow customers into bigger customers are not the same as the tactics required to retain customers longer. It is usually more expensive—although more profitable—to grow a customer than it is simply to keep one.

To visualize this situation, let's go back to the quintile chart of actual customer value that we first considered in Chapter 2. Suppose you were to overlay the *actual* value chart on top of a representation of *strategic* value. For now don't worry about how to obtain the information about each customer's strategic value; just assume that the data on individual customer strategic valuations is available to you. The redrawn quintile chart, with actual values overlaid on strategic values, will provide a Customer Valuation Typology that looks something like this:

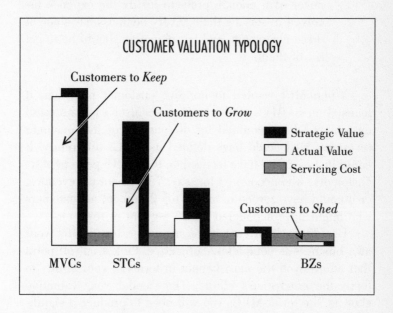

In the quintile chart shown above, we have labeled three principal types of customers, based on our objectives for the customers in each group—whether we want to keep them, grow them, or get rid of them. To make our discussion easier, we will use acronyms.

MVCs: *Most Valuable Customers* are those with the highest LTVs. They represent the core of our current business. Our objective is *customer retention.*

STCs: *Second-Tier Customers* are those with the highest unrealized potential. These customers could be more profitable than they are now, and our objective is *customer growth.*

BZs: *Below-Zero* customers are those who will probably never earn enough profit to justify the expense involved in serving them. Every business has some of these customers, and our objective should be to *get rid* of them.

When MCI wanted to improve customer retention, it focused on its MVCs—the top 5 percent or so of its retail customers who accounted for 40 percent of its consumer revenues. MCI could have defined its MVCs differently. It could just as easily have focused on the top 15 percent of its customers, who accounted for, say, 75 percent of revenues, or it could have zeroed in on the top 2 percent of customers who might have accounted for 25 percent of revenues.

Deciding which customers are in the top tier for your own business is completely subjective. Pick a cut-off point that affords you the most benefit in terms of your ability to focus the enterprise's efforts. The steeper your valuation skew is, the fewer MVCs you will need to produce a significant enterprise benefit from a customer retention program.

Next are the STCs, or second-tier customers. It is often true that the customers with the most unrealized potential are those who lie just below the MVC level. While an MVC is more likely to be giving the enterprise a fairly high share of its business already, an STC often is not. The STC often resembles an MVC in all respects except that it is giving the firm a lower share of current business. Therefore the

STC usually offers the firm a greater *potential* opportunity for added profitability and customer growth.

Defining and quantifying a customer's strategic value is more difficult than calculating actual value, because in order to acquire information about your share of a particular customer's business, some kind of dialogue interaction with the customer is almost always necessary. Later in this chapter we'll discuss this issue in more detail, but for now what's important is that even if the enterprise has no information at all on strategic value, it is still likely that those customers with the most growth potential are just below the top tier. An airline, for instance, will find that many of its own STCs are actually MVCs on a competitive airline.

In addition to MVCs and STCs, there will almost certainly be a few customers in the bottom tier of any firm's customer base who cost more to serve than they will ever return in profit. Servicing customers individually always involves some cost. Customers rarely come free. Almost inevitably, some customers will be worth less than nothing to the firm, and we have designated these below-zero customers as BZs.

By identifying BZs early on, a firm can minimize wasted marketing efforts and pointless sales expenses. A conventional definition of customer LTV would deduct servicing costs from the profit of a customer before calculating the customer's actual value. We illustrated servicing costs separately in the Customer Valuation Typology to show that though we might think of all customers as having some positive value, even if minuscule, the bottom line is that some customers simply do cost more than they are worth.

Detecting Anomalies

By creating a "taxonomy" of customer types based on their needs and their valuations, the 1:1 enterprise can spot opportunities for additional profit fairly quickly. For instance, US West Direct could benefit substantially by simply reviewing all its growth-oriented customers regularly, as a class, and comparing their Yellow Pages spending relative to their total marketing budgets. Growth-oriented customers should have reasonably similar ratios, at least within the same or similar industries. Any significant exceptions—any anomalies—point out opportunities for further sales initiatives.

Note that if US West had not already differentiated its customers into particular needs-based types, then hunting for anomalies would hardly be worth the effort. What makes the tactic so powerful is that the company already knows that different customers spend greater or lesser amounts of their marketing budget on the Yellow Pages for a variety of reasons—and it knows *which* customers, individually, are subject to *which* reasons.

As straightforward as this might seem, even companies with highly sophisticated databases and information systems often do not take advantage of the opportunities presented by anomalies in their customer base. A colleague of ours recently expanded his small management consulting business from a sole proprietorship to a corporation with several partners. His business grew quickly, and he gave each of the new partners a corporate American Express card on the same business account.

After his credit card bill doubled, then doubled again,

an American Express representative called to inquire about the increased size of the bill and ask for some financial information on the consulting firm, which our colleague easily provided over the phone. It was a polite and efficient inquiry on American Express's part, clearly designed to identify any credit risk in advance of a problem. Within two months the bill doubled again, and another call came, asking for additional information, once again easily provided over the phone. However, deciding he ought to have a backup plan, our colleague got a Diners Club card and gave it to his travel agent with instructions that all air travel henceforth was to be billed on that account, while he and his partners would continue to charge hotel and ground expenses to AmEx.

He has not heard from American Express again. He and his partners are still charging hotels and meals all over the world to American Express, but no air travel. AmEx *has all the information needed* to show that the level of travel activity has actually increased, while AmEx's own share of this customer's business has plummeted. Moreover, AmEx is clearly capable of detecting anomalies like this, because the credit people called more than once, even engaging their customer in a dialogue that revealed a complete, honest picture of expanding business needs.

But while the *credit* people at AmEx are quick to use individual information, the *marketing* people obviously are not, perhaps because marketing is simply not oriented toward share-of-customer activities. Or, like the MCI Marketing Department, perhaps the AmEx organization is so focused on acquiring new customers and selling new programs that no one in the firm is rewarded for growing existing customers into bigger ones. Whatever the reason, the result is that AmEx is losing a simple, straightforward chance to retain its share of customer with our colleague and others like him. Diners Club, of course, has a similarly straightforward opportunity.

Our consultant colleague is an anomaly for both AmEx and Diners Club. The growth-oriented investor disproportionately spending money on non–Yellow Pages advertising is an anomaly for US West Direct. A "top 50" car wash customer who suddenly comes in much less frequently is an anomaly. A banking customer with a home loan but no checking or savings account is an anomaly. Having the ability to detect anomalies in your database of customer transactions is critical to pursuing a share-of-customer strategy no matter how simple or sophisticated the database is. But transactional information by itself, even though it may be highly detailed and sophisticated, is often insufficient to infer true share of customer.

Using Dialogue as More Than a Feel-Good Mechanism

As with determining a customer's individual needs, determining a customer's strategic value is often difficult without first engaging the customer in some kind of dialogue or interaction to inquire about other business potential. There may be ways to find out, using records of publicly filed mortgages, that a retail banking customer has a home mortgage at another bank, but this will not be nearly so efficient and straightforward—or so timely and accurate— as asking the customer directly. And how would you find out that a customer has a computer and modem at home, or that she is an up-and-coming medical student, without some sort of interaction? Even if information like this could be purchased from third-party sources, putting it to use for your own enterprise has serious enough privacy implications that it should give you pause.

On the other hand, the more dialogue a firm has with a customer, the more opportunity exists to get an accurate picture of this potential in a way that maximizes the customer's own collaboration in your effort. Any good salesperson knows that the most important pieces of information to acquire from a customer in a meeting are the customer's estimate of future buying needs and information on which competitors the customer is dealing with at present. An increasing proliferation of sales force automation tools is making it easier to record and act on exactly this kind of information.

In the charge card business, a firm may know that its very best customers tend to be upscale frequent travelers who transact thousands of dollars a month in airline, car rental, hotel, and restaurant charges. Someone like our colleague, who transacts a lot of hotel and rental car charges in a variety of cities but little or nothing in airline travel might be presumed to be giving the charge card company a lower share of his business than many other similar customers. *Unless,* of course, this particular customer's travel agent uses a different AmEx account—one that has not been integrated into the customer's other records at American Express—or unless he travels primarily in a corporate aircraft.

The point is that while transactional records can provide substantially more insight than many companies today are prepared to use, the only sure way to nail down a customer's genuine *strategic* value is to engage the customer in a dialogue of some kind.

Even some industries characterized by seemingly universal and perfect transactional records must rely on dialogue with individual customers to understand the why of a particular customer's behavior. In the United States, for instance, every drugstore reports its prescriptions filled, with individual doctor information included, to a central clearinghouse of information. This data is then made available in substantial detail to pharmaceutical companies, who are engaged in relationships with doctors to try to encourage them to prescribe the company's drugs. The doctors doing the prescribing are, in essence, the customers of the drug companies.

Because of the availability and comprehensiveness of this data, not only can a drug company see which of its own drugs are being prescribed by an individual doctor, but it can also see exactly which of its competitors' drugs are being prescribed. On its face, this appears to be an absolutely perfect, quantified share-of-customer record for every individual doctor-customer, available to every pharmaceutical company. But the truth is, very few anomalies in the transactional data can actually be explained by the data alone. Instead, a doctor who prescribes one antidepressant instead of another, for instance, must be contacted by the drug company's detail people if the firm is to have any hope of increasing its share of customer with that particular doctor. While the database includes exhaustive "what" data, it does not include "why" data.

Thus, dialogue with an individual customer serves two principal purposes for the 1:1 enterprise:

1. *Needs specification* The customer tells the firm what sort of product he wants, and where and when he wants it.

2. *Strategic value analysis* The customer gives the firm an indication of the *additional* business he might be able to give it.

Strategies for Keeping Customers vs. Growing Them Bigger

Not only do the customers most worth keeping differ from those most worth growing, but the strategies used will be different as well.

There are at least four separate strategies for improving customer retention, and each is effective in its own way, depending on the nature of the customer base and the enterprise's capabilities. The following are retention-improving strategies, roughly in order of their increasing effectiveness:

1. Customer recognition

2. Loyalty purchasing

3. Product quality and customer satisfaction

4. Customization and collaboration

1. **Customer Recognition** One of the first initiatives many firms consider when wrestling with the issue of retention is customer recognition. If we know a customer is an MVC, why not "recognize" that fact with some sort of special treatment? This approach can be specially effective in a high-end personal-service business. The MCI Customer First program began

essentially as a simple customer recognition program.

Inter-Continental hotels and resorts produces personalized luggage tags for its most valuable customers—baggage tags that discreetly but immediately identify a guest as a Six Continents Club member. When a bellhop sees such an emblem, he knows that the baggage owner is an MVC, and he pays immediate special attention to this customer.

The San Diego Padres baseball team recognizes and rewards its most valuable fans. Relying on a program developed by Looking Glass, a database marketing consultant headquartered in Denver, the Padres ran a survey in the newspaper offering two free tickets to anyone who filled it out and sent it in. They received some 6,400 replies, including 400 personal letters, some running to several pages of typed suggestions and questions for the team. The survey respondents were then recruited into a Padres fan club, and formed into groups based on a loose mix of customer needs and valuations. Gold-level members hold season tickets, while silver-level members are retirees. Women fans are known as "madres," while other groups are now being created for fans with kids and singles. Some of the fans who wrote letters were called personally by the Padres' management, and more than one was treated to dinner by the owner.

The elements of a customer recognition program should be both personal and practical. It does no good to "recognize" someone as an MVC by using a form letter. If a customer is valuable enough to be an

MVC, then he is almost certainly valuable enough to warrant some level of actual human contact, or at least a zero-defects, customized letter.

Best-Interests Marketing

There is a business practice we call "best-interests" marketing which should be included as an element of any customer recognition program. Basically, best-interests marketing involves putting a customer's own best interests at the forefront of whatever policy or marketing program is being executed. For example, phone companies and banks should review the accounts of MVCs and recommend the best plan for each customer. While best-interests is a business practice that makes sense when dealing with any customer, it requires a level of personal care and attention as opposed to a standardized one-size-fits-all program that is often impractical to apply to levels much below that of an MVC.

Consider the successful home builder who sells an infrequently purchased, very expensive product and must therefore rely, principally, on referrals to drive his business. Most builders warrant the homes they construct for a period of one year. After the first year following construction, the owner and not the builder is responsible for any further repairs or adjustments.

New homes are complicated products with many small things that can go wrong at various times.

Even a home built by the best is likely to be filled with little problems that require adjustment. So there are two ways a home builder can treat a one-year warranty. He could wait for the deadline to pass, hoping that his customer (who will never buy another product from him again anyway) doesn't think to call him in to fix anything until after the expiration. This is likely to be the least costly course of action, at least in the short term. Or he could call the new home owner in the fifty-first week, just a few days before the warranty expires, and offer to stop by to inspect the house with the owner, in order to spot any additional problems that might have been overlooked. While this customer may not ever build another home, he is certainly likely to refer others to the builder, right?

Besides the longer-term benefit that best-interests marketing can provide in terms of customer retention and referrals, it will dramatically improve the rank-and-file attitude within the enterprise with respect to how customers should be treated. A well-managed firm will train even lower-level employees to make decisions according to some overall criteria designed to further the enterprise's mission. "Ladies and gentlemen serving ladies and gentlemen" is the mantra at the Ritz-Carlton, for instance, and the thinking and training behind this phrase go a long way toward explaining this company's well-documented excellence in service, customer satisfaction, and complaint recovery. The enterprise that practices best-interests marketing will infuse its culture with the principle that the customer comes first, above everything else.

2. *Loyalty Purchasing* Another, quite different way to increase customer retention is to buy it. MCI was purchasing their customers' loyalty when it changed its acquisition offer from a cash payment to a staged rebate.

Loyalty purchasing is what frequent flyer programs are all about. Because they have escalating awards rates with mileage earned, frequent flyer plans are good examples of how to gain greater customer loyalty as individual customer volume increases. Moreover, by providing extra-special services to very frequent flyers—like priority upgrades and special check-in lines—an airline can make it more attractive for such a flyer to stay loyal than to sample a different airline, where he won't be treated like an MVC.

Sometimes it is sufficient to buy a customer's loyalty just long enough for the customer to become more comfortable with the enterprise. If the enterprise can learn a customer's tastes and preferences during this period, and in the process get a customer to spend time and effort investing in the relationship, then it might be able to transition from the bribery mode to the Learning Relationship mode—which is clearly the most effective strategy for maintaining any customer's long-term loyalty.

Buying customer loyalty is the first instinct at most firms when they are faced with significant customer attrition. But as a tactic it has limited long-term utility. It is easily matched by the competition, and it often smells to customers like just another cheap marketing promotion. In the long run, purchasing a customer's loyalty is not much different from reducing the price to attract new customers.

Even frequent flyer programs, with their escalating rewards structures and a highly attractive "currency" (mileage), provide only a short-term retention advantage in the face of predatory customer acquisition efforts. American can steal United's best customers by (a) identifying them individually, either through a marketing promotion or by partnering with another travel firm, and then (b) selectively "upping the ante" of privileges, mileage bonuses, or upgrades—but just for these particular MVCs. United's only defense against such loyalty "share stealing" would be to raise the ante itself, and the struggle once again would descend to the level of price cutting and margin squeezing.

A more lasting form of loyalty could be fostered by any airline that cracked the code on creating Learning Relationships with MVCs, based on remembering each customer's individual specifications or preferences, and then customizing its services to these needs. Right now United (and American and the other major airlines) treat their top-level frequent flyers better than other passengers, but they still treat all top-level passengers the same way, as though they all have the same tastes and needs.

3. *Product Quality and Customer Satisfaction* There is, of course, no substitute for quality. No customer will return for more of a bad product, so having product quality at least on a par with the competition is essential for a 1:1 enterprise. In Chapter 7 we'll come back briefly to the issue of product and service qual-

ity, but for now what we are really interested in is customer satisfaction. Customer satisfaction is the opposite of customer dissatisfaction, and dissatisfaction is one sure route to defection. Keep in mind, however, that customer satisfaction by itself is usually not sufficient to generate loyalty.

Many firms go to some length to measure their customer satisfaction index (CSI), surveying customers and asking them to rate the product to indicate whether they are "very satisfied" or "very dissatisfied." Whether or not this feedback mechanism is used as part of an overall quality improvement effort, some companies go so far as to incorporate CSI into the overall management of the business, constantly comparing one division to another, this year to last, and so forth. Among firms that do rely on CSI measurements, there is a widely held belief that the only kind of customer satisfaction that really counts is the "top box"—the highest possible satisfaction rating. Studies have shown that it is not enough to achieve satisfaction ratings that are merely good (satisfactory satisfaction?). Only stellar performance seems to have any measurable benefit in terms of customer loyalty at all. Large numbers of customers who are satisfied but not *very* satisfied will still leave the franchise.

Despite a firm's best intentions, using CSI as an explicit component in setting employee compensation often produces unintended and distorted results. A friend of ours recently bought a new Toyota from a dealership in his own area which advertised its very high CSI ratings. As our friend was signing the papers, the salesman called his attention to a question-

naire on customer satisfaction. Explaining first that
the dealership's revenue and his own personal compensation both depended on how the customer rated
his overall satisfaction, the salesman slid the survey
across the desk and asked (wink-wink) whether our
friend hadn't been *very* satisfied with the overall
sales experience. The survey came with a postage-
paid envelope, but the salesman encouraged the customer to fill out the survey right then, right in front of
him, if he'd like to save himself the trouble of finding
a mailbox later, and if he really was (wink) *very* satisfied.

Top-box customer satisfaction is clearly important, but perhaps not for the reason that seems most
obvious. The fact is, other research has shown con-
clusively that customer satisfaction can be accurately correlated with customer loyalty only if it is
measured *relative to the competition.* If your customer shows top-box satisfaction, obviously he is
telling you he is at least no less satisfied with your
firm than he is with a competitor. But the most direct
way to measure customer satisfaction's real impact
on your business is to measure the competition's
customer satisfaction as well.

Ray Kordupleski, most recently AT&T's director
of customer satisfaction, began examining customer
satisfaction at AT&T more than a decade ago, and
his efforts yielded some genuinely groundbreaking
research. For several years after being given the as-
signment to improve AT&T's overall business results, Kordupleski pondered a dilemma. While the
firm was measuring all sorts of variables to calculate
share of market and to identify cost efficiencies,

AT&T's customer satisfaction scores apparently had no correlation to market share, growth, or profit.

A typical dilemma—and one that seemed to recur various ways everywhere—was that while customer satisfaction for one product in the Pennsylvania market was reported at 97 percent, and the index for the same product in New York was only 78 percent, the Pennsylvania business was actually *losing* market share while New York was *gaining*. Moreover, among all markets in the U.S., Pennsylvania reported the *most* satisfied customers, while New York's customers were the *least* satisfied. If anything, it seemed that AT&T was losing customers in spite of getting better and better. How could that be?

This is a commonly voiced problem among a variety of businesses. Quality-control managers' inability to link increases (or decreases) in customer satisfaction directly to market results has led many to question whether customer satisfaction programs really pay off at all in financial terms.

Kordupleski reached three conclusions in his research to explain AT&T's puzzling customer satisfaction statistics: First, the only kind of satisfaction that really counts is the top-box, "very satisfied." Second, and this was critical to AT&T, while price contributes to the overall value proposition, a variety of other factors, from service quality to responsiveness, also figure in determining a customer's relative satisfaction. In other words, it was clearly realistic to satisfy a customer with a quality product even if it sold at a *higher* price.

His third conclusion, however, was that customer satisfaction is useful for explaining competitive business results only when it is measured *relative to the competition's scores.* Even today this principle is completely overlooked in all the hand-wringing over the financial benefits of higher customer satisfaction scores. For most companies the satisfaction scores simply measure the wrong thing. But Kordupleski showed that when *relative* customer satisfaction was measured, the correlation with business performance was actually quite remarkable. In the case of AT&T's business phone "install" rate, for instance, even a small uptick in relative satisfaction was a four-month leading indicator of share growth.

Now, of course, it was easy to explain the Pennsylvania–New York paradox. New Yorkers rate *everybody* lower than the more tolerant folks in Pennsylvania, because they are predisposed to be more demanding of their vendors and less forgiving as customers (is this a surprise to anyone?). But if New Yorkers rate AT&T's competitors *even lower* than they rate AT&T, then market share growth will still occur.

4. *Customization and Collaboration* By far the most effective strategy for keeping customers is the Learning Relationship, based on individual customer collaboration and customization tactics.

Reliable, dependable customer retention occurs only when a customer is *committed* to the enterprise, relative to its competitors, and the best way to ensure this is to collaboratively link individual customer feedback to the customization of products and services. If you can convince a customer to spend some time or energy teaching your firm how to cater better to his or her individual tastes, then you can keep this customer loyal for a longer period, out of the customer's own self-interest. The more time and energy the customer expends in teaching the enterprise how to customize to his own tastes, the more trouble it will be for the customer to obtain the same level of customized service from a competitor.

The Learning Relationship turns a widely known precept around and looks at it from the customer's perspective. Every company knows that learning more about customers, even individually, will be beneficial to the firm's marketing efforts. That's why customer databases are so popular with marketers. The more you learn about your customer base, the better prepared you will be to sell things into it, and to defend it against competitive predation. Learning Relationships, however, are based on the deceptively simple idea that when a customer spends time *teaching* your firm, the customer himself develops a stake in the benefits of this learning. Getting an individual customer to teach the firm about his own particular needs is a completely foreign idea for any business not accustomed to thinking of its customers as individually interactive. We'll discuss the customization and collaboration strategy in more detail in the next few chapters, as we begin to examine the broader implications of Learning Relationships.

Customer retention strategies overlap somewhat with customer growth strategies, but they are not the same. Just as an enterprise can buy a customer's loyalty, it can also buy an increased share of customer. An STC who gives you 50 percent of his business can often be enticed to give you a greater share if you offer him a premium or rebate, but the strategy here is not to spiff a transaction by selling one more widget, but to make a strategic, competitive inroad by *cross-selling*.

Cross-Selling to Increase Your Share of Customer

The most important and immediately beneficial way to increase share of customer, at least for most companies, is by cross-selling. It is astonishing how little effective cross-selling takes place among large firms, and yet when the firm centers itself around the customer rather than the product, cross-selling will dramatically, and naturally, increase.

One common error made by a multidivision company seeking to transform itself into a 1:1 enterprise is to isolate the 1:1 marketing initiative within a single division. But 1:1 marketing is inherently *customer*-oriented, while most companies' divisional structures break along product or functional lines. In a multidivision firm, the divisions usually sell to overlapping customer bases, doing business with a single customer in several different divisions. But most such organizations place responsibility for testing the efficacy of various marketing programs and competitive strategies with the division heads who, after all, have profit-and-loss responsibility. Other business functions are split into divisional pieces and evaluated separately, so why not this one? Why not treat a single customer as if he is more than one customer, by splintering him across divisions?

One reason a customer-centered approach to doing

business is so compelling is precisely because it enables an enterprise to leverage a single customer relationship into a variety of additional profit streams, cross-selling many different products and services to a customer in a coordinated way. Enterprisewide cross-selling is not possible if the pilot project is limited to a single division, or if 1:1 marketing is being tested on a single product. If your enterprise wants to prove the viability of a 1:1 initiative, you need to assign it to a set of *customers,* not products—and probably not divisions.

> *It's hard to remember sometimes, but the 1:1 enterprise knows the competition is* outside *the company, not inside it.*

Look how difficult it is to cross-sell something as logical as advertising and promotional services. In the advertising industry the last decade has seen a number of large, multinational advertising agencies acquiring other firms to add "below the line" services, such as direct mail, sales promotion, or public relations. Even though these disciplines are related to one another fairly closely, the functional skills required to execute each are often quite different, so each discipline is usually represented and championed by a separate set of experts within the larger agency structure. Mass media advertising executives are notorious for selling *against* the direct marketing, sales promotion, or public relations operation in their own company, in order to protect the highest possible media spending level—even though the agency's margin on a client's direct marketing budget is almost always substantially higher.

In contrast to the great difficulty most firms experience when it comes to cross-selling, the process of "cross-buying" is often practiced by smart, well-managed customers. Wal-Mart, a paragon of supply-chain discipline, will routinely negotiate a steeply discounted rate with one division of a supplier, and then apply that rate aggressively to products bought from the supplier's other divisions.

At most companies today, enterprisewide cross-selling, if it is encouraged at all, usually has to be organized on an ad hoc basis, with multidivision committees or "swat teams" meeting informally to exchange contacts and leads. Chubb Insurance, for instance, used to be organized into several different divisions, each of which sold a different line of insurance products to businesses, from marine, to directors and officers liability, to business property and casualty. A single firm often became a customer of only one Chubb division, while other divisions had products that would also be appropriate for the customer. So the firm conducted regular integrative meetings at the corporate level which were designed to discover any potential for cross-selling additional products to each division's new customers examined one customer at a time. Chubb called its process "cross fire," and the firm used it to ensure the maximum possible business from every customer.

Recently, however, Chubb reorganized itself around groups of customers, such as high tech companies and small businesses, so each customer is sold the type of insurance that meets his needs. Thus, "cross-fire" meetings have been replaced by a stronger customer organization altogether, making all lines of business available to each customer in each of the customer groups.

Anyone familiar with the difficulties of "team selling," when a complex system or set of products is being sold by a single company to a large buyer, can easily identify with the difficulties of cross-selling between one division and another, or even one department and another. Cross-selling activities are hard primarily because the firm's organizational structure and executive compensation plan explicitly limit the scope of responsibility of any single manager to things within his own division's jurisdiction—whether his division is organized by product category, or by channel, or by function—and this is the primary obstacle to overcome in implementing most customer growth strategies. To move customers from the STC category into the MVC category, cross-selling is critical.

What to Do When Customers Cost More Than They're Worth

BZs are those customers at the bottom of the customer hierarchy who cost more to service than they will return in value. Every enterprise usually has at least a few BZs, and for some businesses the population of BZs can actually outnumber the population of MVCs and STCs.

The most frequently encountered BZ is not the high-value customer who defects, but the low-value customer who is prone to consume high-cost services. In a business-to-business situation, the enterprise can usually identify some layer of low-value customers who are continually solicited for products, often using direct mail or telemarketing rather than a direct sales force.

In addition to this layer of smaller customers, there will also be some apparently higher-potential customers who just do not wish to collaborate. They either don't want additional services, or don't need to know anything about the project's development, or perhaps they don't care about any sort of product or service quality that can't be quantified. Sometimes they may not even care much about the professionalism of the product or service being bought. If you have a direct sales force, we guarantee that every single one of your salespeople knows such a client—a client that no matter how many times you serve him well nevertheless insists on bidding out the next project once again, in order to beat another tenth of a point out of your margin. Most firms continue to solicit business even from BZ customers such as this, simply because that's what firms do—they try to *get* customers.

US West Direct knows that once a customer is identified as a "non–growth-oriented maintainer" it almost never pays to make a personal sales call. With just a few exceptions, the odds of winning any spending at all are too small to pay for the cost of the salesperson's time. This is a classic example of how to identify a BZ in advance, using a needs-differentiation taxonomy. If a "maintainer" calls in, then US West will certainly take the order; but the company also realizes it doesn't pay off, in the long run, to spend time and energy deploying salespeople to try to win more business from such customers.

In handling such situations, US West's own corporate culture sometimes gets in the way. Descended from the AT&T monopoly, the company has a deep-seated "all our customers are equal" philosophy that often shows itself within the firm's unionized sales force. This corporate bias can be found at a variety of utilities, local phone companies, cable TV companies, newspapers, and other businesses that are, or were recently, monopolies—either by government edict or through natural market forces.

The problem with such a bias, of course, is that customers clearly are *not* equal. They aren't equal now, and they weren't equal during the monopoly days either. A deadbeat still gets a dunning letter, even from a monopoly, while one who pays his bills does not. A large business gets more personal treatment, even from a monopoly, than a little one. Particularly in dealing with BZs, how the enterprise handles its heritage is a critical success factor. The truth is, it's actually *more fair* to treat different customers differently. A customer who invests more in your firm is certainly owed a greater level of service and attention, and by treating customers individually the enterprise can usually raise the general level of service for nearly *all* customers. In Chapter 14 we'll look more closely at this and other cultural obstacles to implementing a 1:1 marketing strategy.

Dealing with BZs is definitely a ticklish problem, fraught not only with internal issues, but also—as First Chicago Bank found out—potentially disastrous PR implications. When First Chicago began charging customers for doing transactions at a teller window that could have been performed at an ATM, the firm's goal was only partly to make up for the higher cost of such manually conducted services. It also wanted to provide a disincentive to those BZ customers who tended to take up more teller-window time and money than they could ever return in profits to the bank. The bank's real goal, in effect, was to find a gracious way to help its unprofitable customers become *some other bank's* unprofitable customers.

When the initiative was announced, it generated a wave of very bad publicity, held up by the press as an example of disservice to customers. Almost all the news accounts failed even to mention that the *only* transactions being charged for were those a customer could have easily performed at an ATM. But as one First Chicago executive later explained,

"Loyal customers win and optimizers change their behavior or find an institution that is willing to ask profitable customers to subsidize them."

A variety of competitors advertised tauntingly that no First Chicago customer would be too small or too unprofitable for *them*. It would be interesting to know whether any of these competitors has actually profited from the new customers obtained in this campaign. As for First Chicago, it reported that the program generated a 230 percent increase in the proportion of deposits made at ATMs within the first month, contributing to a substantial decrease in the firm's operating costs per customer.

In the end, it might be appropriate to rethink the three objectives of any business, and to add a fourth: Businesses exist to

1. Get customers

2. Keep customers

3. Grow customers

4. *Fire* customers

But remember that whatever steps you take to make your BZs more profitable could easily be held up to public scrutiny. Don't put yourself in First Chicago's position. Go out with the full story to all your customers first, and put a press release out that explains the program's rationale (And why not? You can't keep it a secret!).

Fencing Off Both Ends of Pitney Bowes's Customer Spectrum

In late 1993 the mailing systems division at Pitney Bowes began wrestling with the issue of a flattening growth rate and lower profitability. By far the dominant competitor in the postal meter and mailing systems category for some seventy-five years, Pitney Bowes enjoyed a U.S. market share of more than 80 percent, and over the last decade the company had branched out into other business areas, such as copiers and dictating equipment. But the division's marketing executives, VP/Worldwide Kathy Synnott and U.S. large business marketing director Tom Shimko, knew that even though market share was high, customers were disconnecting in ever greater numbers.

Shimko was assigned to tackle the problem, and began studying the historical data to develop a valuation model for the firm's customers. By law, Pitney Bowes is required to know the locations of all its postage meters, which it only rents, and never sells outright. So even though it wasn't all computerized, by linking elements of the historical data with the results of recently administered customer care surveys the company created an algorithm for estimating customer LTV, and then rank-ordered all 1.2 million customers, top to bottom. It discovered that more than two-thirds of the value of the customer base could be accounted for by less than 10 percent of the customers—roughly the top 100,000 accounts. In addition, the firm found it had the biggest retention and profitability problem within the lowest 25 percent—accounts principally sold and serviced by telemarketing and direct mail. Within this group, annual additions were offset significantly by cancellation rates that ran as high as 40 percent.

So Shimko set up two customer portfolio management operations, covering both the company's best and worst customers. Just as MCI fenced off its best customers for special treatment, Pitney Bowes fenced off both ends of its customer spectrum, and then differentiated these two groups by certain other variables designed to serve as proxies for customer needs.

The retention team, assigned to the low-value "churners," went straight to work trying to reduce cancellations. Unlike a bank or a phone company, Pitney Bowes incurs a substantial expense both in acquiring and in disconnecting a customer—particularly a small customer. A low-end postage meter can be operated in a do-it-yourself fashion, but the equipment itself first has to be delivered and, if the customer disconnects, it must then be picked up again.

So one thing the retention team did was tactical, to put off this expense. They used the database tags to identify no-growth accounts with the highest probability of attrition, and telemarketed to them at the two points in time when cancellation was most likely—as they received their first invoice, and at the end of their first contract year.

Strategically, what the retention team found was that retaining a higher proportion of small-business customers was largely a matter of selecting prospects more carefully to begin with and then offering sign-up deals that were tied to longer-term relationships. Instead of ninety days of free service, the company tried a number of staged offers, much as MCI had done—the first thirty days free, followed by a rebate at the end of the contract year, and so forth. Again these offers converted fewer prospects, but the converts were more loyal. At the end of the first year, attrition in this group had fallen by 20 percent and, while market share had improved, the firm actually did it by recruiting *fewer* customers than in the previous year.

Within the portfolio of small businesses being monitored by the retention team was a host of niches and subgroups with distinct and different needs for postage meters. So the firm launched a "professional office" program to help thousands of business professionals with their use of the mail—a dentist program for dentists, for instance, as well as other programs for doctors, accountants, lawyers, and so forth. Each initiative involved prestructured do-it-yourself mailing ideas and promotions.

While the retention team focused on the low end of the customer spectrum, the loyalty team focused on higher-value customers, in what Shimko termed a "less-to-gain, more-to-lose" scenario. A decline in churn was relatively easy to measure at the low end, but the benefits of making an already valuable customer even more loyal and profitable would be difficult to quantify, and would require a longer planning horizon. Nevertheless, in tracking interactions with these higher-volume MVCs, the company learned a number of things that improved its selling process. For instance, it found that selling to influencers tended to generate better, more dependable results than selling to decision makers. One reason for this, Shimko suggested, is that a decision maker at a large firm is more likely to take a numbers-oriented, nothing-but-the-facts approach, while an influencer (i.e., the secretary or the mail room manager most responsible for using the equipment) is more easily persuaded by the idea that a firm will stand behind its equipment and be available to help whenever help is needed.

The firm benchmarked other companies, then developed a number of customer care initiatives, including user-group seminars, special supply offers, a restricted toll-free service line, on-line identifiers so every employee would recognize an MVC, and even a newsletter, where Shimko promoted the firm's brand identity to MVCs at a fraction of the more traditional advertising cost. The company also identified the most elite customers within its MVC ranks—a scant 1,000 enterprise customers, less than 0.1 percent of the base, accounting for some 12 percent of the business. Most of these super elites were already identified as key accounts by the company's sales organization, but now their views on additional product and service needs were carefully solicited by the marketing department and used to define gaps that could be filled ahead of the competition.

The overall effort at Pitney Bowes required two departments to coordinate their efforts. The product marketing department continued to manage line profitability, new-product launches, and intraline positioning, while the newly established customer marketing department was charged with maximizing customer LTV and share-of-customer. Shimko found he could reshuffle existing resources and set this new function up at little incremental cost to the organization. So, while product marketing continued to be evaluated based on the year-to-year sales performance of each individual product, customer marketing is now being evaluated based on year-to-year revenue and profit growth in the customer portfolios being managed.

Customer Differentiation as the Basis for 1:1 Marketing

Pitney Bowes's experience succinctly captures the essence of the differences between traditional, product-oriented marketing—i.e., aggregate market competition—and the kind of customer-driven competition practiced by the 1:1 enterprise. Traditional marketers have always focused on *getting* as many customers as possible, while the 1:1 enterprise focuses not just on getting them, but *keeping* and *growing* them as well—and not just any customers, but the *most valuable customers.*

Shimko, now Pitney's vice president for U.S. marketing, found that these two dimensions of competition don't really conflict with each other. There's no reason not to have both a product marketing department *and* a customer marketing department. Customer differentiation is one of the 1:1 enterprise's most important disciplines, in navigating its way into this new dimension of competition. To be successful, the 1:1 enterprise must be capable of making explicit decisions with respect to which customers are worth keeping, which customers can be profitably grown, and which are not worth having to begin with.

And customers are happy with this. They don't resist. Customers don't *want* to be treated equally. They want to be treated *individually.* In the long run, treating customers individually will pay much higher dividends than treating products individually.

. . .

Understanding the differences that exist between one customer and another is only part of the 1:1 enterprise's task. No matter how detailed we are in describing all the ways customers can be individually differentiated, the success of any strategy designed to profit from *understanding* these differences depends on *behaving* differently toward each customer based on this understanding.

To be successful, an enterprise must *match* the right customers with the right products and services. The traditional competitor produces a range of products first, and then tries to make it as easy as possible for each customer to match himself with the right product. But in the Interactive Age, customers can make their needs known to an enterprise even before the product is made.

Using computer technology, an increasing number of firms are now cost-efficiently customizing individual products to individual customer specifications—making each product to order, with particular features, configurations, or styles. It is customization that completes the "feedback loop" with an individual customer, allowing a 1:1 enterprise to create Learning Relationships. Mass customization is simply a customization process that has become cost-efficient and routine.

We've now finished our discussion of customer differences. In the next few chapters we take up the subject of how the firm *behaves* toward each customer—the product or service it delivers, and how it invoices, packages, promotes, and delivers that product or service. Mass customization is the first topic.

THE ASYMMETRICAL BRASSIERE

How to Profit from Mass Customization

The free enterprise system has nearly choked us all with choice. Increasingly efficient manufacturing technology has made a withering assortment of products available to us, with different colors, shapes, sizes, features, benefits, textures, versions, configurations, styles, and tastes. But rather than giving us satisfaction, the amount of choosing we have to do in everyday life can actually be a burden. In an effort to reach highly targeted niches, and to provide a competitive product in every finely tuned category, traditional marketers have flooded the marketplace with a plethora of variations on every theme. Offering greater choice can be an effective strategy for a producer, but for the busy customer who wants just what he wants, choice can actually prove to be a stumbling block to purchase.

Customization—making a product to an individual customer's order—allows the enterprise to treat different customers differently *without* requiring them to wade through a burdensome number of selections. Until recently, however, customization was, almost by definition, too costly a process for all but the most expensive and upscale products. But with the kinds of computer power available on the assembly line today, an increasing number of firms are finding they can *cost-efficiently* customize their products and services in mass quantities, a process known as mass customization. The real power of mass customization is that it links the enterprise's behavior with a particular customer's individually specified needs, allowing the firm to create a Learning Relationship with that customer.

The Burden of Choice

When you see an ad in the newspaper that screams "Thousands of sofas to choose from!" don't you get a bit exhausted? After all, you have only one living room. For today's picky consumer, combing through thousands of alternatives to find the one right item is a wearying, but not unusual, experience.

Even for services and products we buy repeatedly, it is often the case that hundreds of varieties are offered, but every week, or every day, we have to choose all over again. Think about how many different ways people order gourmet coffee, for instance. At Starbucks and other gourmet coffee bars, all the products are made to order. Every customer's individual specifications are accommodated quickly and efficiently. There are many different varieties, and every customer has his or her own favorite drink. *Everyone* receives a customized product—so what's wrong with this?

What's wrong is that every day, every time a customer comes in, she has to *re-specify* how she wants her latte. She can order it the same way every day for weeks or months, but she will almost certainly have to re-specify every time. Not only is this a lot of trouble, but with each purchase she takes the same risk, that this time the service person won't catch all the details of her specification, or that her drink will be mixed up with someone else's and she won't discover it until she's out the door and down the street. She has to check the bag *every time* to ensure that she has the extra lid, because she likes to switch lids when she gets to work and keep the drink hot longer.

Okay, but what's the alternative here? Didn't we just finish a whole section analyzing how customers are different? Surely customers aren't all going to be happy with the same thing, the same service, the same price-value trade-off. If customers really do have different needs, then the more diverse these needs are, the more product variety must be offered to them, right? Certainly our customer prefers having her made-to-order latte rather than a more standard drink, and if there weren't a demand for thousands of different styles of sofas, there would be no warehouse advertising them this way.

So, are we suggesting that customers would be happy with more simplicity and less choice?

Actually, yes. The fact is, customers don't really want choice. That is, they don't want to have to choose. What customers want, whether they are consumers or businesses, is for you to *know* what they want, and when and how they want it.

There is, of course, an important difference between the

sofa warehouse and the gourmet coffee shop. The sofa buyer physically reviews dozens, maybe hundreds, of furniture items, to pick out the one or two she wants. Perhaps the furniture is loosely arranged by style or price, and perhaps a helpful salesperson can steer her to the right general area of the store. The sofas, however, have already been manufactured. If she doesn't find the upholstery she wants, she can order it from the factory, but the advantage of taking one off the floor is that she can have it in the house in days or hours rather than months.

The coffee customer, on the other hand, *always* gets her product made to order. But every time she buys it she has to instruct the enterprise again, repeating the product specifications she has already given the firm dozens of times previously.

Specifying and Remembering

These examples illustrate two fundamentally important principles that must be applied to turn customization into a competitive advantage.

1. *Design interface* In a make-to-order world, the enterprise needs a convenient but accurate way for a customer to specify exactly what he or she needs. If the design interface involves strolling around a three-acre warehouse to find the right sofa, or waiting eight weeks for the made-to-order product, it is not very convenient for the customer, nor is it particularly cost-efficient to the firm (think of the inventory cost of maintaining thousands of sofas).

2. *Customer specification memory* One of the first principles for doing business as a 1:1 enterprise is that you should never require your customer to tell you the same thing twice. The enterprise can make it irresistibly convenient for a customer to continue doing business only if it actually *remembers* what each customer has specified individually.

These are the two aspects of customization that must be correctly mastered in order to turn the act of customization itself into an effective competitive tool for getting, keeping, and growing customers. Clearly, the sofa warehouse has an inadequate customization interface, while the coffee bar fails to remember its customers' product specifications. Either of these problems is enough to derail a 1:1 enterprise. Only a firm that is able to overcome both issues will be capable of turning customization into a defensible, long-term competitive advantage.

Think of the act of choosing as a kind of barrier between your customer and you. The more alternatives you ask the customer to choose from, or the more times you require a customer to make the *same* choice, the bigger this barrier is. Direct marketers have known this since the beginning of mail order shopping. One sure way to *reduce* the response on a solicitation mailing is to offer several detailed options and require that the respondent choose from among them. No one knows exactly why response goes down when choice is introduced, but it probably has to do with turning a simple, one-step decision ("Am I going to respond to this offer or not?") into a multiple-step decision ("Okay, I think I like this, now, let's see, which option is right for me?").

When Nissan flirted with mass customization in the early 1990s, they were reported to have offered as many as eighty-seven different types of steering wheel from which to choose. But their customers tended to like only a few of them, and what they disliked was having to choose from such an unnecessarily time-consuming array of options.

Barista Brava: Serving Customers Not Just Coffee

Let's return to the Starbucks coffee outlet, and think about the firm's design interface and customer memory. Clearly, Starbucks is able to customize its various products to individual specifications. Its design interface is very simple, requiring only that a customer specify her product verbally when ordering.

However, because Starbucks is not set up to *remember* those individual customer specifications, from day to day the customer has to start all over again with every purchase. The customer must specify on Monday, then re-specify on Tuesday, and then re-specify on Wednesday, and so forth. She might buy the same thing every day for weeks or months at a time, but each purchase must be preceded with a repeated product specification. In effect, every time the customer interacts with Starbucks, she must again choose the particular product that will satisfy her own personal taste, from among the hundreds—or thousands—of products being offered.

Barista Brava, however—an up-and-coming Starbucks competitor—works differently. Barista's service people work in teams of two or three and do everything. They take a customer's order, prepare it, and serve it to the customer.

The Barista customer enters the establishment and chooses whether to enter the line for drip coffee or espresso. This is Barista's sole concession to the kind of division of labor that dominates most manufacturing models.

Each team is led by a *barista* (Italian for "bartender") who watches the line to see which customers are coming in to the store. Like a maître d' at a fine restaurant, part of the *barista*'s job is to *remember* his customers on sight, so when a customer gets to the head of the line, her coffee is already prepared just the way she has always ordered it.

George Harrop, Barista Brava's owner, takes pride in the fact that one of his baristas once served twenty-eight customers in a row without having to ask a single one what he wanted!

"We're in business not to serve coffee, but to serve customers" is Harrop's constant refrain. And he knows that remembering customers' individual tastes, saving them the trouble of re-specifying (and avoiding all the risks that go along with this), is the simplest, most straightforward way to serve them well.

Of course, a regular customer who orders a *different* type of coffee every time will see no benefit, because she has no "regular" order to be remembered—but the overwhelming majority of heavy gourmet coffee consumers tend to stick with a preferred type of coffee. Or, a *barista* might remember more than one "regular" order for a single customer. She might come in twice a day, always ordering a decaf latte before work, and a double espresso after lunch.

Customization vs. *Mass* Customization

The competitive advantages of customization can be genuinely immense. When a customizing firm uses the right
design interface and remembers its customers' individual
specifications and interactions, a truly powerful relationship
can be developed with individual customers. This is made
possible because an enterprise takes an *integrative* approach to competition, one customer at a time—linking the
individual customer's interactions with previous knowledge
of that customer, and then using this learning to drive the
company's actual production process. In short, the customer
tells us what he wants, then we deliver it that way to that
customer—treating each different customer differently.

It's one thing, however, to create a database of individual customer information and feed it constantly with updates based on interactions with customers. It seems another thing entirely to orient an enterprise's actual
production and service delivery processes to such individual demands. For any firm that has developed a cost-efficient method for producing high quantities of a standardized product or service, customization can loom as a
prohibitively expensive obstacle to becoming a 1:1 enterprise.

But this is where the third capability of computer technology comes into play. In addition to making routine interactivity possible and radically improving the cost-efficiency
of computerized databases, computer technology has also
been applied more and more frequently to logistical and
assembly-line processes themselves, allowing firms to man-

ufacture and deliver customized products with increasing efficiency.

Customization occurs when an individually tailored product is delivered to a customer. *Mass customization* occurs when the process of customizing products is engineered into a routine. Joe Pine, author of the benchmark book *Mass Customization: The New Frontier in Business Competition* (Boston: Harvard Business School Press, 1993), defines mass customization as the cost-efficient mass production of goods and services in lot sizes of one.

In order to become a mass customizer, a business must modularize its processes, so that it is not so much engaged in producing an end product or service as it is in producing *elements* of the product or service that can then be assembled in different combinations, based on what individual customers request. Pine says that modularizing a firm's production process to become a mass customizer is somewhat analogous to building toys with Lego building blocks. Lego blocks come in just a few standard sizes and shapes, and each block is equipped with a coupling mechanism that allows the user to join it easily with any of the other blocks. A child can assemble an infinite variety of toys by arranging this finite number of Lego blocks in different ways. Rather than thinking of mass customization as the actual making of a product, visualize the process as the assembly of premanufactured units, not unlike Lego blocks.

Mass customization like this can be made more and more effective by reducing the "granularity" of the modules, thus exponentially increasing the number of possible production outcomes. Unlike the niche marketer, the mass customizer doesn't manufacture all the potential combinations of a product and then wait for some customer to request one—in many cases there are so many possible combinations that it would be literally impossible to do so. Rather, the mass customizer waits to receive a request from an individual customer, and then creates the product or delivers the service to order, assembling it from a combination of components.

Another key to developing a mass customizing firm is to form an organization that *learns* from each new customization initiative. The mass customizing organization must be capable of routinizing the act of customization by remembering the steps that had to be taken for each new, previously not encountered request. Pine says the most effective organizational structure for a mass customizer is somewhat similar to that of a continuous improvement firm—a workforce of multidisciplinary teams, constantly on the lookout for opportunities to make incremental improvements in product or service quality. But he says it is different from continuous improvement in one key way: The continuous improvement organization is driven by observing the engineering, production, and delivery processes, and comparing the results of these processes to the desired final product. But the mass customizing organization is driven by observing and remembering individual customer requests, and comparing them to what other customers have requested.

One way to point out the difference between customization and mass customization might be to take a good look at how the Ritz-Carlton tailors its services to individual customers. The Ritz-Carlton hotel chain trains all its associates—from those on the front desk to those in maintenance and housekeeping—in how to converse with customers and handle complaints immediately. In addition, it provides each associate with a "guest preference pad" for writing down every preference gleaned from conversations with and observations of individual customers.

As part of its widely renowned total quality program ("Ladies and gentlemen serving ladies and gentlemen . . ."), Ritz-Carlton refers to any type of customer complaint or comment as an "opportunity." If you happen to be in a Ritz-Carlton hotel and overhear two employees talking about the "opportunity" they had with the guest in Room 315, keep in mind they might be talking either about a guest who needed more towels in the room, or one who became extremely irate when his phone didn't work correctly. Every such opportunity is entered into a database that now contains individual profiles of more than half a million guests. Employees at any of the thirty-one Ritz-Carlton hotels worldwide can gain access to those profiles through the COVIA travel-reservation system.

What the Ritz does is simply remember what its customers tell it to do, and then the hotel chain tailors its service individually, based on this learning. If, for instance, you were to check in to the Ritz-Carlton in Marina del Rey and ask for a firm pillow, they would note this fact and, next month, when you checked in to the Ritz-Carlton Buckhead in Atlanta, you would have a firm pillow in your room even if you forgot to request it again. Whether you request a computer desk in your room, or a minibar without liquor, or a cube of ice in your white wine from room service—any uniquely personal request, suggestion, or complaint is noted and *remembered*. The Ritz prides itself on customizing its stays to accommodate the individual tastes of travelers.

However, despite the fact that the company is unquestionably one of the highest quality service providers in the business (winning the Baldridge Award in 1992), the Ritz-

Carlton hotel chain is a customizer, but not a *mass* customizer. If a Ritz-Carlton concierge is asked to find a good dry cleaner for a particularly unique kind of clothing, for instance, he will figure it out and ensure that the customer gets what he wants. Then he'll enter the request in the customer's preference profile. But the next time another customer asks for something similar—say, a different type of leather cleaning—the concierge on duty at the time will have to *reinvent* the process, as will concierges at all the other Ritz-Carlton properties when and if they face similar requests.

The Ritz-Carlton's design interface is simple—very similar to Barista Brava's or Starbucks'. Its memory of customer needs is also excellent, using a regularly updated database accessible to every operating unit. But its process for actually delivering customized services needs to be changed if it hopes to become a truly cost-efficient operator. To be a genuine mass customizer, the organization must be able to learn and adapt, not only to the individual needs of particular customers, but to the service delivery and production processes themselves.

Mass Customization in Practice

Dell Computer is a firm we first visited in Chapter 3, as an example of how a 1:1 enterprise would look on the 1:1 Enterprise Strategy Map. It sells personal computer systems in the direct-to-consumer channel—that is, by mail, phone, and package delivery. Dell offers a certain finite variety of CPUs, monitors, printers, and other elements, but altogether these elements can be combined into more than 14,000 useful configurations. Although Dell offers catalogues to customers to assist them in picking out their products, Dell knows that trying to portray all the ways its systems can be configured would overwhelm any catalogue.

Rather, when a potential customer (or a current one) calls in to Dell, the service representative first interviews the customer with respect to the type of use he plans for the computer. The representative is careful to match his questions, as closely as possible, to the level of knowledge and understanding the caller displays. A first-time computer buyer may be asked whether he plans to use the machine for anything other than word-processing and spreadsheet analysis, for instance. After the interview, Dell recommends a system configuration that will meet the customer's needs.

Dell's system clearly illustrates the importance of a simple, useful design interface that focuses on the customer's needs rather than on the product's capabilities. The phone interviewer is trained to compare this particular customer's needs with other, similar needs expressed by other customers, and to match those needs with the appropriate configuration of computer. The company's order fulfillment system is set up so that each system is configured on a make-to-order basis, using modular elements.

It may be easy to see how Dell does it. After all, the company is really just an order fulfillment operation, assembling and shipping premanufactured components—something like electronic Legos. But mass customization is sweeping a wide variety of businesses where it doesn't always look quite so easy:

■ Levi's Personal Pair women's blue jeans are made to order, and sold at a price about 20 percent higher than the price for a regular pair of premanufactured jeans bought off the rack. After taking a customer's measurements in one of its fifty-six North American stores, the store clerk modems the fitting information to the firm's factory, where the custom-fit jeans are manufactured in any of more than 10,000 different sizing combinations.

■ Bally Engineered Structures, Inc., a Pennsylvania manufacturer of heavy refrigeration systems and related items, has converted its operation to mass customization. It used to have a standardized assembly process for the items ordered by customers—mostly refrigerated rooms and walk-in coolers. The components of its products, such as floors, foam panels, and refrigeration units, are modularized so that a customer can now order any one of more than 10,000 units rather than having to pick from the standard twelve units the firm used to produce.

■ R. R. Donnelley's Digital Division is capable of printing individually different documents, with color, picture, and print changes made digitally, as the press runs. No manual intervention is required in the process, and no buttons need to be pushed. The division specializes in print runs of 5,000 or less. Donnelley's customized printing operation is located in Memphis, the FedEx hub, specifically so a customer can request printed documents via phone or on-line, and then get them shipped out that very night. Small runs of brochures are ideal for Realtors who want to publicize individual houses, for instance. In a "drive-by shooting" the Realtor takes a picture of a home with a digital camera. After receiving the digital image by wire, Donnelley combines it with other information transmitted from the Realtor, and brochures with this house, or dozens of houses, are printed in small quantities and available literally *the next day*.

■ "My Twinn" is the name of a baby doll that is custom manufactured in Littleton, Colorado, to resemble the child who owns it! Facial features, hair style and color, and eye color are all open to tailoring, based on specifications and the child photos sent in with the order.

■ Ross Controls mass customizes pneumatic valves, using interactive computer-aided design to allow its industrial customers to specify and continually upgrade their valve systems. One customer, GM's Metal Fabricating Division, is buying 600 integrated valve systems, each individually customized for a particular stamping press, and each performing better than a standardized valve at one third the cost.

■ Morley Companies, Inc., headquartered in Saginaw, Michigan, operates five business divisions, including a travel incentive company. Morley's standard practice is to customize every aspect of each customer's experience right down to the kind of beverage stocked in the client's hotel room upon arrival—be it diet Coke, spring water from Europe, or Jamaican Blue Mountain coffee.

■ Indigo America, Inc., in Massachusetts, prints brochures and product packaging to individual, mass customized specifications. Imagine going to a football game at Penn State, for instance, and seeing Joe

Paterno's face on the Coke cups or hot dog wrappers—or getting baseball cards made that feature each member of the Little League team.

■ Datavision mass customizes videotapes, using a rack of CD-ROM drives to load individual video modules on each. For a car company sending out video demos of a new model, for instance, the company could cost-efficiently turn out thousands, or hundreds of thousands, of individually customized tapes—tapes that promote trunk room to golf players, safety to parents of small children, and so forth. Each video could show cars with the exact colors, styles, and option packages the customer is most interested in—provided that the car company remembered to note these things on the customer's recent visit to a showroom. The video could even include a short message from the customer's own dealer and service manager. Datavision can do all this today and put videos in the mail for less than $5 each.

■ Lenscrafters can mass customize eyeglass lenses in about an hour, while the customer waits. Remember when you used to have to wait weeks for the delivery of a new lens prescription? Now the Miki Corporation, a Japanese eyewear firm, has taken eyeglasses a step further. At Paris Miki, a prototype store now open in Paris, a person not only specifies the lens prescription, but can also design the actual frame, and tailor its shape and lenses to any one of thousands of configurations.

■ Lutron Electronics, in Coopersburg, Pennsylvania, is a worldwide leader in lighting controls. Just a few of the customization possibilities include specifying colors for things like dimmers, switches, and cable/phone jacks to match the room where each is installed.

■ Personalized Books, in Millstadt, Illinois, can mass customize children's books. After taking a child's name and some other details, the firm works them into a standard story. The text appears integrated with color illustrations, just as any other children's book. The child's photo can also be incorporated into newborn storybooks.

One of the secrets behind the success of mass customization is simply that it allows a customer to *participate* in the actual design and development of his own product. As a result, the customer is much more likely to be satisfied with the overall performance of the product.

French Rags mass customizes upscale women's knitwear. The company, based in Los Angeles, became a mass customizer not because it wanted to create a competitive advantage for itself with its customers, but because of its need to survive in the face of what it considered an outright hostile distribution system. Brenda French, the ambitious founder and owner of French Rags, found herself at the mercy of an unresponsive, costly, and difficult retail store network. She was producing knitwear for women and shipping it to department stores where, she maintains, many of the buyers and merchandisers didn't even understand the product. For instance, she used to get an inordinate number of returns from stores where her merchandise had been displayed on hangers and stretched out of shape despite the clear instructions in her shipping documents to avoid hang-

ing the clothes. Even today French can turn bitter and angry when she recalls her problems trying to deal with the
"kids" who had powerful positions as buyers for large retail
chains, but couldn't seem to grasp the nature of her product.

In 1989, on the verge of bankruptcy, she began cutting
back on product distribution. But as she withdrew from the
retail market she received more and more phone calls from
a loyal band of repeat customers, each wanting to know
where to obtain more of her knits. So she bought a German-
made Stoll knitting machine (a computerized loom), and
French began taking orders nationwide through a series of
"trunk sale" events. She hired sales representatives—
largely from the ranks of her most pleased current customers—who were willing to host week-long sales events to
which current and new customers were invited. A customer
can go to such an event, pick out a pattern she likes, and
specify the color, style, and size of the dress. Then French
Rags makes the product to order and delivers it.

French Rags's design interface is, like the coffee bar,
human to human. Brenda French still buys the yarn herself,
from the same source in England where she has been buying for years. It is the same colorful yarn that made her
designs so popular to begin with. Now, however, this yarn
gets fed into a digitally controlled loom, and her products
are not premanufactured and shipped out to be inventoried
at a variety of retail stores, but instead made to individual
customer orders.

Levi's highly successful design interface was designed
by Custom Clothing Technology Corporation. According to
Sung Park, CCTC's young, entrepreneurial founder, one of
the most interesting customization tasks for clothing manufacturers in the future will be women's foundations—brassieres. His firm is now at work on a project to understand

the immense complexities of this subject, including the fact that all human beings are fundamentally asymmetrical—that is, no one's left side is an exact mirror of his or her right side. Some people are more asymmetrical than others, and since all brassieres today are manufactured as left-right mirror images, this has significant implications for the comfort and look of foundation garments.

CCTC is now trying to map out and understand all the different variables that could go into fitting a brassiere. The next step, if the project goes forward, will be to create a workable design interface—a fitting procedure that accurately and efficiently captures these variables, in order to match them digitally with the new capabilities of a digital production line.

The Custom Foot: Learning Relationships That Work

Designing a business around the customization proposition, rather than designing customization into an existing business model, brings a fascinating array of opportunities.

Just opened in Westport, Connecticut, and soon to be in a variety of other locations around the country, The Custom Foot is a new chain of custom footwear stores. The store sells men's and women's shoes, made to order, hand-crafted in Italy, in any of a wide variety of different styles. The shoes are mass customized not just to individually chosen styles and features, but to individually taken measurements as well.

A Custom Foot customer comes in and spends seven to

ten minutes with first one foot and then the other placed on a scanner device that takes a perfect measurement of each foot's contours. After this computerized measurement is taken, a salesperson manually takes additional measurements, using a tape measure and a traditional shoe-sizing tool. Jeff Silverman, the company's CEO, says the manually taken measurements are never actually used, but his research shows a substantial proportion of customers have more confidence in the product's fit if manual measurements are taken. (The computerized scanner device looks like no more than a tilted mirror. No actual scanning activity is visible to the customer.)

The customer then sits for a few more minutes at a computer console, answering specific questions about the type of wear she has experienced on her current shoes, and so forth. These questions are incorporated into the manufacturing process to ensure a better-wearing, better-fitting product. An additional set of marketing questions is included, in order to generate relevant, customer-specific information for the firm's customer database. By answering these additional questions, the customer earns a discount on her purchase. To reassure the customer on her privacy, the company explicitly promises never to permit the use of any customer-specific information outside its own business.

About 250 styles are "carried" in The Custom Foot's retail store, most as physical samples, but some just as photographs. The store has no actual inventory on hand for sale at all. The customer can pick out a style, then specify several different kinds of sole, different types, quality, and expense of leather, colors, and other features. Altogether, not even counting the fact that each customer's feet are measured independently of each other, a total of 12 million different configurations of style and features are available to be specified.

After the customer has picked a combination of style and features, the store modems the information directly to its manufacturing facility in Italy, where the shoes are hand-crafted to individual order. Within about three weeks, the shoes will either be sent back to the store for pickup or delivered to the customer's home, at her option. The range of prices for these shoes goes from about $100 to $250. They are no more expensive to purchase than any other good pair of adult shoes.

Silverman's goal, however, is more ambitious than simply creating a well-fitting, customized shoe. The company will soon invite the customer to bring to the store a picture of whatever shoe design he or she wants, clipped from a magazine, or even from a competitor's brochure or catalogue. Then, if The Custom Foot doesn't already have that particular style in "stock"—that is, if his manufacturing facility has not already created for itself the capability to make a shoe substantially the same as the one the customer has brought in—he will make it from the illustration. In this way his firm will have a continuing supply of new styles for its customers to choose from—a steadily increasing digital "inventory."

Eventually, Silverman plans to allow customers to "rate" different styles of shoes found on the store's shelves, so that the firm will have a richer and more useful database of customer tastes and preferences. With a rating system database, the store will know not just what shoe a particular customer has bought, but what shoe the customer also liked but didn't buy, at least not this time around.

You might think that even though no switches have to

be manually thrown on the assembly line, producing and delivering customized shoes *must* cost more per unit than standardized products. After all, somehow the right products have to get matched with the right customers and sent along to the right stores. But mass customization provides a number of cost-savings all down the value chain. There are usually little or no inventory costs, for example, and product returns and wastage are lower. These savings are so significant that as the cost of computer technology continues to plummet, a totally new production dynamic will soon appear:

In many industries, mass-customized products will soon be less expensive than standardized, premanufactured products.

Regardless of costs, however, the process yields important competitive benefits to The Custom Foot. First, there is the Learning Relationship. Once the enterprise has an individual customer's foot measurements and preferences in its computer, it will have an immense advantage in securing that particular customer's future shoe purchases. Even if a competitor offers an identical customized product, using identical mass customization technology, the repeat customer will find it more convenient to buy from The Custom Foot again, rather than having to re-specify and get remeasured. In fact, it is not unusual for a customer to come to The Custom Foot for her first custom pair of shoes and immediately order more pairs, in different styles, but made to exactly the same fit. Finally, a decent-looking pair of shoes that don't hurt the feet!

The Custom Foot calls each customer after every sale, to ask if everything is satisfactory with the shoes. The firm knows that even though a customer is likely to have a better-fitting shoe than she's ever had before, there may still be an issue to discuss. So they want to ensure they discover any complaints early, and they incorporate as much feedback and learning as possible—that is, as much as each customer cares to give them—into the customer database.

According to Silverman:

> Our business is not selling shoes. The products we offer, while of the highest quality, do not constitute our real business. The Custom Foot is, plainly and simply, in the business of satisfying the very particular size and style needs of our customers. We plan to create Learning Relationships with our customers so that once we've satisfied them we never ever lose their business. I mean *never*! And we're going to do whatever it takes to ensure we continue to satisfy each of our customers, individually.

Despite The Custom Foot's ambition to make whatever design a customer requests, there is an additional issue that sooner or later the company will need to wrestle with: the "badge value" of shoes. Many people do buy their shoes at least partly because of the name on the shoe. A particular Custom Foot design may look exactly like a Ferragamo, but the *name* Ferragamo won't be visible anywhere, and with some customers this will cause an insurmountable problem.

Perhaps the solution to this would be to go into another line of business, as a contract-customizer for designer names. Instead of (or in addition to) mimicking the style of a designer shoe, The Custom Foot might be able to talk individual designers into allowing the firm to sell their designs—with names attached—in mass customized sizes.

There is, however, a much bigger business opportunity here, beyond becoming a contract manufacturer. It might be easier to visualize this opportunity by first reviewing the recent history of the airline industry.

When the airlines began computerizing the reservations systems to speed the processing of passengers and ensure that planes were filled efficiently, a whole industry was created around computer reservations systems (CRSs). These operations soon became highly efficient purveyors of information more or less independent of their airline owners. Now, after just two decades of computer progress, nearly every airline has dropped its CRS into a separate subsidiary so it can sell its reservations-taking services to other companies, including competitive airlines. It is now widely known that American Airlines' SABRE reservations system actually generates a higher, more reliable profit than the airline itself.

What if a firm such as The Custom Foot were to set up licensing agreements with a number of other shoe manufacturers, allowing these manufacturers to customize their own shoes using measurement information first taken by The Custom Foot? Ultimately, by pursuing this strategy, The Custom Foot could become the SABRE system of the shoe business.

Imagine: Five years from now you get out your Lands' End catalogue and call them up to order a pair of hiking shoes. The customer service rep then asks you for your Custom Foot ID number, so the shoes can be manufactured to fit your feet.

In this scenario, whose customer are you really?

These examples perfectly illustrate how the 1:1 enterprise must link production and delivery processes to what it learns from particular customers. By gaining insight into an individual's own particular needs and preferences, and then producing a custom-made product or service in response to those individual needs, a 1:1 enterprise locks the customer into a long-term, highly durable relationship. In such a relationship, much more is involved than mere price. And the value of the business is not found in the actual products being manufactured, but in the firm's knowledge of each individual customer's needs and product specifications.

Streamline: A Home Shopping "Agent"

Streamline is a Boston company in the business of customizing each of its individual customers' weekly shopping trips. The company offers customized home delivery of a variety of products and services, including groceries, pharmaceuticals, office supplies, laundry and dry cleaning, and even rental videotapes. Once you've signed up for the service, Streamline installs a staging area cabinet in an accessible area of your home—perhaps your garage. The cabinet includes a refrigerator-freezer, a dry storage compartment, a dry cleaning hanger rack, videotape storage box, and other compartments. The entire staging area can be locked; you have one key and Streamline has the other.

The company charges a $49 set-up fee, and $30 a month for subscribing to the service. This covers a once-a-week delivery service, but additional deliveries can be ordered on an ad hoc basis for an extra charge. Streamline buys wholesale and delivers retail. Streamline's groceries come to the home at the same price as they are sold in most supermarkets, its dry cleaning is no more expensive than that provided by most dry cleaners, and the selection of videotapes is as wide as might be found at any good video store.

Once a week the company delivers whatever groceries and other items are on your list at that time. Obviously, because of the staging area, you don't even have to be home to receive the delivery. Streamline just leaves some things at your house and picks other things up, such as videotapes to be returned or more laundry and dry cleaning to be done. You come home later, unlock the staging area, and put the groceries and other items away. You no longer have to get dressed to go grocery shopping, and you don't have to figure out whether to do it with or without the kids, before or after soccer practice. You can "shop" simply by reviewing and updating your Streamline shopping list—at midnight or at five o'clock in the morning if you find it convenient.

What makes Streamline's story compelling as an example of a 1:1 enterprise is its simple and effective *design interface*, and the way it uses its *memory* of individual customer interactions and feedback to generate Learning Relationships and lock its customers to it.

The design interface is remarkably straightforward. When you sign up for the service, the firm sends a representative to your home with a handheld bar code scanner and a laptop, for an "installation." The rep scans all the grocery, liquor, health and beauty aid, pharmaceutical, and other products in your home, to create your own ready-made shopping list, usually totaling 150 products or more. Some customers want this list provided digitally for their home computers, and the company also makes it available as a printed, faxable page. If a customer needs a fax machine,

Streamline will provide one wholesale. So any customer who wants to can use a PC and modem or a fax machine to send in a shopping list that has been updated to reflect this week's added items.

But most Streamline subscribers simply phone their orders in, speaking to a customer service representative on Streamline's end who can call up the household's list and update it while the customer is on the phone. In any case, the process takes just a few minutes, and replaces the two or three hours each week that the customer used to have to spend shopping and running errands.

The company's memory of each individual customer is the driving force behind its business. In addition to maintaining a record of each customer's shopping list, the firm regularly asks for individual customer feedback to improve the accuracy of its service with respect to that customer. Every customer is asked to rate the service on a scale of one to ten each week. While the average rating is very high, the firm carefully monitors each individual customer's ratings over time. If a string of tens is followed by a nine, for example, Streamline knows this may indicate a problem needing attention. Additional feedback from customers is encouraged, and might involve anything from asking for riper tomatoes next time to advising that the driver backed over a shrub during the last delivery.

Every week Streamline compares a customer's current shopping list and recent feedback with what it already knows about the customer from previous transactions and feedback. Thus, the company gets continually smarter about each of its individual customers, and it sends a revised and updated list back to each customer automatically, along with order confirmation. As each relationship develops,

Streamline accumulates a large amount of additional knowledge, and it continues to improve its service to that individual customer.

Tim DeMello, founder and president of Streamline, says each customer's feedback enables his company "to begin the Learning Relationship" with that customer. "We learn that they like starch in their shirts and they want them on hangers. We learn they like their bananas green. We learn that their children like to watch Disney videos."

According to DeMello, about half this learning takes place within just the first three to four weeks of each relationship, but even after that, the firm continues to learn additional, useful things about a customer for many months. During the first few weeks—the "rapid learning" phase—customers are encouraged to call in and speak with Streamline representatives to update their orders and deliver feedback verbally rather than on-line or via fax. This verbal feedback enhances the richness of the initial learning, and ensures that Streamline rapidly acquires as much information as possible about the customer.

As Streamline compiles a more and more complete record of an individual household's consumption rate for various products, it puts some products on an "automatic replenishment" basis—that is, it schedules the delivery of a product at some regular interval that approximates the rate at which the household consumes it. Toilet paper, or dishwasher soap, or any other product used with a predictable frequency can, after a while, be put on automatic replenishment.

It is easy to see how the nature of Streamline's basic relationship with a customer will evolve, from responding to the needs the customer remembers for herself, to taking care of all the things the customer no longer has to remember. It won't be too long in any given relationship before the company will have the capability to remind a customer to check that she hasn't run out of particular products. Either when a customer calls her order in to the Streamline customer service center, or perhaps when the customer signs on by modem to update her shopping list for this week, we could see Streamline providing a message back to the customer:

Take a minute to check your supply of eggs and sandwich meat, because our records show you may be running low.

Of course, to gain such an insight into any customer's habits requires a long period of increasingly accurate *interactions* with the customer, but that just means it is an even more powerful competitive advantage for Streamline. Like the car you teach how to drive, when you do business with a company like Streamline, you are constantly teaching it how to better serve you, individually. As time goes on, what may happen is that Streamline will send the customer a shopping list every week rather than vice versa. The customer would make any changes he wants, and then retransmit the list back to the company.

DeMello's vision for his firm includes two important directions for success. Operationally, he is constantly looking for ways to make a customer more efficient at ordering—basically, improving the design interface associated with the Streamline service. DeMello knows that for Streamline to maintain its competitive advantage with individual customers, he has to be able to accommodate a wide variety of customer-specified modes of interactivity. So he wants to ensure that the firm can participate in whatever interactive medium a particular customer might prefer. Although the primary mechanisms for interacting with customers today are the phone and fax, he wants to make the PC-modem interface more efficient, and he is considering connecting with customers on the Web. In addition, he wants to have Streamline counted in on any additional forms of interactivity, including whatever the cable television providers or local phone companies might be considering. DeMello feels that one of the key convenience issues in the future will be equipping a customer to interact more efficiently with his company from any room in the house, not just from the computer console or the fax machine.

Strategically, DeMello says his firm's real interest is not just "to be a consolidator of consumer products, but to acquire and own each individual customer relationship." Deepening each relationship is the firm's objective, and delivering products is just one means for doing so. Streamline is constantly on the prowl for additional items to be delivered, and DeMello welcomes feedback from customers about additional products or services they'd like to have—flowers, shoe repairs, and so forth. As a result of this feedback, the company is already offering fully prepared meals, and many customers now order two such meals each week, delivered with the groceries.

In addition to actual products and services for delivery, DeMello would like to offer additional, informational services to his customers, which would allow the company to "drill down" into each customer's individual preferences. Streamline could offer nutritional information and guidance related to a customer's grocery purchases. It could provide helpful information on a "look-up" basis: "What's the best way to apply floor wax?" Or it could assist the customer in keeping track of her own household's needs—storing menus and invitation lists, for instance, so a customer could look up what she prepared for the dinner party last spring, and whom she invited. Streamline plans soon to offer ready-made Christmas cards, and to maintain each customer's individual address list on its own database.

Streamline's business is made possible by the computer's capabilities to facilitate interactivity with individual customers, to remember what those individual customers have said, and then tailor the firm's behavior accordingly. The firm's entire business proposition is built around treating each different customer differently. Streamline represents a totally new business—really, a whole new category of business.

It comes as no surprise that such an initiative has important implications for the way products and services have traditionally been distributed in the world of standardized production and one-way mass advertising. Early on, Streamline offered its home delivery services to several retailers, but was rejected out of hand. ("Why would we want to *deliver* products to customers? We have a great store here, where we can display our merchandise and influence purchase behavior. Customers who come in for some things usually buy other things on impulse.") So, rather than using the supermarket or the video store as a supplier, then marking up the cost of the products to cover delivery expenses, Streamline resorted to buying wholesale and delivering retail.

DeMello says he would have preferred to operate the delivery business as a stand-alone service, something like Peapod, the groceries-only delivery service headquartered in Chicago. Peapod is affiliated with Jewel in Chicago and Safeway in San Francisco. Consumers are charged a fee for each delivery, in addition to the monthly subscription fee for belonging to the service. It has been a considerable burden for Streamline to set up the systems necessary to run a grocery business, a dry-cleaning operation, and a video-rental firm, as well as making efficient deliveries. However, he says, the consumer demand was clearly there, and when it became clear he wasn't going to secure cooperation from any existing stores, he didn't hesitate. Now, rather than offering a complementary service to a supermarket, similar to Peapod, Streamline has *become* a supermarket, albeit a very different kind of supermarket—and a very real competitor to the very supermarkets who rejected his original offers.

Streamline, like French Rags, found that the distribution system was simply set up for a totally different business model. To create their own businesses as 1:1 enterprises, both DeMello and French first had to invent new distribution models. If there is a moral to this story it may be this:

Disintermediation is the best revenge.

In business since 1995, Streamline's share of customer averages 85 percent for groceries, and virtually 100 percent for dry cleaning, yielding an annual revenue per household of some $6300 per year, more than double the per-customer revenue generated by Peapod.

Clearly, when it comes to using customization to keep and grow customers over the long term, Streamline's strength is its simple design interface and its constantly improving memory of individual customer specifications. The real power of customization is not its manufacturing efficiency, not the reduction in inventories, not the operational benefits. Rather, the true advantage of customization comes when it is integrated into an enterprise's ongoing relationships with its customers.

Because of advances in information technology, our whole economic system is rapidly changing from a produce-and-sell model to a make-to-order model. In the produce-and-sell system, choice is a prerequisite to meeting individual needs. The more choice available, the more finely tuned the products on offer can be. But in the make-to-order model, the factors that count are (a) the interaction with the customer (how do we know what to make?), and (b) remembering the customer's specifications (so he doesn't have to tell us again). *Both* these factors count—the design interface and the specification memory. No 1:1 enterprise can ignore either.

When the relationship with an individual customer is driven by a constantly improving knowledge of that particular customer's individual needs, we have a Learning Relationship. In the next chapter we'll dissect the Learning Relationship to see what makes it so powerful, and to decide which business situations offer the most potential for it.

SMART RETREADS

How to Keep Your Customers Forever, and Increase Your Margins Too

hink of your life as a consumer. There must be a retail establishment somewhere—maybe a deli, or a CD store—where you really like to shop, because someone there always seems to know exactly what you want. So now visualize going into this store and having them screw something up, with the result that you leave feeling a little angry. If it were any other store, you think to yourself, you'd take your business elsewhere. But the reason you don't go elsewhere is it would be too much trouble, right? You'd have to teach someone at another store everything about your personal tastes that the person at this store has already learned.

The basic strategy behind creating a Learning Relationship is put yourself on the other side of the equation:

Give your customer the opportunity to teach you what he wants. Remember it, give it back to him, and keep his business forever.

In this chapter we're first going to examine the requirements for applying this strategy in a variety of situations. But we're also going to look at how Learning Relationships can be used, not just to increase customer loyalty, but to improve unit margin. After all, if we increase the desire on the part of a particular customer to remain loyal, then we should also be able to improve our margin—on *that* customer's business.

Customization and the Learning Relationship

The reason customization is such a powerful competitive strategy is partly—but only partly—due to the customer's increased satisfaction with a better-tailored product. The enterprise will not necessarily realize a sustainable advantage just from the fact that a customer can get a product tailored perfectly to his own specifications. That is, once the technology is adopted by everyone and a number of competitors offer customization, then a customer will be able to get satisfaction anywhere, so the competitors are once again reduced to commodity margins.

What gives customization its real strength is that *customization allows a firm to create a Learning Relationship with a customer.* It is this Learning Relationship that will keep a customer in the franchise even after everybody has adopted a 1:1 approach. There are two requirements for creating a Learning Relationship:

1. The firm must be a successful, cost-efficient customizer, with an effective *design interface* and an accurate *customer-specification memory,* as we outlined in the previous chapter.

2. *The customer will have to expend effort* in order to teach the firm these specifications.

When an enterprise gains new knowledge of an individual customer's own specifications or needs, two activities are taking place: The firm is *learning,* and the customer is *teaching.* What creates genuine loyalty is the interaction of both these activities. The customer's effort to teach an enterprise, when the reward for that effort is a more individually satisfactory product or service, is what makes a customer loyal. The customer is, through his own effort, increasing the *value* of the enterprise, to *him.* With respect to this individual customer, the Learning Relationship ensures loyalty and protects the firm's unit margin as well.

The Custom Foot remembers the way your feet are shaped, and the way you prefer your shoes to look and fit. The Ritz-Carlton remembers you prefer a firm pillow. Streamline remembers you like your bananas green and your shirts on hangers. In each of these cases, a critical factor involves the level of effort or time the customer herself dedicates to the "teaching" process. In The Custom Foot's case, the customer must come in for the measurement, spend some time answering questions about how her last pair of shoes fit, pick out the right style, and make suggestions with respect to her preferences in leather quality or type of sole. The entire process, from beginning to end, requires a good twenty minutes in the store. Of course, twenty minutes doesn't seem like a lot of time to spend in a store. In fact, to buy shoes at some other store, the customer would almost certainly have to spend the same amount of time, pulling on different shoes to see what the fit was like, trying to match a preferred style with an acceptable sizing.

But at The Custom Foot, the customer needs to spend twenty minutes in the store *only* the *first* time. On this initial visit, the firm gathers all the information, *and then remembers it.* Even if a competitor were to offer identically customized shoes, with identical technology, after the customer has come in once to specify her shoe size and preferences with The Custom Foot, she will have to think twice before switching brands.

In Streamline's case, while the customization process doesn't require as much initiative on the customer's part, it takes place over a period of time that must be repeated before a competitor can provide the customer with the same level of convenience (again, assuming a competitor were to arise in the first place). Every week, when a customer updates her shopping list and provides feedback on the previous week's delivery, she makes it that much more difficult for a competitor to reproduce the level of convenience she will now be getting from Streamline. It might take several months for Streamline's computers to get a good fix on a customer's consumption rate of paper towels or dishwasher soap, but over time, as it accumulates a more and more accurate picture of this particular customer's needs, the benefit of remaining with Streamline continues to increase—for that customer.

Not all customizing firms have learned to *remember* the way their customers specify the product, and for them it is easy to believe that customization is not much of a loyalty-builder at all, but simply one more expensive product enhancement. For instance, Burger King promoted itself for years as a "Have it your way" hamburger chain, but relatively few people take advantage of this service even today, precisely because Burger King doesn't *remember* how any particular customer wanted it the last time! It's always more trouble to specify what your way is than to simply say "I'll have a number three."

But it's not difficult at all to imagine how Burger King's business would function if it were to allow customers to identify themselves with membership cards or PIN codes. This would enable the company to remember what "your way" is, for each customer. Customers could even specify different kinds of meals for themselves. If Burger King had such a capability, it could soon hear a customer come to the counter and announce "I'll have *my* number three, please."

Suppose a Starbucks and a Barista Brava were next door to each other, with no appreciable difference in the quality or price of their products. In one store, regular customers have to re-specify their drink every day, while in the other they do not. In the Starbucks outlet, the re-specification process is not only a little time-consuming, but it always entails some risk that the server will not understand the order correctly that day. No such wasted time or risk is involved at Barista Brava. For the Starbucks customer, it is just as easy to order coffee at Barista Brava tomorrow, while for the Barista customer, it is much more difficult to order coffee at Starbucks tomorrow. Which outlet's customers will be more loyal?

There are many examples of businesses that could easily gain an advantage by simply remembering the things their customers teach them. For instance, a retail bank that really wanted to save its customers from telling it the same thing twice would never make a customer fill out his own loan application. After all, the bank itself already has the information! Name and address, account numbers, balances—all this data is already stored electronically inside the bank's own computers somewhere. It's only a question of using information technology to save customers the time and trouble of looking up routine information.

This is exactly the capability Bank of America plans soon for its NCR-designed data warehouse. A Bank of America customer who calls to apply for a loan will have his application filled out for him, as the bank uses an integrated customer database to access his average three-month balances in a variety of accounts, his credit card payment history, and his other loan performance variables. The only thing the customer will have to do to complete the application is fill in the information Bank of America does not have access to—the loans and accounts the customer has with other financial institutions, the bank's competitors. Once Bank of America puts this program in place, an existing customer will find it much more convenient to apply for a loan at "B-of-A" rather than going to a competing bank, where he will have to fill out all the paperwork himself.

Or consider the ATM. It would be hard to think of a better device for interacting, customizing, and creating Learning Relationships with individual customers—yet most banks completely overlook its power. At least one New York City bank, for instance, a bank renowned for its computer expertise and its early, decisive use of ATMs to extend its market dominance, identifies every customer who comes to its ATMs by requiring a card and PIN code. Then this bank asks every one of these *identified* customers the same question: "What language would you like?" In a cosmopolitan city like New York, it's a good idea to offer a variety of languages—including even Korean and Arabic. But once you've put your own bank card into the machine *shouldn't the bank know exactly who you are?* Why would the bank have to ask you that question more than once or maybe twice?

In fact, if you access your own bank's ATM, and you have a fairly uniform pattern of usage, why can't the bank remember this pattern and use its memory to shorten your transaction and make it more convenient?

Welcome, Mr. Smith. Do you want your usual $200 cash, no receipt? Yes _____ No _____

We once suggested to some banking executives that the ATM should remember a bank's regular customers and their habits. One of the executives asked if it wasn't overkill to program in such a high degree of customization for every bank customer. After all, he said, it makes a lot of sense to figure out how to program this kind of memory into an ATM to save time for a very high-value customer, but what about the small-balance, high-cost "below-zero" customer?

Think about the dynamic here. While the BZ is standing at the ATM trying to figure out whether he can afford to make a $15 withdrawal, who do you suppose is likely to be waiting in line behind him? In Chapter 6 we asserted that mass-customized products and services would soon prove *less* expensive to produce and deliver than standardized, one-size-fits-all products and services. It should be easy to see that an ATM that customizes itself to *every* customer, whenever any recognizable pattern emerges, would be able to process many more transactions per hour through the same machine.

Overcoming "Quality Equality"

Two implications are worth noting here, and each has to do with the way an enterprise links its customer interactions to its production and service delivery processes. First, in order to produce coffee drinks in the way that it does, Barista Brava had to reorganize its processes, so that instead of an order taker relaying instructions to a kitchen worker, the coffee drinks are in fact prepared by integrated teams of order takers themselves. This allows feedback from individual customers to be integrated directly into the production process. In French Rags's case, the assembly line production process (that is, the digitized loom) is integrated with individual customer style and color specifications, so that there is a seamless connection between customer and product.

If Burger King were to launch a customer-identification system designed to remember individual customer preferences, in order to capitalize on the "Have it your way" idea, the enterprise could realize a significant advantage only by integrating this customer information into the actual production process. As was the case with Barista Brava, this would almost certainly mean a major reengineering of the production process itself. While it isn't at all difficult to imagine a McDonald's undertaking such a task, it is almost certainly beyond the capabilities of the current Burger King, with its more loosely controlled franchise system and its irregular, undependable service quality.

This brings us to the second important implication: product and service quality. The strategies that underlie 1:1 competition for customers are based on the premise that the enterprise's product and service quality are at least on a par with its competitors. No customer ever returns for more of a sub-par product.

We use the term QQP as an abbreviation for the kind of quality necessary to compete as a 1:1 enterprise. QQP stands for *Q*uality of product, *Q*uality of service, and fair *P*rice, each of which is important for ensuring that an enterprise can in fact compete in a 1:1 fashion. It is not necessary for a 1:1 enterprise to have superior product or service quality, simply a quality for each that puts it on a par with its principal competitors. This may in fact be the only kind of quality that can be sustained in an age when every firm is focused on quality improvement.

As we first suggested in Chapter 5, a dilemma that worries increasing numbers of managers is that even though the firm's customers report high—sometimes outstanding— levels of customer satisfaction, attrition can still be rampant. Product and service quality are no longer sufficient to differentiate a firm. As a result, in most industries firms are now facing a problem some consultants label "quality equality"—when every serious competitor's product and service quality is already at a very high level.

We don't mean to trivialize the amount of work or dedication that goes into quality improvement efforts. In fact, the continuous-improvement model provides important advantages to any firm wishing to transform itself into a mass customizer, as we said in the previous chapter. What we *are* saying, however, is this:

No matter how much work you put into quality at your firm, you will never be able to prevent your competitor from putting the same level of effort into his own quality.

In their excellent book *The Discipline of Market Leaders: Choose Your Customers, Narrow Your Focus, Dominate Your Market* (Reading, Mass.: Addison-Wesley Publishing Co., 1995), Michael Treacy and Fred Wiersema proposed three distinct "value disciplines"—operational excellence, product leadership, and customer intimacy. The authors point out that a firm must focus on only one of these value disciplines—in order to succeed in a competitive marketplace. But while all three disciplines offer a competitive advantage in the short term, only customer intimacy can actually create a long-term, sustainable competitive advantage. This is because no matter how excellent your enterprise is at operations or product leadership, unless you also enjoy some type of monopoly power over supplies, or research facilities, or intellectual property, you simply cannot prevent your competitor from executing every bit as well as you do.

But if you create a customer-intimate firm—a 1:1 enterprise that learns individual customer requirements and then executes to those requirements, improving each individual customer relationship over time—you can create a literally insurmountable barrier to competition, *for one individual customer at a time.* Providing product and service quality equal to your principal competitors is still essential. But the next round of competitive success will go to those enterprises that can establish *relationship* quality. As a 1:1 enterprise, if you have a Learning Relationship with a customer, you can rely on that customer to resist the entreaties of any competitors who do not already know his specific needs as well as you do.*

In a somewhat similar fashion, the 1:1 enterprise does not have to offer the lowest price—merely a fair price. By "fair" we mean not exorbitant in relation to the quality of the product and service. The range of prices you charge for your products and services has to be more or less similar to the range of prices charged by your principal competitors. However, the more individually tailored the product becomes, the higher a value the customer will place on both the product and the convenience of not having to re-specify it. Over time, this will create a willingness on the part of the most loyal customers to pay a *higher* price.

The Learning Relationship is not a difficult concept to understand, and it is surprisingly easy to apply in a wide variety of business situations, from small proprietorships to large industrial enterprises. After you order flowers for your mother's birthday, the 1:1 florist reminds you next year, in advance of her birthday. The 1:1 travel agent remembers that you prefer window seats, four-door sedans, and hotel rooms with data ports. The bookstore's frequency marketing program links the record of your purchases, so eventually the company will know that you prefer mystery novels, or self-improvement books, or romance fiction. And on the Web, companies like Amazon.com can do this without requiring a frequent buyer card.

---

* The Treacy-Wiersema definition of customer intimacy does not exactly parallel our definition of 1:1 competition. They rely on a number of aggregate-market rationales, and aggregate-market initiatives by themselves will not yield a defensible competitive advantage in the same way that true 1:1 marketing will. However, some aspects of their customer-intimacy argument do incorporate some of the same customer-specific dynamics we use in the 1:1 model.

Something important to note here is that Learning Relationships, as we have defined them, do not depend on emotional attachments. The kind of relationship marketing we are advocating has little to do with creating a fondness on the part of your customer for your product or brand. Rather, we are simply talking about *convenience*. What we are suggesting is that by remembering customer preferences and tastes, and by always picking up in a customer dialogue where you left off with this particular customer the last time, you can in fact create a "barrier of inconvenience"—a reason for that customer never to want to deal with your competitor again, provided only that you continue to deliver QQP, or product and service quality at a fair price.

This does not mean that emotional attachments don't often play a role in maintaining customer relationships. They do, and the 1:1 enterprise is better able to capitalize on such attachments than any other kind of firm. After all, *everyone* you talk to at a 1:1 enterprise will remember your name and what happened the last time you interacted. But emotional attachments are not the primary mechanism at work in securing customer loyalty. Convenience is.

Using Learning Relationships to Increase Profit Margins

It is a well-known economic axiom that in traditional, aggregate-market competition, increased unit volumes can be achieved only by accepting declining unit margins.

If a company sells 100,000 widgets this quarter, and desires to sell 110,000 widgets next quarter, then—all other things being equal—obtaining this additional sales volume will require a lower price, a coupon, a rebate, an incentive bonus to the sales force, an advertising campaign, or some other expenditure. Unit costs also decline with volume, but most firms operate competitively only at production volumes that already reflect a significant flattening in unit costs. No firm can continue to compete if it is producing and selling only 1,000 widgets per quarter, for example, because the unit cost of producing and distributing this small a number of widgets is prohibitive. Therefore, since all viable competitors will already be operating at reasonably comparable unit costs—i.e., at very nearly the lowest unit costs possible—no single competitor can increase its sales volume without suffering a decline in unit margin.

But the 1:1 enterprise will find it is able to *increase* its unit margins with increased sales volume, when that sales volume is measured on a per customer basis. That is, by collaborating with individual customers, interacting with them, and tailoring specific products and services for them individually—by creating Learning Relationships with individual customers—*a 1:1 enterprise can increase its unit margins over time.*

Start with the proposition that any firm's best, most loyal customers are generally more willing to pay the regular price, and less likely to be constantly looking for the best possible price-off deal. That's one reason we think of them as our best customers. When the florist sends a note reminding you of your mother's birthday, and offers to deliver flowers again this year to the same address and charged against the same credit card you used with the florist last year, what are the chances that you will pick up the phone and try to find a cheaper florist?

Every company tries to limit low, introductory prices to

brand-new customers who might not be comfortable with the product yet—"strangers" who need a little extra enticement to try the product *the first time.* By using Learning Relationships to increase customer loyalty, however, the firm no longer has to rely on price discounting—the only genuinely effective currency available to the aggregate-market competitor—to purchase a constant stream of new customers (many of whom are usually not so "new" at all).

The biggest cost of discounting to attract new customers is price dilution. Even though you advertise primarily to attract new customers, you already have a set of current customers, and many of them are (or would have been) willing to pay the regular, full price for your product or service. When you advertise a special price to attract *new* customers, your established customers also take advantage of it, although they were *already* going to buy from you at the regular price. This is price dilution.

An MVC is more valuable to the firm because he buys more frequently, or in greater volume, or over a longer period of time. Charging a best customer a nondiscounted price is not unfair to the customer. Your firm and its products simply have a higher value to your best customer, provided that you remember the customer from transaction to transaction, the same way the customer remembers you.

The primary reason a repeat customer is willing to pay the regular price is that it is *easier* for him to buy from you. It is more convenient—for *him.* He's bought from you before, perhaps many times. He already knows the quality of your product and service. He is already familiar with how your product is priced, bundled, delivered, warranted, and serviced. He's been satisfied in the past with your firm. If he were to buy now from a different firm—one he has never bought from—he would be taking a certain risk. The product might not be consistent, or it might not be as consistent as he already knows yours to be. It's more trouble to evaluate a new supplier than it is to continue doing business with a current one. Your customer knows how to find you—you're in his phone book, or on his list of acceptable vendors. When he wants another product, he simply deals with you again. No need to qualify a stranger, no need to search for a new source, no need to waste time evaluating things and making a new decision, trying to quantify the trade-offs among price, quality, and promptness.

Fred Reichheld paints a fascinating picture of the increasing value of customers who remain loyal for longer and longer periods. In his excellent book, *The Loyalty Effect: The Hidden Force Behind Growth, Profits, and Lasting Value* (Boston: Harvard Business School Press, 1996), the most authoritative book ever on the economics of customer retention, he meticulously examines a wide range of businesses and industries to document the benefits of retaining customers longer. While there really are too many useful ideas and concepts in *The Loyalty Effect* for us to do it justice with a quick summary, suffice it to say that loyal, long-term customers entail lower servicing costs, generate increased revenues, refer other customers more frequently, and are willing to pay a price premium. For companies that can calculate unit margins on a per customer basis, it should be clear that the highest-margin customers will be MVCs. In other words, MVCs give a firm not only a higher *volume* of purchases, but a higher *margin* on each unit purchased as well.

It should be clear, also, that virtually all the factors that contribute to the MVC's willingness to pay a higher, nondiscounted price are magnified several times over when we add to the equation the convenience of a highly customized

Learning Relationship, developed with the customer's investment of effort over a long period of time.

Let's go back once again to our magazine circulation director, first seen in Chapter 2. The magazine offers introductory prices to new subscribers as an acquisition tool, while collecting higher rates from readers who have already subscribed for a year or more. It costs only $35.90 to get the first 52 issues of the magazine, but when resubscribing for the second and subsequent years, the price increases to $75.90. As a practical matter, this differential in pricing is one reason magazines (and other subscription-type services) tend to lose customers early on to "churn." Customers sometimes quit and then resubscribe, using a slightly different name, or their spouse's name, just to get the introductory rate again.

Since new customers get all the good deals,
savvy customers always want a company to think
of them as "new."

But magazines could virtually eliminate churn if they were to become genuine 1:1 competitors, linking their product delivery process in a feedback loop driven by individual customer specifications—that is, if they were to create Learning Relationships with their individual subscribers. Imagine that a magazine could somehow track which stories were scanned or read in detail by a reader, and then each week deliver a magazine that was individually customized and increasingly relevant, *to that reader.* Suppose a reader were to subscribe to the magazine, and then every week find that the issue he receives in the mail is better and more focused than before on the issues he personally finds most interesting. If this were how the magazine subscription worked, then after subscribing for a year the reader would be receiving a very "smart" magazine, tailored to his own individual interests. When asked for more money on renewal, he would have to think seriously about whether it makes sense to quit and start again, just to get the introductory price. A second-year subscription to the magazine might cost more, but now it would be worth more too.

This, of course, is a completely hypothetical idea for subscription magazines. A paper magazine that comes in the mail cannot "track" what stories an individual reader spends time on. There is no customer feedback mechanism for a magazine, at least as magazines are currently manufactured and delivered. It's not hard to visualize how a "smart" magazine could be delivered in an on-line format—indeed, this is exactly the business proposition of a number of online services today—but few people want to spend time sitting in front of a computer screen to browse through a weekly magazine. Magazines are for reading on trains and planes, or for picking up from the coffee table for no particular reason. On the other hand, since digital printing technology already makes mass customization of printed documents feasible, and since researchers today spray microchips onto the surface of a newspaper to track how long a subject holds the paper in his hands, it may not be long before someone figures out how to mass-customize magazines embedded with microchips to provide individual reader feedback.

Are we too far out for you? Well, think of the Streamline subscriber who has stayed with the firm for a year or so, until all her shopping needs have been thoroughly tracked. Streamline would then know exactly how to select the right tomatoes for her pasta when she orders them, and what videos to recommend for the children. She would rely on the company to remind her when she's forgetting something.

It's obvious that it's in the long-time customer's self-interest to remain loyal, but this also means that Streamline could structure its fees so that once a customer remains with the firm for a certain period, the price *increases*. The way it would be implemented, it would almost certainly look more like an introductory discount for new customers than an up-charge for longer-term customers. Perhaps the $30 per month subscription fee could be raised to $45 per month, but left at $30 monthly for customers in their first year. Or perhaps, after the first year, customers would be charged a "data handling" fee, or an automatic replenishment surcharge.

One thing is clear, however:

Once a customer's individual needs have been taught to a 1:1 enterprise, the value of the enterprise to that particular customer increases dramatically.

There is undoubtedly some point at which even a loyal customer would decide the firm's charge is too high, and the higher the price charged, the more likely Streamline's business will be threatened by competitive imitators. But clearly, the enterprise can justify the higher price as the product becomes better tailored with every interaction and the relationship therefore becomes more valuable to that customer. This is quite different from the dynamic that drives pricing in traditional aggregate-market competition, where the loyal customer is being charged full price for the *same* product that the enterprise sells to new customers at half off.

Think again about the dynamics of The Custom Foot.

Once a customer has had her feet scanned and individually fitted to shoes, it takes no effort at all to order the next pair, to be fit the same way. The customer doesn't have to select from whatever sizes are available in the back of the store, doesn't have to try any shoes on, doesn't have to get measured again, *doesn't even have to come in to the store!* A repeat Custom Foot customer could easily order her next pair of shoes, or her next dozen pairs, over the phone, based on Custom Foot's catalogue (in Custom Foot's case, the firm will even work from a design in someone else's catalogue!). This is quite a bit more convenient than having to visit a physical site, even for a few minutes, and pick from what's there already. It is not at all unreasonable to expect a large proportion of customers to be willing to pay extra for this level of convenience.

Independent Purchase Events vs. Conditional Purchase Events

A simple way to visualize this principle at work is to return to the "marketing space" we first postulated in Chapter 1, when we suggested that customer-driven competition should actually be thought of as operating in a different dimension from aggregate-market competition. We mapped a horizontal bar and a vertical bar onto a hypothetical marketing space defined by the number of needs being satisfied vs. the number of customers being served.

Let's return to this marketing space and imagine that it contains a large number of "purchase events"—each square in the space can be thought of as a different customer satisfying a different need at a different time. As far as the aggregate-market competitor is concerned, these purchase events are completely independent of one another. That is, whether one customer buys the product or not is completely independent of whether another customer buys it. So the aggregate-market competitor's view of the business situation is this:

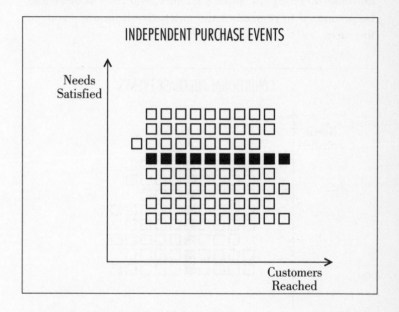

The aggregate-market competitor wants to "line up" as many customers as possible who are satisfying a particular need—a need that the firm can fill. It is because these purchase events are independent of one another that the aggregate-market competitor is forced to reduce price in order to gain more transactions. Because the customers are all treated to the same product at the same price, the market clears at whatever price the aggregate-market competitor must offer to attract the last, most marginal, least interested, new customer.

But the customer-driven competitor—the 1:1 enterprise—is looking at this same marketing space from a different perspective. From this perspective, rather than being independent, the purchase events are conditional. They are all undertaken by the same customer, and the *customer* can be presumed to remember the enterprise from one event to the next.

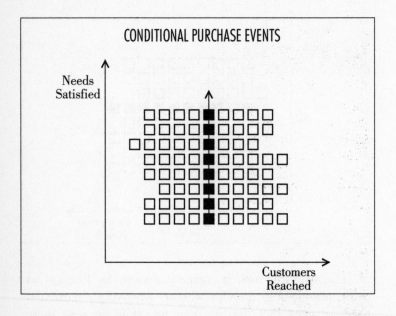

CONDITIONAL PURCHASE EVENTS

Needs Satisfied

Customers Reached

The 1:1 enterprise should ensure that the purchase events undertaken by any single customer *remain* linked together by the enterprise, so that each successive purchase event becomes more convenient for the customer.

Learning Relationships: Not So Easy All the Time

As compelling as the benefits of Learning Relationships are, this radically different business model cannot be applied in the same way by everyone. Companies such as home builders, real estate brokers, and appliance manufacturers—firms that do not interact frequently with end users—often don't transact enough to make a Learning Relationship viable over more than a short-term period. But each might find it beneficial to develop such relationships with general contractors, and each will enjoy more referrals from one-time customers by catering to these customers' individual needs. In *The Loyalty Effect,* Reichheld points out that one of the principal differences between a profitable home builder and an unprofitable one is that the more successful business enjoys a much higher referral rate. In any enterprise characterized by infrequent, high-ticket purchases, referrals are a critical differentiator.

Similarly, makers of products like paper clips, whose revenue or profit margin per customer is too low to justify building individual Learning Relationships with end-user customers, might nevertheless find it advantageous to cultivate Learning Relationships with office supply chains that interact directly with end users or purchasing agents. In Chapter 12 we'll discuss in more detail why and how a firm might go about creating Learning Relationships with the members of its distribution chain rather than with its end-user customers.

Producers of commodities such as wheat or natural gas,

which cannot be customized easily, or commoditylike products bought mainly on the basis of price, will have a particularly difficult time establishing Learning Relationships with their customers. They can really gain from this approach only by first expanding the definition of their "product." We'll see a lot more about this strategy in the next chapter, but one example we could use to illustrate the principle is the initiative being pursued by Bandag, the truck tire retreader.

Bandag sells retread rubber for truck tires to more than 1400 dealer-installers worldwide, each of which has the machinery to buff a tire down to its casing, evaluate the casing for any flaws that might make retreading impossible, and attach new tread rubber in any of a variety of tread patterns. However, the retread rubber Bandag sells is essentially a commodity, comparable in cost and quality to its competitors' products.

The company already employs information technology to simplify the customer interaction. After buffing the old tread off a tire, a dealer's inspection will occasionally reveal a flaw in the tire casing, rendering it unsuitable for further retreading. Often the flaw is a manufacturing defect, giving the tire owner a warranty claim, and Bandag encourages its dealer to invoice the manufacturer for the claim on the customer's behalf, collect the payment, and return the refund directly to the customer—oops, make that "client."

Starting with its largest, most committed national accounts, Bandag has also begun offering much more comprehensive fleet-management help to create deeper Learning Relationships. It has plans, for instance, to inject radio frequency microchips (RFI chips) inside the tread rubber of newly retreaded tires (the chips may in fact be "built in" when the rubber is manufactured by Bandag). The RFI chip will not only indicate tire pressure and temperature, but it will count a tire's revolutions, allowing the Bandag dealer to determine the actual mileage on a tire simply by "reading" the chip electronically from a distance. Thus, the customer will no longer have to rely on visual inspection, the truck driver's memory, or manual tread-depth measurements to determine when a particular tire needs to be taken off the vehicle and retreaded. Over time this process will give Bandag a base of highly accurate fleet-performance data. Soon the company will be able to report to a fleet owner on his fleet's performance, relative to other, similar fleets in terms of operating costs and tire efficiency, pointing out things done well since the last report, and areas for continued improvement.

The more experience the company builds with any single fleet owner, the more learning about this particular fleet's operating characteristics will be applicable to the relationship. In effect, each fleet-customer in this business will be teaching Bandag, its retread vendor, about the fleet's own individual needs and tire usage patterns, and the parameters of its operating costs.

Learning Relationships and the Customer Base

While a Learning Relationship is attractive to an enterprise because of the loyalty it engenders in a customer, what makes it attractive to the *customer* is its convenience. The principal driver of a Learning Relationship's benefit, from the customer's standpoint, is that it saves the customer time and energy in specifying his own individual needs. When a customer's needs are more complicated or unique—that is, when they are different from the needs other customers have—they are likely to be more difficult to specify correctly, and it will be more convenient *not* to have to specify. So, a Learning Relationship's level of benefit for the enterprise is directly proportional to the amount of needs-based differentiation in the firm's customer base:

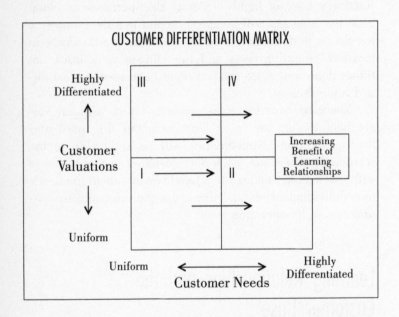

The direction of benefit, for a Learning Relationship, is *biased* in favor of needs-based differentiation as opposed to valuation-based differentiation. The more needs differentiation there is within the customer base, the more benefit can be realized from a Learning Relationship. An ATM that remembers a customer's regular transactions will earn just as much loyalty from the $15 BZ as from the $200 MVC or STC.

This doesn't mean that valuation skews are unimportant or irrelevant. As we'll see in Chapter 13, the most logical, cost-efficient way for an enterprise to make an orderly transition from aggregate-market competition to customer-driven competition is to prioritize this transition on a customer-by-customer basis. And while there are some business processes and customer transactions—such as the ATM service—that are better customized to *everyone,* there are others for which the expense of customization can be paid off more efficiently by allocating the benefits first to an enterprise's higher-value customers. Thus, the more skewed a customer base is in terms of valuations, the easier and more cost-efficient this transition strategy is likely to be for the enterprise.

Even purchase frequency, in the end, boils down to a needs-based difference rather than a valuation-based difference. Although a customer who purchases an item more frequently is likely to have a higher value to the enterprise, from the customer's standpoint it is neither frequency nor volume that makes the convenience of a Learning Relationship attractive. Rather, *it is the amount of effort the customer must expend in respecifying with each purchase.* Reducing that level of effort provides a benefit to the customer, and this benefit raises the real value of the enterprise to the customer, driving both loyalty and unit margin—with that customer.

From the standpoint of creating a loyal, higher-margin relationship with any particular customer, the Learning Relationship simply does not depend on differences in customer valuation. For the most part, the customer won't know and won't care how valuable he is to the enterprise relative to other customers.* What *is* important is the amount of needs differentiation.

This is why companies that sell commodity products have more difficulty establishing Learning Relationships. The customers of a gas station, an airline, or a wheat broker all need the same basic thing. For the most part, they want to meet the same basic need. Bandag figured a way out of this dilemma by expanding the definition of its "product" to include not just the commodity of truck tire retreading, but the service of fleet management.

In the next chapter we'll discuss a systematic way to minimize the disadvantages of a customer base that is not well differentiated by needs. We'll show how to increase the diversity of customer needs by peeling back the layers of a product to reveal the entire customer need set in all its true complexity.

---

* Although many customers will not care about this relative worth to a company, the most valuable customers are more likely to care—probably because they believe their value should give them some clout. We once witnessed a gentleman on an airplane who complained, and wound up his expectation that his problem would be resolved with the justification that he had paid full coach fare! The flight attendant was unimpressed. "We can't tell the difference between somebody who pays full fare and somebody who pays discount," the flight attendant told the man, probably to make the point that everyone is important to this airline. The man said, "Oh? Then would you discount my ticket? Because *I* can tell the difference!"

EXPANDING THE "NEED SET"

8

How to Customize, Even If You're Selling a Commodity

The basic trick in establishing a Learning Relationship is to look for all the little opportunities to remember differences among customers. Every piece of identification, timing, delivery, or product specification is a possible mechanism for establishing a Learning Relationship. The enterprise should see itself in the business not just of remembering a customer's specific needs for the basic product, but also the goods and services that surround the product—things such as how the customer would prefer to be invoiced, or how the product should be packaged, or even what additional products or services might also be indicated because the customer wants the basic product.

In this chapter we present a systematic process for expanding the definition of what any individual customer needs—from basic product to the product-service bundle and beyond. The reason an enterprise should want to do this is that a broader definition of the customer's set of needs will lead to more complex differences among customers. This in turn will enable the enterprise to benefit by remembering these differences and create Learning Relationships with its customers. In effect, by expanding the customer need set, the enterprise is "replotting" the customer base in the Customer Differentiation Matrix—moving it steadily to the right, in the direction of benefit for the Learning Relationship.

Of course, every business can benefit from doing this; the benefits are not limited to commodity sellers. A pharmacy, for instance, should remember not only its customers' prescriptions, phone numbers, and addresses, but their family relationships, their allergies, their doctors, and their insurance carriers. The pharmacy should make it so convenient for a customer to buy from it that the customer never wants to go to the trouble to teach any other druggist. Indeed, there is at least one high-end pharmacy now picking off the very best drugstore customers around the country, operating via toll-free phones and next-day package delivery.

Merck & Co., the pharmaceutical firm, purchased Medco Containment Services, Inc., in 1993 for $6.6 billion, precisely in order to be able to create Learning Relationships with individual drug consumers and their physicians. Relying on Medco's comprehensive database of individual medical records, Merck can remind individuals on blood pressure medication, for instance, that their prescription is low. The company even works with pharmacists and physicians on behalf of specific patients to recommend pharmaceutical alternatives to surgery.

Getting Your Customers to Want Different Things

The left-right bias of a Learning Relationship when it is viewed on a Customer Differentiation Matrix means something very important to your customer strategy. If your customer base is mired in quadrants I or III, on the left side of the matrix, then your chances for creating Learning Relationships are dim. In quadrant III you may be able to "buy" the loyalty of your most valuable customers, at least in the short term, with some sort of frequency-marketing or key-account program that disproportionately rewards them. In the long run, however, you'll find yourself in a bidding war for these MVCs, not unlike the market-share battles going on constantly in industries such as airlines, long distance, and credit cards.

Therefore, every firm should want to move its customer base, over time, to the right of the Customer Differentiation Matrix—toward greater and greater needs differentiation. You want your customers to want different things, so that by catering to their desires you can make them more loyal and increase your margins.

The most loyal customers are those who come to rely on the unique convenience of dealing with a firm that remembers them. But if a customer base is characterized by customers who all want the same thing, then we have a problem. If there's nothing unique to remember, then what's the benefit for the customer?

Obviously, every customer *likes* to be remembered and recognized. We're not saying that recognizing customers and simply calling them by their names isn't an effective and helpful service enhancement, and this applies whether your customers are consumers or other businesses. Often, however, what really cements a customer's loyalty is not the emotional reward of being recognized on sight, but the convenience benefit of having a variety of other things remembered.

When the enterprise sees its customers as having relatively uniform needs, what is often happening is that the firm is viewing its customers through the lens of a fairly uniform set of core products. But even a commodity product is actually a bundle of physical goods, ancillary services, delivery times, invoicing schedules, and other features that are rarely commodities at all. The truth is the "products" we sell are generally much more complicated than we give them credit for being.

A product or service can, in fact, be pictured somewhat like an onion, with layers and layers of ancillary services and other product features surrounding a core product. The more layers are considered, the richer and more complicated a product will become, and so the more diverse the firm's customer base will be in terms of what each customer needs from the "product." By focusing on these additional layers, an enterprise can replot its customer base into a position that is characterized by relatively more needs differentiation.

The trick is to visualize the product in the broadest sense possible. It helps to visualize your product not just as a product, but as an object that provides a service. Then ask yourself: What is the service my product is providing? It's easy to see how The Custom Foot can create a Learning Relationship with a made-to-order custom-fit shoe. The shoe performs its function better, and has more value to the customer, when it fits both the customer's physical foot and aesthetic tastes. Every foot is unique, and every customer has a different idea of what sort of style looks best.

But what are the services that a tape or disk-drive backup system provides to a customer? If Iomega were to include in its software an automatic reminder screen to help its customers remember they should back up their data, where does this feature fit in the description of the product itself? If videotapes and costume items are offered to help role-playing boys have more fun playing make-believe games with their Lego sets, then what role is Lego playing?

In its broadest possible sense, the product-as-service can be thought of in terms of three successively complex levels:

1. The **core product** itself includes its physical nature, if it is an actual product, or its component services and executional elements, if the "core product" is actually a service. Customizing the core product includes:

   ■ configuration

   ■ features or capabilities

   ■ fit and sizing

   ■ color and style

   ■ timing or frequency

2. The **product-service bundle** includes the services and features that surround the core product. Customization of the product-service bundle includes:

- invoicing, billing, and cost control (from the customer's standpoint)

- packaging and palletization of the products

- logistics and delivery

- promotion and marketing communication

- help lines and product support

- service operations

3. The **enhanced need set** includes any related customer needs that might be combined with the product-service bundle to enhance the overall set of needs that the product addresses. Customizing an enhanced need set includes:

- related products or services

- strategic alliances with other firms serving the interests of the same customers

- collaborative opportunities

- "value streams" following a product or service sale

For an enterprise attempting to create Learning Relationships by differentiating customers according to their individual needs and then catering to those differences, it might help to view the product and its enhanced need set as a diagram, like this:

THE EXPANDED CUSTOMER NEED SET

CORE PRODUCT	PRODUCT-SERVICE BUNDLE	ENHANCED NEED SET
Configuration	Billing, invoicing, cost controls	Related products
Features	Packaging, palletization	and services
Fit, sizing	Delivery, logistics	Strategic alliances
Color, style	Promotion, communication	Collaborative
Timing, frequency	Help lines and product support	opportunities
	Service operations	Value streams

As the customer's need set is expanded, the definition of the product itself becomes more complex, and with a more complex product the enterprise can make customization more beneficial. At each successive level of product complexity, the enterprise has another opportunity to remember *something* that will later make a difference to a specific individual customer.

When a company like The Custom Foot or French Rags makes a clothing item to an individual customer's order, tailoring it to an individual style or color combination or to a particular size, the company is customizing a core product. The same is true of Dell Computer, which customizes its product configuration to each individual customer's order, or of Streamline, which provides household product deliveries to order.

In each of these cases the enterprise's core product or service can be customized to the different needs or tastes of different customers. Every example involves a customer base that is already well differentiated in terms of customer needs—clothing and shoes, computer systems, household shopping needs, as well as an enterprise capable of making literal changes to its core products through mass customization. What about when a firm's customer base appears to be made up of customers with more uniform needs?

To create Learning Relationships with customers who have more uniform needs, we have to expand the need set. As we do, customers will become more diverse in the way they individually define their needs, and this will have the effect of "replotting" the customer base farther toward the right on the Customer Differentiation Matrix.

Customization Is the Key

Expanding the need set is not sufficient, by itself, to guarantee increased customer loyalty and higher margins. It is always helpful to improve the level of service you give customers, but you can't prevent your competitor from doing just as thorough a job as you. Instead, the key is to focus on *customizing* to each individual's own different needs.

The question to ask yourself, as we take a tour through each of these product and service ideas, is this:

What products and services can you offer now that will cement the loyalty and improve the margin on your customers even if your competitors offer the same products and services, *customized the same way, at the same price?*

Believe it or not, the answer to this question is: plenty. But customization is the key. Simply improving the quality of your product or service, while definitely advantageous in the short term, will not necessarily yield a competitive benefit over the long term.

Customizing Your Services

Every product and service comes with a bundle of ancillary services. An enterprise can focus on how its products are packaged or palletized. Purchase orders and RFPs can be stored and recalled when necessary, to save a customer the trouble. A consumer goods company selling to retailers should be able to palletize its products in different ways to meet the different specifications of its various retailer customers. Sam's, the Wal-Mart–owned warehouse club, requires packaged-goods companies to sell their products in extremely large sizes, partly in order to justify the low per unit prices that are Sam's hallmark. But some of these companies, unable to accommodate this requirement on their own assembly lines, package their cereals or soups or frozen foods in the standard sizes, ship the containers to another location, and then shrink-wrap several packages together to make up the required sizing for Sam's.

One of the simplest ways for any business-to-business firm to customize its product-service bundle is simply to remember how and when *each customer* wants to be invoiced. A credit card company with corporate cards, a phone company, or any other firm that sells a high-transaction product or service to other businesses might consider offering some customers the opportunity to tailor the invoices to weekly totals rather than monthly. Or a firm could provide the invoices on a quarterly summary basis, or even offer to allow the customer itself to specify which time periods to invoice at one time. The same, of course, goes for geographies, divisions, product lines, and every other conceivable invoicing breakdown.

Companies with products that are already fairly customized can benefit by customizing these ancillary services even further. An outdoor signage business, for instance, might consider that its service is highly customized to begin with. After all, an advertiser can buy as much or as little outdoor advertising as desired, covering virtually any period of time and any geography. A customer can even "ride the boards" to pick out particular locations to be included in the showing, or excluded from it.

The companies that buy outdoor advertising the most frequently are advertising agencies, who buy a range of media products for a variety of different clients. While the agencies' clients all want different kinds of outdoor exposure from the ad agency, the agencies themselves all need the same basic thing from the outdoor firms they deal with—as wide a range of out-of-home media as possible, so they can serve the diverse interests of their advertisers. This is similar to the difference between bookstores and book publishers (bookstores sell different titles to each customer, while publishers sell the same titles to each bookstore).

One simple idea would be to send invoices out in accordance with each agency's individual client billing cycles. One advertising agency buyer reports that if one of her clients wants to buy outdoor that starts on any day other than the first of a month, she and her client get extra invoicing from the outdoor company and complex reconciliation problems later with the client. A two-month "showing" that begins on, say, the 25th of the month, will generate three monthly invoices, not two—from the 25th to the end of the first calendar month, then the entire second calendar month, and then from the 1st to the 24th of the final calendar month. The situation is made even more aggravating because the advertising agency's own billing cycle to its clients begins on the first or the fifteenth day of the month, depending on the client.

Providing cost recaps, statements, and other financial reports on software spreadsheet programs *chosen by the customer* is another way to create a Learning Relationship, especially for a business-to-business marketer. Most business customers are concerned with cost management and control. Making it easier for the customer to manage the costs your firm represents, and facilitating the customer's "teaching" you about his own cost parameters, will increase your value to the customer and the customer's value to you. The trick here is to ensure that the customer's most recent costs or performance variables can be tied back to that customer's history, so you add value by pointing out areas for improvement.

Operational Entanglement

More and more firms are finding that by using information solutions they can increase the capabilities of their customers to interact with them, and this interaction by itself can provide a powerful bond. In many cases it enables the customer conveniently to perform some of the same ancillary services for himself that the enterprise would otherwise have had to perform for him. We've borrowed the term "operational entanglement," which we first heard at National Australia Bank, to refer to the operational services in a product-service bundle performed by the customer rather than by the enterprise. An enterprise should concentrate on enabling its customers to perform more and more of these operations, in order to create an increasingly customized, and high-quality, relationship.

Every time a customer uses an ATM to transfer money from savings to checking, for instance, a task that just a few years ago would have required the services of a teller, the customer is collaborating with the bank. Collaboration allows the customer to do an increasingly sophisticated job of product and service specification—providing convenience for the customer and customer loyalty for the marketer. The ATM customer is operationally entangling himself with the enterprise.

If a firm sells to governmental units, or if a product is sold to companies that do business with governmental units, then it's a safe bet that plenty of detailed, written forms and applications are required—equal opportunity compliance forms, registrations, filings, and so forth. Any firm that deals with these issues should include the filings as a part of its service. Just tell us what we need to know about your firm and we'll file the forms for you. If your business is hauling toxic waste, prepare and file your customer's environmental impact statements. Or you might offer to maintain and update an inventory of all the potentially hazardous materials on your customer's various work sites.

FedEx puts computer terminals in the mail rooms of its largest customers so they can book, track, and pay for their own package shipments without ever having to get on the phone to call the company. Ultimately, this means that these big customers are becoming part of FedEx's extended enterprise—collaborating with FedEx to help it sell more package deliveries to themselves, conveniently and inexpensively.

What FedEx and other package delivery services could also do is get themselves operationally entangled with package *recipients*, by assigning unique "addressee numbers" designed to save a shipper time and prevent mislabeled packages. If you receive a package but haven't yet been assigned an addressee number, they could leave a message assigning you one. In the future, when someone plans to ship a package to you, you could either spell out your name, address, zip code, and phone number, or just give them your addressee number instead.

The bond trading department at CS First Boston recently installed a system making it possible for its institutional customers to trade their bonds directly, using the Bloomberg platform. After a customer installs the system, the broker's prices for U.S. treasury securities, Repurchase Agreements (Repos), commercial paper, and other products become available for immediate access. Currently, 350 of the firm's Repo clients use the software, and 100 of them execute transactions regularly, representing almost 25 percent of the firm's total daily transactions. The most immediate advantage to CS First Boston is that this very labor-intensive process is now less labor-intensive.

So far so good, but what advantage will CS First Boston have if its competitors also install the system? Little, unless the firm uses its on-line system to *customize* its relationships with individual institutional customers, saving them more time and energy every time they sign on. If a customer accessed his trading screens and the first information shown had to do with the markets and maturities that *that customer* usually trades in, based on the customer's previous interactions on the system, then the customer would be more resistant to venturing out onto competitive systems.

This is indeed the direction in which the firm is moving. CS First Boston's vision is that of an electronic system providing a single totally *customized* point of entry for executing electronic trades, even in the billion-dollar range—a point of entry that reaches all the way down to the clearing bank and involves almost no human intervention. Not only will this reduce costs, but it will lock in the loyalty of the company's institutional customers.

Selling Related Services

In addition to the services and operations that naturally accompany a core product, most products and services can easily be associated with other, related needs on the part of a customer. When a customer purchases a new house from a building contractor, it is a safe bet he will need insurance, mortgage financing, legal help, and so forth.

In many cases, catering to an enhanced need set is simply a matter of providing "extra" services to meet the obvious needs a customer has, based on the simple fact that the customer is already buying something you produce. If you run a dry cleaner, why not offer to hold on to the extra buttons and material swatches that come with a new suit or dress? That way, when the clothing needs to be repaired, the customer doesn't have to dig through drawers to find these items himself. Or offer a "hands-free" used-clothing donation service for your customers. "Tired of those dresses? Bring them in, we'll appraise them and donate them to a charity, and then we'll deliver the tax receipt to you."

Hotel La Fontana, in Bogota, Colombia, caters to the international business traveler. If you have a trip to Bogota planned, the hotel will set up your appointments in advance for you. Just tell them the names and numbers of the people you want to meet with. There is also a lawyer on staff for the benefit of business guests with last-minute legal issues, including everything from customs regulations to transfer taxes.

There is a scene in the movie *Miracle on 34th Street* in which a little girl climbs onto Santa's lap at Macy's to say how much she really wants a pair of skates for Christmas. Santa assures her she'll get just what she wants but, just as the store's toy manager steps within earshot, he quietly tells her mom to go to Gimbel's, Macy's archrival. Gimbel's skates will better protect her little girl's ankles, he says. Ready to fire this insubordinate Santa on the spot, the toy manager is interrupted by a previous child's mother, who had been given similar advice with respect to her son's request for a toy fire engine. She tells the shocked manager how delighted she is that "a big outfit like Macy's" can put the spirit of Christmas ahead of its own business, and she says she will be a regular, loyal Macy's customer from then on. As the manager returns to his post, he finds six more delighted mothers waiting to see him, each of whom has the same message.

There is probably no simpler statement of the difference in philosophy between traditional marketing and 1:1 marketing than this:

*The focus of the 1:1 enterprise is not to find more
customers for its products, but to find more products
for its customers.*

Santa's point in *Miracle on 34th Street* was to satisfy the
customer absolutely and totally, and that should be your
goal too. But beyond this, the deeper any firm is able to
penetrate a particular customer's needs, the more likely that
firm will be able to cement a Learning Relationship with the
customer, earning the customer's loyalty not just out of grat-
itude, but because it is more convenient for the customer to
remain loyal. As long as she is certain her own interests are
being protected, the customer will trust the enterprise with
a greater and greater share of her business.

To the aggregate-market competitor, the customer database is a "fishing pond" stocked with potential targets for
the firm's products. The 1:1 enterprise comes at this proposition from the opposite direction—stocking the *customer's*
"fishing pond" with other products and services that are
likely to be needed by that individual customer. What is
surprising is how such a simple, commonsense philosophy
could be so little practiced.

A professional colleague of ours had difficulty making
time to furnish her living room and dining room. Finally an
Ethan Allen design consultant came to the house armed
with tape measure, catalogues, fabric swatches, graph paper, and tiny magnetic furniture to experiment with placement. Together the designer and our friend measured and
drew out the walls, fireplace, archway, windows, and doors.
They tried out furniture placement and picked out two sofas, a dining room table and chairs, lamps, end tables, secretary, armchairs—two entire rooms of furnishings. But
Ethan Allen did not offer quite the right rug for the living

room, and this meant that no furniture could be ordered immediately, because the upholstery fabrics could be specified only after the rug was selected. Realizing that her firm didn't have the rug to satisfy the customer, the designer got up to leave, asking the customer to be sure and call when she *found the right rug*. Weeks later, the customer finally took the time to shop for a rug, and found a breathtaking ten-by-fourteen Oriental style—in a great store that also sells sofas, dining room tables and chairs, end tables, secretaries, window treatments. She spent about $15,000 with this store, over and above the rug.

What the designer should have done, of course, is use her knowledge of this customer's tastes, needs, and preferences—knowledge acquired during an intense face-to-face consultation lasting more than two hours—to find her a rug, even if it was another brand that came from a different store. This designer *should* have found the rug even if she didn't mark it up, although this customer was so pressed for time, she probably would have gladly paid a fee just to avoid having to sit for another two hours with someone else.

If the needs of a customer are for products or services that are not within the realm of an enterprise's core competency, then the firm should create strategic alliances with other firms that cater to the related needs of the same customers. This "find products for customers" idea—even if it means going outside the firm's own core competency—is perfectly captured by the philosophy that permeates USAA, the widely acclaimed San Antonio–based insurance company. In the 1930s it was nearly impossible for a military officer to obtain reasonably priced auto insurance, so a group of officers formed United Services Automobile Association, later known by its acronym, USAA. This company handles every customer transaction by phone and mail, and continues to offer its services almost exclusively to active and former military officers. But it has moved far beyond auto insurance, carving out a network of other businesses, such as life insurance, homeowners insurance, specialty vehicle lines (motorcycles, boats, RVs, planes), and mutual funds, as well as a sprawling set of alliances with merchandise providers, home mortgage companies, credit card issuers, and so forth.

Retaining ownership of its own customer relationships has been critical to USAA's success. A member who calls to request information on, say, a second mortgage for his home will soon be connected directly to a USAA partner company—not a subsidiary, but a strategic ally who has met USAA's strict quality and service criteria. USAA's customer database will be linked with the ally's database, and updated in real time as the transaction progresses. At USAA, finding products for customers is just one aspect of the firm's quality-service customer-driven philosophy.

Alliances like this work best with non-competitors, especially when the enterprise is trying to meet the needs of a large number of customers. However, in serving the interests of any particular, individual customer, even dealing with a competitor can sometimes be appropriate. A commercial bank, faced with a corporate customer that doesn't want 100% of its business in the hands of any single bank, might consider recruiting particular competitors into the relationship.

The more valuable a customer is, the more it pays for the enterprise to take responsibility for satisfying the customer's needs, even if it means going outside the enterprise's core products and services. Another friend of ours is a busy professional who shops from catalogues for her children's clothes and places two orders a year with one particular company, totaling well over $1000 a year. It should be fairly easy for the cataloguer to predict this MVC's needs, as she is obviously ordering for two children who progress logically in size each season.

Last fall she placed her semiannual order, late at night, as usual. The sales associate, obviously plugged in to a sophisticated computer system, advised the woman about item availability and anticipated shipment dates. Everything was ready to ship, except those little black oxford shoes, which had sold out and were now discontinued, a big disappointment to our friend, as they were to go with the black formal outfit her son would wear to a wedding the next month. But the sales associate told her not to worry. "These little shoes are pretty easy to find," she said, trying to be helpful. "Just stop by any Wal-Mart and pick up a pair there."

Our friend suggested a different idea: "Why don't *you* 'just stop by Wal-Mart' and pick up a pair and put them into my shipment? If I had time to go to Wal-Mart, I wouldn't pay your prices, and frankly, I'd just go ahead and get everything there instead." Of course, this customer's special request did not compute, since she looked no different to the order taker than any other customer. This cataloguer is in the business of selling products to whatever customers they can get to call them up. They don't see their business in terms of finding products to meet the needs of the customers whose needs and interests they already know about—not even MVCs.

Strategic alliances don't have to be forged with separate companies—they can be created between diverse divisions within a single firm. As a 1:1 marketing strategy, creating such alliances has important implications for team-based selling. The marketing objective is to keep customers longer and make them into even bigger customers. But the managerial obstacles can be immense, particularly within companies organized into autonomous divisions with decentralized P&L responsibility.

Cross-selling the products manufactured by one division to the customers of another division is the simplest of all marketing strategies. Yet, due to entrenched distribution and commission systems, it is often one of the most difficult to implement organizationally. The most constructive way to deal with this type of problem is to deploy the marketing effort through "customer managers," whose expertise lies not just in the products offered, but in the complex and varied needs of the enterprise's customers.

Collaborative Opportunities

When a customer teaches a firm what he wants, or how he wants it, individually, the customer and the enterprise are, in fact, collaborating on the sale of a product. The more a particular customer teaches the enterprise (provided the firm is equipped to deliver whatever is specified by the customer), the less likely that customer will be to defect.

Some products and services yield collaborative opportunities naturally, especially high-end services and custom-manufactured products. But for businesses that see their customers as having more or less identical sets of needs, it is often necessary to focus on ways to create collaborative opportunities by expanding the need set.

Consider the regional Bell operating company (RBOC), seeking to protect its monopoly franchise from competition now that the regulatory barriers are coming down. Most RBOCs think of their local monopoly operation as a commodity service business. That is, a customer picks up the phone, dials a number, and gets connected. The customer wants the connection to go through quickly and correctly—oh, yes, and cheaply—since it's just phone service. But how much more is there to a phone call?

Quite a bit, actually. And figuring out how to *tailor* the enhanced need set to the individual requirements of individual customers is the key to customer retention and margin growth. Remember: Only genuine *customization* can guarantee customer loyalty and improved margins.

Let's contrast two different approaches, one taken by an aggregate-market competitor focused purely on customer satisfaction, and one taken by a 1:1 enterprise focused on customization and Learning Relationships. In *The Loyalty Effect*, Fred Reichheld suggests that the RBOC should focus on product quality and customer satisfaction when trying to retain its business customers, zeroing in on special services designed to attract and hold them. For example,

> *Small businesses are always eager to retain their old phone numbers when they move to new locations. It makes it easier for customers to stay in touch, and prolongs the usefulness of old advertising and promotional material. To earn the ongoing loyalty of this very attractive segment, one local phone company is developing the capacity to offer the same phone number regardless of a company's location. Another local phone company is working to provide its best customers with a full range of value-added services, such as call forwarding, cellular, long distance, and charge card, all combined on one billing statement.*

In the escalating battle for customers that now characterizes the local and long distance business, the latest strategy is, in fact, exactly such "bundling" of services, providing consolidated bills and suites of phone services, such as on-line connections and even e-mail, all wrapped into a single relationship.

It would be a great strategy, too, except for one thing. If a new competitor *matches* a phone company's service, as it would certainly do when entering the market, then the small business customer no longer would have any overwhelming reason not to defect. If, say, Time Warner were to introduce local phone service for small businesses using its cable TV network, it would almost certainly do so in a way designed to mimic the most attractive service features of its local phone company competitor. So, if the small business can switch to Time Warner but still keep its historic phone number when moving, and if it can still get the same kind of consolidated phone bill as provided by the local phone company, then where is the original firm's advantage?

The traditional answer to this dilemma is that while the advantages of product and service innovation are real, they are only temporary. Business authorities and consultants who give this answer suggest that the local phone company should continue to innovate, continue to provide a steady stream of better and better service in order to stay at least one step ahead of its presumably slower and less nimble competitors. A corollary to this suggestion is that execution will always become the defining competitive advantage. There simply is no way to prevent a competitor from matching your product, service, and price, so you must be better at execution, execution, execution.

But there *is* a way to prevent a competitor from matching your innovation with respect to its impact on particular customers, one customer at a time: customization.

If, *in addition to* devising generally applicable service enhancements to be delivered the same way to every customer, a Bell company were to focus on *customized* services—products that would be used or consumed differently by different customers—it would have a chance to create Learning Relationships with its individual customers. This would have the effect of locking in each customer's loyalty *even if* the phone company's competitors offered the same exact product innovation!

The trick is to design products and services, within the enhanced need set, that a customer and marketer will have to *collaborate* on, in order to implement them or get a benefit from them. When phone service is linked with computer power, it is actually quite rich with such collaborative opportunities. One of our favorites would be speech-recognition speed dialing similar to the product Sprint offers today for its Foncard customers. The customer simply dials the toll-free number Sprint assigns him, then speaks the name of the party he wishes to call. He can store up to ten names on the service by first dialing the associated number, and then speaking the name into the phone to teach the Sprint computer how he says it.

Imagine if an RBOC were to offer this kind of speech-recognition speed dialing—perhaps with up to 50 or even 100 names available to each customer rather than just the ten that Sprint offers. A customer using his phone would simply speak a name into it (probably after dialing a standard prefix, such as 99*) and then the RBOC's computer would dial that number. Every time a customer with this service calls a number not yet on his register, he would simply push a different Touch-Tone combination of numbers and speak the name into the phone once or twice, to register the name.

After a few months of entering numbers and names like this, a customer will have taught the phone company's computer quite a bit. Moreover, he will have taught the company this without ever having to do anything as onerous as filling out a survey or answering a questionnaire. This customer no longer has to remember everyone's seven-digit phone number, nor does he need to remember anyone's two-digit speed-dial number. He needs to remember only if he's ever looked this number up to dial it before, because if he has, then chances are he's already entered it in his speed-dial register.

With this continuously customized product, the local phone company has created a Learning Relationship with its customer. This relationship will be nearly impervious to competitive predation, even from identically capable rivals! If Time Warner were to come into the local phone market and offer the same service—speech-recognition speed dialing—the customer might be tempted, but he can't forget that to get up to the same level of service he's already achieved with his local phone company he'd have to spend another several months reteaching Time Warner's computer what he's already taught the RBOC's computer.

A few of the RBOCs do offer speech-recognition speed-dialing today, but they charge substantial fees for the service. Any firm interested in creating Learning Relationships to maximize customer retention ought to be subsidizing this kind of collaborative service, at least for its highest-value customers. Here's a heretical thought: Maybe the RBOCs should even consider *rewarding* their very best customers, giving them some kind of incentive to use their individual speed-dial registers. After all, the more use a customer makes of the service, the more resistant the customer will be to competitive offers later. (In fairness to the RBOCs, current government regulations may restrict this type of initiative—but the strategic lesson should not be lost.)

What makes a collaborative product like this so important, in terms of increasing a customer's loyalty and unit margin, is that the customer must invest time or effort in the collaboration. As is the case with Streamline, which learns a customer's shopping habits in increasing detail over a period of months, this kind of product from a phone company would simultaneously cement a customer's loyalty and ensure the firm's unit margins. One can imagine a future in which a computer will be able to recognize a spoken name and look the number up from its own database. At this point, the advantage of speech-recognition speed dialing will be undercut, because less investment on the customer's part will be necessary to customize the service. But even so, there will still be some advantage to being able simply to speak a friend's first name and get connected.

An RBOC could lock in a business customer by focusing on the product-service bundle, including the way calls are invoiced. Most businesses manage their phone costs the way they manage other costs. Sometimes phone expenses are allocated to different departmental budgets, or billed to clients. Think of a law firm or a large consulting practice trying to allocate billable phone calls to individual clients and nonbillable ones to various departmental budgets. At present, many such firms have complex account codes wired into their centrex systems, so every outbound call is preidentified by the caller.

But the management of any firm's telecommunications costs would be much easier if the phone company would simply provide the bill on a spreadsheet program, either via disk or on-line, rather than on a paper invoice. If it were doing this, the phone company could easily customize every firm's bill, based on how that firm has used previous spreadsheets to allocate costs. It could save the firm the expense of running a complex centrex system, and it could create Learning Relationships with its business customers as well, earning their loyalty in spite of competitors who match this service.

Imagine a law firm's accounting department taking the first such spreadsheet bill from its phone company and identifying all the phone calls to be billed to clients, by individual account. After doing this, the accounting department returns the revised spreadsheet to the RBOC, and the next month's bill comes with the costs already allocated, wherever repetitive phone numbers would indicate. Now all the accountants need to do is manage the exceptions, each month returning an updated spreadsheet to the RBOC. Over time, the RBOC's bill would become smarter and smarter, with respect to the ways this particular firm is allocating its phone expenses.

Value Streams

Some firms have nothing to offer their end-user customers to entice them to want relationships. A firm that produces a single product, infrequently purchased, is in this kind of situation. In such cases, the firm should concentrate on creating a "stream of value" behind every product sale. Usually a value stream involves some type of service to follow on after the actual product sale, but it could also involve an interaction designed to generate income later from customer referrals. The home builder who, in order to satisfy customers and generate more referrals, calls his customer the week before the one-year warranty expires and offers to inspect the home for any persisting problems is in fact creating a value stream behind the sale of the home.

Or consider the home furnishings manufacturer who sells infrequently purchased items to consumers, through retail outlets. How does such a firm create a relationship with the purchaser of a couch, or a rug? One way to do it is for the company to own its own retail outlets, so the customers come in to see the firm directly. Ethan Allen, for instance, would have no problem establishing contact with its end-user consumers (that is, they *should* have no problem, but they aren't now in the business of creating electronic, corporate relationships with individual customers beyond the interpersonal relationships between designers and customers).

Drexel Heritage, on the other hand, is a furniture manufacturer that owns no retail outlets and has no direct contact with its own end users. This firm should create a stream of value behind its products. Why not sell every couch with a free cleaning included after twelve months? Send this card in and we'll make an appointment to come to your home and clean your couch—or your rug, or your ottoman, or your new bathroom sink—making it look as good as new once again.

Zane's Cycles in Branford, Connecticut, offers a lifetime warranty on every new bicycle purchased in the store. Before you think of this as an expensive form of customer coddling, consider the implications in the bicycle business, where large purchases are infrequent, but servicing, auxiliary products, and options can add up.

What if you ran, say, a fine men's clothing store? People come in and buy dress shirts, shoes, and designer suits that cost anywhere from $500 to $2000 each. It's certainly good business practice to keep track of your customers carefully, remember their fittings and preferences, and assign a salesman to each. But why not a dry cleaning and repair value stream? Buy your suit from us and for an extra $150 we'll take care of all dry cleaning, pressing, and repair for the first three years.

The value-stream tactic is often used to encourage warranty card registration, particularly by software vendors whose products are bundled into the personal computer hardware of the OEM (original equipment manufacturer). Send the registration in and the company will give you ninety days' free advice and help in putting the software to work. Lately, because in any software business the installed base is everything, many vendors are actually giving away the basic product in order to maximize their initial installed base and make money on upgrades and other services. That's why Microsoft gives its Web page builder, "Front Page" away, and Sun practically gives Java away as well— each of these companies wants to make money on the value stream.

Look for software vendors in the future to *pay new customers to take their new products.* It is only a matter of time before a new basic software product is not only given away free, but comes with extra compensation—perhaps in the form of additional free services, coupons, magazine subscriptions, credits, or even (dare we suggest it?) a free computer—in order to induce customers to install the software, get used to it, and become loyal. Then *sell* them the upgrades.

Putting It All Together

By applying these strategies, you can view your customer base through a series of increasingly discerning lenses. As your view of it becomes more refined, you can pick out more of the differences that distinguish one customer from another.

While we've used different examples to illustrate the core set of needs, or the product-service bundle, or the enhanced need set, most firms don't need to limit their efforts to any single one of these techniques. So let's now put it all together by taking a hypothetical example from an industry in which a company is likely to have rich customer data but poor customer needs-differentiation, to see how that firm could approach its customer need set to create Learning Relationships and loyal, high-margin customers.

The example we'll use is the consumer credit card business. Most consumer credit card issuers use their massive customer transaction databases merely to differentiate their customers by value (and some don't even do much of that!). But the types of transactions reveal a wide variety of needs, some of which could be better defined by incorporating dialogue too. Let's assume you operate a credit-card-issuing firm. You have rich data, but the only thing you've really done with it in the past is score your customers by their value to you. What do you do to begin differentiating them on their needs?

Core Product

The first step is to look at the core needs an individual has for the card. It should be apparent that people's attitudes toward using their credit cards are quite diverse, and any credit card company will probably already have a wealth of research on this. But the trick here has three elements:

(a) Understand a few of the more significant of these particular, individual needs

(b) Create products or services that address these needs

(c) Know *which* individual customers have *which* needs, in order to offer the right products to the right customers without overexposing any single customer to a whole range of largely irrelevant services

The type of needs-differentiation found most frequently in the credit card business today is based on analyzing the transactions undertaken with the card. A few forward-thinking issuers (led by American Express) will actually offer different services and products to customers whose transactions involve heavy travel, for instance, as opposed to frequent merchandise purchases. But while transactional analysis by itself is helpful, the real power of needs-differentiation will be found in those individual customer needs that can be revealed only through actual dialogue interaction, the way US West Direct did with its Yellow

Pages advertisers, or Iomega or Lego could do if they wanted (see our discussion of these ideas in Chapter 3).

To take one example, any credit card issuer's customer base will probably include a high number of consumers who want to discipline their spending and saving. So, in addition to identifying this as a discrete customer need, your firm must do research enabling you to identify a customer who has this need in some cost-efficient way. This could be accomplished with a quick, incentive-based survey enclosed in the billing statement, but it could probably be done more effectively by asking one or two questions of a customer whenever you receive an inbound customer service call.

Second, you need to design a product or service you could offer to keep such customers loyal. How about a "save while you spend" option, allowing a cardholder to designate a percentage of her bill to be tacked on and socked away? If she signs up for this service, then for every hundred dollars she spends on your credit card, she'll be billed $105, and the extra $5 would go into a designated mutual fund account, or even a tax-free annuity. She should be allowed to choose the savings rate—electing to be billed $110, or $150, for instance—and also the investment vehicle.

Product-Service Bundle

The overwhelming majority of consumer credit cards are produced in standardized "packaging," yet the packaging could be highly customized. Because a customer carries the card with her everywhere and must take it out and show it to others in order to use it, there is a "badge" element to a credit card product that is exploited by premium cards. Lots of people already prefer showing a gold or platinum card so much, they are willing to pay a substantial premium to do so.

So why not sell your credit card as a vanity card? One bank today lets customers choose a design created by a celebrity. But why not allow customers to pick from hundreds—or thousands—of card logos, designs, colors, and so forth? We do it with checks, so why not credit cards? Ultimately, you could probably *sell* a customer a software disk allowing her to use a PC to design her own unique card, which you would then produce for this customer alone.

Or in terms of billing and service operations, why not collaborate with your customers by delivering customized bills to them electronically? Imagine the utility of a credit card if your customer could download the bill automatically into a spreadsheet program—her choice of Excel or Lotus or Quicken—with all the items she'd charged, ready for tax accounting, family budgeting, or whatever. She ought to be able to redesign her own bill, upload it back to your firm, and then have future invoices come in that fashion. She should be able to integrate your bill with her checking account and savings account records, which until now she has maintained on a separate program.

Enhanced Need Set

Finally, think about all the potential strategic allies that could help your credit card firm satisfy a deeper and deeper set of needs for each customer.

Affinity cards are an obvious idea for any card issuer
that wants to make customers more loyal—provided that it's
the right affinity group. A number of banks already customize the financial characteristics and the physical appear-
ance of the cards to meet the different needs of smaller and
smaller groups, from national charities to university alumni
associations and even antique car hobbyists. So imagine
how loyal a bank's cardholders could be made if the local
Girl Scout troop, for instance, went door-to-door selling Visa
cards as well as cookies. "Sign up for our Visa and for every
$100 you spend, Troop 5121 will get 25 cents." Or the local
PTA could do this, or a hospital, or the YMCA, or a nursing
home, or a volunteer fire department.

Most credit card companies are already in the value-
stream business—but almost without exception they address the same value streams, the same way, to every customer. Every customer is solicited for credit card loss pro-
tection, every customer is offered special deals on
merchandise, or airline frequent flyer tie-ins, and so forth.
But few card issuers go to much length to match particular
value streams with particular customers.

Just one obvious ally, for instance, could be the telephone companies—companies that are already beginning to
dabble in the transfer of money through the Internet,
through phone debit cards, and the like. But to do this right,
you need to tailor the value stream, or the related product
offering, to the needs of individual customers.

Phone debit cards are particularly big in Europe. Say
you have a customer in Frankfurt planning a business trip
to Istanbul. You could offer him a 60DM phone debit card
for use on the trip, including the debit card in the ticketing
documents themselves and billing him automatically

through his travel agent account (provided that he is putting his air ticket on your card), by creating an alliance with the airline's reservations system.

There is an interesting business opportunity for any firm willing to "decommoditize" other firms' offerings in order to help them create better, more customized and longer-lasting relationships with their customers. One such firm may be the Relationship Marketing Group, recently launched by Mary Naylor, the entrepreneurial founder and president of Capitol Concierge.

Capitol Concierge provides a variety of conciergelike services to the inhabitants of office buildings in and around Washington, D.C. If your building or your firm is served by Capitol Concierge, you can call "your" concierge at any time and ask him or her to find a gift for your husband, or figure out the most convenient Italian food restaurant in a particular area, or book a limo, or pack a box lunch, or arrange a messenger, or detail your car, or plan a reception. Widely known as a 1:1 marketing firm, Capitol Concierge employs a sophisticated calling center and customer database to *remember* every request you make as an individual. In that way, the company can remind you not only of upcoming birthdays or anniversaries, it can also zero in on the kind of concert or opera tickets *you* most prefer, based on your previous communications and transactions with the firm.

Naylor formed Relationship Marketing Group to offer such conciergelike benefits to the customer bases of other companies, essentially as a way of allowing these clients to enhance their customers' need sets. By packaging such services under the umbrella of another brand name, RMG is able to decommoditize the product or service otherwise offered by that brand. Mercedes owners who lease their cars may soon find they can use Naylor's services themselves, through a Mercedes-owned contract. Alamo Car Rental may soon offer this type of benefit to its more elite frequent car renters. And any one of the airlines should see this service as a way to broaden the differentiation of needs within its own customer base.

If you own a credit card issuer and you want to find the next level of service to offer your more elite, higher-value customers, you might want to consider attaching a conciergelike service enhancement—even one provided by a third-party contractor.

One more thing is important to remember about creating Learning Relationships with customers. The customization that makes such a relationship effective must take place within the enterprise's own system. If the customer retains the customized information himself—for instance, if the speech-recognized speed-dialing capability resides not in the phone company's computer but in the phone owned by the *customer*—then the leverage that the firm has over the customer relationship could vanish.

It *could* vanish—*unless* the firm can also capitalize on yet one more asset that interactivity places at its disposal: the knowledge of how other customers, with similar needs, want to be served. This is the subject of our next chapter.

COMMUNITY KNOWLEDGE

How to Anticipate *What Your Customer Wants*

Up to now, we've concerned ourselves with the idea that a genuinely customer-centered firm should remember what a customer has specified in the past, not only to guide the firm's future dealings with that customer, but also to give the customer an incentive to *teach* the firm about specific individual needs. This converts a sale from a one-time event to a continuous iterative process—a process that is increasingly satisfactory for the customer, as the enterprise's Learning Relationship with that customer improves. Competition in the 1:1 enterprise is a matter of scope versus scale. To the 1:1 competitor it is not the *scale* of customer base served, but the *scope* of relationship maintained with an individual customer that determines success. In the battle for one customer at a time, the successful competitor will not be the one with the most customers, but the one with the most knowledge about his individual customer's needs.

Some people will recognize the Learning Relationship as providing an agentlike service to the customer, acting in the customer's own individual interest, as it "learns" what that interest is through successive interactions.

But what if the customer were to maintain his own record of specifications and purchases himself? If the RBOC's invoice allocation spreadsheet is produced by the customer's own centrex system or if the record of a customer's usage of household products is maintained in his own PC rather than in Streamline's computer, then this would severely undercut the competitive advantage that customization gives to an enterprise. There could be several Streamline services, and each week the customer could simply bid them out, one against another, reducing the level of competition once again to a transaction-by-transaction battle over price.

However, there is a way for the 1:1 enterprise to avoid this vulnerability, and it derives not just from the scope of a firm's relationship with an individual customer, but from the scale of its customer base—a scale that cannot be matched by a customer-maintained agent. We call it the principle of "community knowledge."

Community knowledge comes from the accumulation of information about a whole community of customer tastes and preferences. It is the body of knowledge that a 1:1 enterprise acquires with respect to customers who have similar tastes and needs, enabling the firm actually to *anticipate* what an individual customer needs, even before the customer knows he needs it.

Knowing What Customers Want—
Even Before They Do

One of the best examples of community knowledge at work is Agents, Inc.'s "Firefly" Web site (http://www.ffly.com). A Web user can visit the Firefly site to get a recommendation for the type of music he might like. At the site, the user is first asked to rate a number of different types of music. He can review as long a list as he would like, and he can even listen to different selections. After the user has rated different pieces and musical groups, Firefly will make recommendations to him for the kind of music and even the particular CDs he might like.

Firefly's recommendations are not based just on this particular customer's tastes. Rather, Firefly's software considers this customer's *community* of other customers with the most similar tastes. A number of other raving Stones fans like this other group too, or this particular CD by another group, so Firefly may suggest these choices to the customer, who never even heard of the CD being recommended.

Clearly, Firefly's premise works not just because of the knowledge it acquires about a particular customer's tastes in music, but because of the knowledge it has acquired from a large number of other customers. There is no way a Firefly customer could receive as accurate—and *anticipatory*—a recommendation without the benefit of this wider range of individual ratings. Besides music, Firefly also rates videos, and has plans to branch into a number of other arenas as well, including finance and investment.

To see how the principle of community knowledge can be applied in other contexts, go back to The Custom Foot. Suppose, when a patron came in, the store clerk were to give her a score card on which she could evaluate some of the shoes now on display. The clerk would ask her to roam the shelves and simply rate a selection of shoes, on a scale of one to five, for whether she really liked the style and might want to buy it, or really detested it and wouldn't be caught dead in the shoes.

The first use for this information would be to watch out for new styles that resemble her favorites. But in addition, if The Custom Foot were to do this with every customer, then over time it would build up an immensely rich database of individual tastes and preferences. It would also be able to match these tastes and preferences with each customer's individual buying behavior. This would enable it to recommend a particular style of shoes to a customer, not because that particular customer had ever expressed an interest in that particular style, but because other customers—customers who have said they like the same kinds of shoes she says she likes—have already bought this particular style.

We have to be clear about what's going on with this particular equation. Using community knowledge is not just proposing things to a customer based on what that customer has said she would probably be interested in. A 1:1 enterprise with a database of detailed individual tastes and preferences is actually in a position to *anticipate* what a particular customer wants, *even before she herself realizes she wants it.*

The power of community knowledge can be significantly leveraged by soliciting individual customer feedback, especially for products or services where individual tastes vary greatly. Consider how the principle of community knowledge could be used to enhance the value of something like an on-line travel and reservations service, for instance. There are very few barriers to launching such a service, so there will probably be many competitors—airline reservations systems, credit card companies, publishers, and providers of other on-line services—all struggling to acquire customers and make them loyal. Anyone who travels frequently has already seen advertisements and solicitations for a number of these new services, from easy SABRE to United's APOLLO On-line.

The first initiative for any of these operations, to keep its own customers loyal, should be customization. An on-line travel and reservations service should remember every individual customer's travel profile—seat and meal preference, frequent flyer numbers, limo or taxi to and from the airport, credit card numbers to use, and so forth. And rather than relying on a lengthy one-time customer questionnaire for this information, an interactive service ought to be able to build a profile as it goes along—that is, the customer should never have to specify the same thing twice.

Every time a user signs on to such a service, she will find it easier to get the reservations and tickets she wants. The first screen should show her most frequently chosen routes in the last few months or weeks, just in case she wishes to click on one of these routes and get right to the business of booking another trip. When the customer clicks on a route, the next screen should show the flights she has chosen most frequently, and so forth. If a customer requests something quite different from what is in her previously accumulated profile—a first-class seat, for instance, rather than her usual coach seat—the service could alert her of that and ask if she wishes to override or change her profile, or to designate and "save" a new profile.

A lot of money will be riding on customer loyalty in this business. The main source of revenue will be not the traveler, but the commission-paying travel provider. The more users any particular on-line ticketing service has, the more buying power that service will have with travel providers. Airlines, for instance, may pay an average commission rate of about 8 percent, but an on-line service that can produce 25,000 frequent business travelers will clearly be able to negotiate a higher commission rate than one with 1,000.

Obviously, to have any hope of success, an interactive travel service must be designed to conform itself to a particular traveler's tastes and preferences as rapidly as possible, to try to lock in the traveler's loyalty by becoming more and more convenient for her. But what happens when a PC software program comes to market, allowing all these variables to be stored in the customer's own computer?

One tactic to lock customers in longer would be to turn the travel service into a community knowledge generator. Travel is such a business of tastes and preferences, it is remarkable that no on-line service has yet latched on to this. The hotels and restaurants we visit, the airports we connect through, the limousine companies we book and resorts we spend time at—nearly everything about the travel experience, except perhaps for the service onboard the airlines themselves, is varied and unique.

Suppose a travel service were simply to ask its frequent business travelers to give it personal feedback on the hotels they use. Every hotel is different, and hotels vary in quality and facilities from city to city, sometimes dramatically even within a single large hotel chain. Suppose the on-line service were to use a simple three-point scale—rate the hotel A if you really like it and the next time you come to San Antonio you want to remember to stay at this hotel. Or rate it B if you were generally satisfied and wouldn't mind staying there again. Or mark it F if you don't like the hotel and don't want to stay there in the future if you can help it. Obviously, when the traveler goes to San Antonio again, the system will help her remember a terrific hotel or avoid a bad one.

But the real advantage of community knowledge is that the system would also be able to recommend the right hotel *for this traveler* in a city she has never even visited! Suppose our traveler were making her first trip to Hong Kong. An on-line travel service that relies on developing a body of community knowledge could propose a hotel for her that has been rated high by *other* people—*people who tend to rate hotels in the same way she rates them.* Such a system could in fact provide help in choosing a restaurant, a car service, a trout-fishing camp, or the lowest-hassle air-ground route to Darwin, Australia. No amount of processing power on the traveler's own PC could *ever* provide this kind of insight; only the wealth of data from the 1:1 enterprise's own customer base can provide it.

Information Tools

The actual method by which massive amounts of data are stored, sorted through, and utilized to draw these kinds of analogies can be more complicated than the typical LTV model. But because of the ever-increasing power of microchip technology, the method doesn't always have to be a "statistical" model at all. Even PC platforms can now support some types of neural network engines, which are fundamentally nothing more than learning by trial and error.

A neural network calculation starts with a hypothesis—say, that people who buy shoe style A also tend to have rated styles B and C very high. The database is combed for people who have rated one or both of these styles high, and the computer checks one customer at a time to see whether the customer has also bought style A. If the customer did buy the same style, then the hypothesis is reinforced as it applies to all customers (or to other customers similar to this one). If it is not, then the hypothesis is altered slightly, in the direction of the most likely error, and retested. Then it is retested again and again. If, for instance, during this process several customers in a row are found to rate style B highly, but not C, then the computer will adjust the formula a bit, draw another customer or group of customers from the database, and run the test again, under the new hypothesis, which will give more weight to how customers rate B and less to how they rate C. Very high-speed, high-capacity computers can perform millions of such calculations per second, which means they can iterate and reiterate on a neural net model that considers literally hundreds of variables, across a million customers or more, in just a few minutes.

So when it comes to applying community knowledge to better understand particular customers, the speed and power of computers enables us to get to the answers faster, and for reasons we may not truly grasp, intellectually. It might turn out, for instance, that a customer is more likely to want to buy a particular style of shoe not because other, similar customers like this style, but because other customers who have said they *dislike* the same kinds of shoes she says she dislikes tend to buy this particular style of shoe. We don't have to understand an outcome before we use it to find a particular product for a particular customer. But the more customer experiences we can test our hypotheses on, the more accurately we will be able to match any particular customer with the product or service that he or she most desires.

Empirical Media Corporation

A young entrepreneur from Carnegie Mellon University in Pittsburgh, Ken Lang, did his doctoral thesis on software technologies that combine neural networking and other machine learning techniques to sort and filter information.*

In 1995, Lang launched Empirical Media Corporation to bring to market a commercial application of his theories, with a product called U-Media. U-Media is aimed at the millions of Internet users faced with a wearying array of news and information choices to sift through. Today, the

---

* When it comes to predicting customer behavior, it is sometimes useful to know how neural networks differ from the more traditional models based on statistical analysis. Statistical models generally require more careful planning and mathematical analysis than neural nets, but the output of a statistical model includes "diagnostic" variables that help a statistician understand how or why the model achieved a particular result. The neural net, on the other hand, just produces an answer, and that's that—no diagnostics, no trail of clues. But neither a statistical model nor a neural net can efficiently process vast quantities of independent variables. The objective of each type of calculating engine is to construct an equation, and an equation made up of several thousand weighted variables has so many possible permutations and combinations that the computation itself can bog down considerably. Neural nets are themselves a subset of a much larger branch of computer technology loosely called "machine learning," and this field offers the best hope for processing and understanding very complex forms of data and information. There are probably hundreds of machine learning and neural net techniques being developed at various laboratories and college campuses around the world.

typical Web user will "bookmark" the Web sites he finds interesting in his travels. There is a spirited competition among Web site operators to create and maintain the most useful "search engine," enabling an ordinary user to find what he wants more easily. But for all but the most intrepid Web warriors, the entire system is still too complex and too daunting to be used easily. Trying to sift for information from the Web is somewhat similar to trying to take a sip from a fire hydrant.

Enter Empirical Media, with its sophisticated machine-learning and neural-network tools. U-Media can be used to customize the ultimate search engine for you—an engine that will conform itself to the information you personally will most want to retrieve based on your stated preferences, your history of interacting, and (important point here) the history of *other* Web users who interact in a similar fashion as you do.

As you use U-Media to retrieve news and information, the button you click to go to the next page or section will actually be a "rating bar"—with a continuous scale of colors, progressing from green to red. Where you click on the bar will indicate your personal satisfaction with the "interesting-ness" of the data or page you are leaving. Because of the richness of the feedback inherent in the rating bar mechanism, the firm will develop a much more accurate picture of a particular customer's preferences than could be developed simply by analyzing a "click-stream" tabulation of the pages viewed by the customer, and it will zero in on this picture at a much more rapid pace.

According to Lang, who understands the implications of this for his venture's future prosperity: "Users will have incentive to stay with our service exclusively because of the time invested in building a personal profile that becomes even more effective with continued use." As a result, the firm plans to offer its basic U-Media service free, figuring that once it locks customers in, it can generate immense revenues both from advertisers who want to reach them and from selling upgraded services at higher prices to longer-term customers.

More than simply customizing its information filtering to the individual feedback of individual customers, however, Empirical Media's machine-learning calculation engine relies explicitly on the principle of community knowledge, which Lang calls "community filtering."

A Warning About Teaching Customers

The truth is, the idea of community knowledge has a direct lineage from one of the most important values any business can bring its own customers: education about what other customers are doing. Most successful enterprises know that they must teach their customers as well as be taught by them. An enterprise brings insight to a customer based on the firm's dealings with a large number of that customer's own competitors. Indeed, most business customers demand this. The enterprise thus serves as a conduit for spreading knowledge within the industry.

However, precisely because community knowledge is such a powerful concept, it is important to stipulate that not everything a customer should know can be derived from other customers. It is also the enterprise's responsibility to teach its customers about new technological developments, and how to use them profitably. In a *Harvard Business Review* article, "Disruptive Technologies: Catching the Wave,"

Joseph Bowers and Clayton Christensen pointed out a startlingly counterintuitive reason that leading companies often fail to develop new technologies that others immediately grasp—they stay *too* close to their customers. IBM, for instance, apparently missed out on the early PC wave because the company's customers, all of whom had purchased large mainframe computers, simply could not conceive of how the PC would revolutionize their own business.

In an era of faster and faster change, the 1:1 enterprise is going to have to teach customers, not just be taught by them. Fred Wiersema, in *Customer Intimacy*, says there are three types of customer coaching: bringing out the product's full benefits, improving the customer's usage process, and breaking completely new ground with the customer. Any one of these types of customer education can come from the knowledge an enterprise acquires by serving other customers.

There is an important caveat here for the 1:1 enterprise. Obviously, if what the firm teaches a customer is generally useful across all the products in the enterprise's own competitive category, then there is no inherent advantage to the enterprise in terms of customer retention. The customer could easily take the education and buy products from the firm's competitors, and this is a particularly acute issue if it is the distributor who is being treated as a customer (see Chapter 12). Automotive manufacturers, for instance, face this dilemma when they try to educate their dealer organizations to give better customer service. The Mitsubishi dealer may also have Chrysler, Isuzu, and Honda dealerships. Any help he gets from one of these car companies will be immediately useful to him in selling any of the other brands.

Businesses have tried to make teaching customers into a more economic business proposition in several ways.

Some charge customers for the teaching. Computer systems firms have an interest in teaching their customers how better to use computers, and for the most part they try to *sell* this teaching—even to their current customers—in the form of systems and business consulting. In such a situation, it goes without saying that the industry expertise and experience acquired by the consultants while working for one customer are usually quite beneficial in consulting for the next.

Other businesses use proprietary platforms of one kind or another, and then invest time teaching customers how to use their platforms. They do this on the dependable theory that once a customer has taken the trouble to learn one system, it won't want to go to the trouble of learning another.

Yet another way businesses teach their customers is by facilitating user groups, conferences, and other mechanisms for putting customers in touch with one another. This has always been a useful mechanism in technology businesses, but in the Age of Interactivity it will become useful for nearly anyone with any kind of complicated product at all. Teaching customers through user groups and cross-customer conferences can be an effective way to expand the customer need set.

Finally, the 1:1 enterprise with a large number of customers can use community knowledge to *lead* a customer to a product or service that the enterprise knows the customer is likely to need, even though the customer may be totally unaware of this need. It might be as simple as choosing a hotel in a city the customer has never visited, but it could also apply to pursuing an appropriate investment and savings strategy, even though the customer may not have thought of it yet.

Traditional Marketing and 1:1 Marketing

What sets the principle of community knowledge apart from more traditional market segmentation?

To answer this question properly, we first have to understand that differences and similarities among customers are simply opposite values of the same variable. What distinguishes the 1:1 enterprise is not *whether* this kind of variable is used, but *how* it is used. To the traditional competitor the initiative is product-focused. The traditional, product-focused competitor zeroes in on what customers have in common in order to sell a product to the widest possible number of interchangeable customers from within an aggregate market. The product-focused competitor simply wants to find the next most logical customer for a particular product.

But the 1:1 enterprise is customer-focused. Competing in the customer dimension, the enterprise uses information about what customers have in common, not in order to find more customers for a particular product, but to deduce the next most logical need that a particular customer will have. The 1:1 marketer uses community knowledge to gain a greater insight into an individual customer's tastes and preferences, and sometimes can anticipate what an individual customer needs even before that customer has asked for it.

Objectivity as a Selling Proposition

Be honest now: When your stockbroker suggests an out-of-the-ordinary stock to you, doesn't the thought flash through your mind that he may be making this recommendation because the brokerage itself has a vested interest in moving the stock?

The relationships that most customers—even the very best customers—have with their vendor partners is one of qualified trust. The more a customer must rely on the judgment or recommendation of a vendor, the more trust is required to sustain the relationship. But no matter how trusting the customer is, he will still want to cut the cards once in a while.

Every customer wants genuinely objective, unbiased advice in a commercial transaction, and every customer knows that sometimes this advice will run counter to the seller's own interests. When our traveler to Hong Kong is given a hotel recommendation by her on-line service, how will she know that the recommendation is a function, not of the service's interest in her satisfaction, but of the bonus commission being paid by the hotel? For that matter, when the Firefly music customer receives a recommendation for a particular CD, how can he actually be sure that the CD isn't being proposed because a particular record company has paid Firefly to push it?

Of course, if an enterprise makes a recommendation that comes *purely* from comparing a particular customer's feedback with the feedback from other customers, then it is indeed entirely objective and unbiased—or, rather, it is entirely "subjective," based on the subjectively felt tastes and preferences of the customer. In any case, it is easy to imagine an interactive future when a firm relying on community knowledge will actually promote the fact that it relies *only* on the feedback it gets from customers to make suggestions.

To amplify this idea somewhat, an enterprise could also provide value to its customers by serving as a host for customer "reviews" of various products, options, and services. "Here are the two hotels you are most likely to prefer in Hong Kong, and for each we've attached the three most recent customer reviews." We'll talk more about facilitating and passing along customer reviews when we discuss various forms of interactive media in Chapter 11.

Agent objectivity is likely to be such a valuable selling tool in the Interactive Age that it will be worth protecting. One common but misguided criticism that Agents, Inc., hears with respect to Firefly is that a Web site like this is subject to "tampering" by interested record companies. What if Warner Records were to enlist all its employees to sign on to Firefly and rate all of that firm's CDs very high? Then, the argument goes, wouldn't these CDs get disproportionate recommendations from Firefly's agent software?

The answer to this, says Nick Grouf, CEO of Agents, Inc., is absolutely not. According to Grouf, Firefly's software is structured in such a way that it makes recommendations first by comparing a user's own interests profile to the profiles of other customers with similar tastes. In effect, for each individual user Firefly creates a "community" of users—an affinity group—and relies heavily on the individual profiles within this affinity group to make its recommendations. So if a customer is not already predisposed to give high ratings to all (or at least most) Warner releases, then it is unlikely the software would try to make a recommendation to him by matching him with the profile of a Warner employee who did. On the other hand, if the customer actually *did* tend to like Warner releases, then the added high ratings of the Warner employees would have no real effect anyway!

Grouf emphasizes that Firefly's software is not based on any kind of "voting" for the best overall kind of music for everyone. Because every user is *individually* identified, it is, in fact, an extremely difficult program to tamper with. What would actually happen, he says, if a large number of record company employees signed on with the intent to "prime the pump" for their properties, is that these employees would be creating their *own* affinity group—composed of Warner Record employees—and Firefly would simply continue to recommend other Warner titles to the members of this group.

Nevertheless, the idea of tampering does raise an interesting point. Part of Firefly's allure for music lovers, and part of Amazon's allure for book lovers, is the fact that users on these sites can leave their own written messages, in effect posting customer-written reviews of various works. Neither site has a foolproof screening mechanism for these reviews to ensure that the publisher or the record company can't bias the reviews toward its own properties. On the other hand, the reviews a user is most likely to trust on the Firefly site will be those posted by other members of his own affinity group—customers whose tastes in music the user trusts because they are reasonably like his own. The same principle could easily be applied by Amazon.

The creation of such affinity groups actually gives sites like Firefly an additional business, as a kind of high-efficiency dating service. At the site, after all, it is possible to strike up conversations with other visitors who share your own tastes in music, or movies. And you can choose not to reveal your identity until you feel comfortable you'd like to meet the other visitor "in the real world"—outside of cyber-space.

But despite the fact that both Firefly and our hypothetical on-line travel service actually *do* maintain their objectivity, how can they possibly *prove* this to the satisfaction of their customers? Addressing this problem may actually create a business opportunity for independent "privacy and bias auditing" by outside firms. We could imagine a future in which Firefly's software and business operation are audited and periodically spot-checked by a company like Arthur Anderson, which would issue a finding that the software's recommendations are, indeed, truly objective. Such an audit might also confirm, for instance, that individual users' preferences are not being passed on to third parties, counter to the site's representations, or that name and address files are actually removed from aggregate data before they are released to outsiders.

The Self-Organizing Customer Base

Community knowledge can yield immense benefits to many businesses, but especially to those businesses that have:

1. *cost-efficient, interactive connections with customers as a matter of routine,* such as on-line services, banks and financial institutions, retail stores, and business-to-business marketers, all of which communicate and interact with their customers directly, and on a regular basis; and

2. *customers that are highly differentiated by their needs,* including businesses that sell news and information, movies and other entertainment, books, fashion, automobiles, computers, groceries, hotel stays, and health care, among other things.

When the goal is to zero in as rapidly as possible on a particular customer's tastes or interests, using community knowledge is likely to be not only more effective, but less costly too.

Consider the typical clipping service, for instance. Whether it delivers its product on-line or not, the service will probably employ a small army of editors and researchers to comb through thousands of articles and printed items, categorizing them and marking them for their relevance. The editorial function is, indeed, the principal "service" any clipping service provides. It might have hundreds or thousands of topical categories, but in the final analysis the firm's editorial efficiency is only as good as the editor who happens to review each particular item.

On the other hand, by using the principle of community knowledge to rate articles, an interactive clipping service could use its customers as editors. The customers themselves will probably do a faster and more accurate job of rating individual items for one another than hired editors would because (a) there are so many more customers than editors, and (b) the customers are much more interested in the particular issues being rated. And don't forget that the customers are already there. In an interactive system, they don't have to be given a professional's salary before they'll provide feedback.

By using customers as editors, a clipping service can

more quickly tailor the news and information items it provides to an individual customer's precise interests. If this process were completely dependent on that particular customer's feedback, it would be a slow, painful process, and every time the customer encountered a new variation in topic, the service would first have to wait for new feedback, in effect making the customer edit *everything* so the service could "remember" the editing. Instead, the idea of community knowledge allows an enterprise to edit a particular customer's interests not just by remembering his previous interactions, but by identifying customers with similar interests, and comparing how *they* have rated particular topics—topics that might be completely new to the original customer.

The same is true of any firm, not just an interactive clipping service. Instead of editors screening articles, a manufacturing company has market researchers deciding on new products. Retail stores have buyers and merchandisers deciding what to put on the shelves. Service firms have program managers. In a sense, however, any enterprise that uses community knowledge is turning the customer base itself into a self-organizing system. In the Interactive Age, instead of serving as an arbiter of which customer tastes and preferences are met, the 1:1 enterprise will become a clearinghouse for them.

An argument could be made that customers will resist being "categorized" like this—that people naturally want to think of themselves as unique, and do not want to have products and services recommended to them based simply on the preferences of other people with "similar" tastes. But traditional marketing presumes many more similarities among customers than this, and most of these similarities are much cruder, based on data like demographics, income, and zip code, which are only remotely connected to any single customer's actual needs.

Whether it's news articles, shoe styles, or hotel service, comparing a system that relies on editors or market researchers to a system that relies on community knowledge is very much like comparing a command economy to a free market.

And in the free market of community knowledge, it is interaction that is the currency.

SURFING THE FEEDBACK LOOP

How to Get More Customer Feedback While Protecting Privacy

The 1:1 enterprise, operating in an interactive environment, relies not just on information *about* customers, but on information *from* them.

Dialogue and feedback are indispensable elements of a customer relationship. Communication *with* the customer (rather than communication *to* the customer) plays an essential, integrating role in the customer-driven dynamic of competition. Each interaction gives the enterprise access to information about that particular customer that would otherwise be completely unavailable. The 1:1 enterprise then integrates this information into its other operations, using the information to drive its behavior with respect to that particular customer by individually tailoring its products and services.

In this chapter we're going to analyze the nature and role of customer dialogue in more detail, including the types of media an enterprise can use to conduct its dialogues with customers, and the kinds of transactions that occur between an enterprise and its customer as they interact.

Customers can be differentiated principally by their needs and their valuations, and this principle tracks neatly with the two most useful categories of information that can be derived from a customer interaction:

1. *Needs specification* In interacting with a firm, the customer can specify his individual needs precisely, whether these needs have to do with his shoe size, or the maximum allowable p.s.i. on a pneumatic valve, or the type of hotel most preferred. Whenever and however a customer interacts, the enterprise has a chance to get a better fix on *that* customer's particular, individual needs. Feedback from a customer of an evaluative nature also falls into this category. When the customer tells the firm whether his new car was delivered clean, or that he'd like the tomatoes riper next time, he is enabling the enterprise to zero in on a more and more precise understanding of what *this* customer actually wants, *individually*. Needs specification, in most situations, is inherently an iterative function. Think of it as ratcheting up the learning curve on an individual customer's personal set of tastes, preferences, and desires.

2. *Strategic valuation insight* While any firm with a reasonably reliable customer database should be tracking current transactions and statistically assessing individual customer LTV on an ongoing basis, in most

cases only the customer himself can reveal to the enterprise what additional, future opportunities for doing business might be offered. Insight into a customer's strategic valuation would include, among other things, advance word of an upcoming project or pending purchase, or information with respect to the competitors a customer also deals with, or referrals to other customers that could be profitably solicited by the enterprise. This type of information can usually be obtained *only* in a direct interaction with the customer, and it is vital to the firm's ability to prioritize its marketing and selling efforts—that is, its ability to allocate the firm's customer investment efficiently.

Marketing executives have always known that using a database to know customers better enables the enterprise to sell things more effectively, so learning about customers has always been seen as positive. When this learning is reduced to the quantum level of the individual customer, however, involving direct interaction with the customer, there is a benefit that far surpasses the firm's increased level of knowledge.

In an interactive relationship, not only does the firm go to the trouble of learning, but the customer goes to the trouble of teaching. It is this investment of time and effort on the customer's part that provides the fuel for sustaining a Learning Relationship, and the increased customer loyalty and higher unit margins that come with such a relationship.

The need for feedback by the 1:1 enterprise provides an interesting juxtaposition with the role of customer communication for the traditional aggregate-market competitor:

*The traditional marketer crafts a message to customers
that is as persuasive and effective as possible, but the 1:1
enterprise will try to elicit the most efficient, most useful
feedback from customers.*

Increasing the "Bandwidth" of Customer Dialogue

There are an increasing number of new and interesting mechanisms for interacting with customers—new interactive media, ranging from the Touch-Tone phone and the World Wide Web, to the computerized cashier's station and the ATM. More interactive devices and media seem to be created every day. It was only recently that without the aid of a genuine computer expert, an Internet user would have been incapable of handling anything more complex than crude, text-based communications. Now anyone can upload and download graphics, audio, and full-motion video, although the signals like video that require higher "bandwidth" (that is, many more bits per second to transmit) cannot always be conveyed in real time.

But just as the microchip has fueled a decades-long revolution in the power of electronic machines to calculate, it is also fueling a revolution in the speed at which vast quantities of information can be sent down a pipeline as crude and restricted as an ordinary copper phone wire. Delivering quality, real-time video via ordinary phone lines was a laughable impossibility only a few years ago, but today's more capable data compression technology—software, not hardware—makes it quite realistic. We are steadily increasing the bandwidth of the communications infra-structure, not just by adding optical fiber and coaxial cable, but also by applying a higher degree of machine intelli-gence to the problem.

As the electronic bandwidth has increased, and as the bandwidth already available is stretched to greater and greater capabilities, the actual mechanics of interacting with customers has become easier. Today, what most firms fail at is not the mechanics of interacting, but the strategy of it—the substance and direction of customer interaction it-self. The typical Web site owner, at least in the initial stages of this medium's life cycle, relies on the Web site to do things that are directly analogous to what a firm needs from nonaddressable, noninteractive media such as print and broadcast.

Most companies' Web sites are nothing more than com-plicated electronic billboards that *convey* information to their "visitors." A site can be highly creative, it can be intricately structured into hypertext, with "hot links" from one topic to another, and from one site to another, but Web sites are still primarily used to convey information in a single direction—from the site operator to the visitor. Most Web site operators are not yet relying on this richly interac-tive medium to conduct rich *interactions* with their custom-ers. One senior analyst from the high-tech venture firm Hambrecht & Quist, interviewed in a magazine about an Internet-based business his firm recently helped finance, said that companies wanting to move beyond electronic bill-boards on the Web "can't just pick up a book on HTML, but they'd better pick up one on 1:1 marketing."

Interacting with a customer individually allows a firm to practice 1:1 marketing, and what this analyst was saying, essentially, was that 1:1 marketing is so different from broadcasting messages to an aggregate population that it might be worth reading about and studying. Interactivity allows a firm to conduct ongoing individual dialogues over brief or extended periods of time, with unique, individual customers. Each dialogue can be different. Each can evolve separately, as and when an individual customer contributes his own thoughts.

Rather than simply ensuring that its broadcast and print messages are *laterally* coordinated across various media, such as television, print, sales promotion, and direct mail, the 1:1 enterprise must be careful that its communications with every customer are *longitudinally* coordinated over the life of that individual customer's relationship with the firm. Today's dialogue with a particular customer must pick up where yesterday's left off.

Not unlike door-to-door selling, when a commercial relationship is characterized by periodic interactive exchanges of information, every step of dialogue must give permission to the firm to continue with the exchange.

Different interactive mechanisms can yield widely different information-exchange capabilities. The bandwidth of a dialogue should be thought of simply as a measure of how capable the design interface is between customer and marketer. It is the design interface that allows a business to learn a customer's product specifications and potential for doing business, and the efficiency with which this kind of information can be conveyed back and forth between the customer and the enterprise is what we will think of as a dialogue's bandwidth. As information technology advances, the potential for increasing this bandwidth continues to grow.

The bandwidth of a dialogue via postal mail is very small, because even though mail is "addressable" to individual customers, it is still a print medium, and involves a lengthy cycle time. So while a business may be able to remember immense amounts of data about an individual customer, using this information to conduct an actual dialogue with the customer through "snail mail" is impractical. On the other hand, postal mail can be effective in delivering detailed written and graphic information, and in executing simple, one-time-only kinds of individualized transactions.

The bandwidth of telephone dialogue is much greater, and is significantly enhanced by Touch-Tone dialing. Using the phone, a business can set up a fairly efficient, real-time design interface between the firm's computer and an individual customer—at the customer's location rather than in a store. Similarly, the bandwidth of a fax message, or fax on demand (Touch-Tone–driven fax response) is even higher. EDI and e-mail have still higher bandwidths, although they, too, depend on the telephone line, with all its limitations.

Face-to-face encounters, such as those in which a Ritz-Carlton guest expresses a personal preference, or the in-person exchange during which a business owner answers questions put by a Yellow Pages sales rep, might seem as though they have the highest bandwidth of all, but even a face-to-face meeting is not always the most efficient form of customer dialogue. While any human-to-human conversation, whether in person or via the phone, will generate emotional feedback and nuances that no stream of electronic data could possibly duplicate, this type of feedback is not needed in every situation.

The biggest limitation for both phone and face-to-face interaction is that the enterprise cannot *track* these as well as it can track electronic exchanges. To be able to improve its relationship with any given customer, the enterprise must be sure that the employee responsible for the voice interaction with that customer is actually capturing its key elements for the company's database. Many firms with direct sales forces have plenty of dialogue interaction with their customers but little to show for it in terms of *corporate* memory. For most such firms, the salesperson assigned a customer will own the "company's" relationship, and this works to the enterprise's benefit only as long as the salesperson remains employed.

We can increase the bandwidth of a dialogue interaction by upgrading either the data-carrying capacity of the communication line or the efficiency of the "dialogue interface," the mechanism used by both the customer and the enterprise to communicate. Customer interactions at a computerized cash register, for instance, or at a video kiosk in the mall, have the potential to carry a richer, faster exchange of information than even a phone conversation between two people, because both the communication line and the dialogue interface can handle a faster flow of information. The line that connects such machines to the company is almost certainly a higher-capacity phone wire, or even an optical fiber. And when you check out at the grocery store, your dialogue interface includes the UPC codes being rapidly and efficiently laser scanned into the store's computer.

On the other hand, a very rich type of dialogue, very high in bandwidth, is necessary when a customer comes in to have her foot sized by computer for a custom shoe, or when a pneumatic valve customer uses an interactive, computer-aided design system to help specify a new valve system. For products that involve significant differences among customers, the bandwidth of a dialogue must accommodate as much automated measurement of these customers' different needs as possible.

Doing an Inventory of Interaction Events

There are so many mechanisms for interacting, and so many reasons to interact, that the first thing the 1:1 enterprise should do is take an inventory of all the current and potential interaction events between the enterprise and the customer. To do such an inventory, it is best to categorize interaction events according to two criteria: the media through which the event occurs, and the content of the event itself.

1. *Media* Every event takes place in or through a particular medium. The medium is the *mechanism* for interacting, whether it's a phone, a face-to-face conversation, or the mail. The 1:1 enterprise must understand all the current and potential media for interacting with customers, along with the strengths and limitations of each. Media that could facilitate interaction between a customer and the enterprise include:

   ■ *Print and mail:* printed material such as postal mail, catalogues, brochures, print ads with response devices, and coupons

   ■ *Telephone (voice):* inbound and outbound voice-based phone calls

- *Telephone (nonvoice):* facsimile and data transmissions

- *On-line hosts:* Web sites, Internet, CompuServe, and other similar systems

- *Direct, face-to-face:* personal sales visits and meetings

- *Point of purchase:* kiosks, card readers, and computers at cashier stations

- *Wireless:* pagers, PDAs, cell phones

Note that this list of media does not actually represent all possible channels of communication available to a firm in getting messages *to* customers— merely those media that are available for communicating *with* customers. Outdoor advertising, magazines, and television, for example, are conspicuous by their absence. That's because, in order for noninteractive media like these to facilitate a dialogue with a customer, they must first be linked with an interactive medium similar to the ones already on the list.

2. **Content** In addition to a mechanism for interacting, every event also has a substantive content to it. That is, every interaction between an enterprise and a customer occurs for some purpose—perhaps it is the customer initiating a complaint, or the enterprise sending an invoice. The 1:1 enterprise must understand what the range of content is for interacting with its customers, whether the interaction is initiated by the customer first, or by the enterprise first:

a. *Customer-initiated interactions:*

- Orders and payments for products and services
- Product or service specifications
- Inquiries and requests
- Complaints or disputes
- Fan letters

b. *Company-initiated interactions:*

- Order fulfillment and product delivery
- Invoicing, billing
- Selling, persuading, promoting
- Informing, educating, benefiting

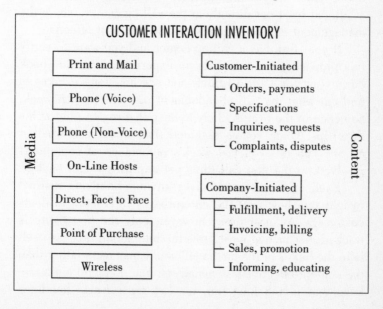

CUSTOMER INTERACTION INVENTORY

Media

- Print and Mail
- Phone (Voice)
- Phone (Non-Voice)
- On-Line Hosts
- Direct, Face to Face
- Point of Purchase
- Wireless

Content

Customer-Initiated
— Orders, payments
— Specifications
— Inquiries, requests
— Complaints, disputes

Company-Initiated
— Fulfillment, delivery
— Invoicing, billing
— Sales, promotion
— Informing, educating

At most companies, the management of customer interactions is not in the hands of people responsible for monitoring and managing the content of the interactions. Rather, it is the responsibility of those who are charged with managing the media mechanics of it. This conflicts with the 1:1 enterprise's need to generate and track dialogue in order to integrate individual customer feedback into various corporate functions.

At almost any firm that has a calling center, for instance, the managers at the center will be preoccupied with media efficiency issues rather than with content effectiveness issues. The figures that are used to evaluate how well a calling center is being managed will be oriented around things like answering times, call abandonment rates, and talk time. But the actual content of the interactive events taking place at the calling center will not be managed well at all—at least not directly at the calling center, where the management of interaction would be the most effective.

If your firm has a calling center and you want to verify this proposition, you can do an experiment: Put this book down (just for a little while!) and see how long it takes to find out what the call abandonment rate was for last week. Someone in the firm is likely to have that report right at his fingertips. Once you've obtained that figure, ask whether anyone can tell you last week's percentage of complaints resolved on the first call (thus not requiring a call back).

Each of these figures gives an important and distinct insight into how well the enterprise is interacting with its customers. At most firms, however, only the first figure is tracked, because at most firms the interaction process itself is in the hands of the media efficiency managers rather than the content effectiveness managers. You may find out as we have that in the long run, it's *less expensive* to handle a problem on the first call than have the customer make several more calls. (Never mind that a first-call-satisfied policy also results in happier customers whose valuations increase.)

Another frequent weakness of such an organizational structure is poor coordination and cross-use of the various media themselves. Usually there will be someone with an expertise in programming and computer networks, for instance, who is charged with setting up and monitoring a firm's Internet presence and Web site. But even though a customer or prospect happens across a firm's Web site and is moderately interested in getting more information, he may not want to spend more time downloading it right there. He may have a more detailed question that really isn't answered in the prepackaged pages at the site.

Since most Web sites are in the hands of managers responsible for the medium rather than the content, there are usually very few links between the site itself and other interactive media. The problem with this is that a single customer may choose to interact via any of several media, and he may choose different media for different types of interactions—the Web site to get the details of how your product is configured, perhaps, and the telephone to make a complaint. But even though he might interact via different media, *he is still the same customer,* and his dialogue should be managed in a coherent way by the enterprise, from medium to medium.

If your Web site, like most, is in the hands of Web specialists, then it probably doesn't make it very easy for a visitor to change media. Again, you can prove the validity of this by visiting any randomly chosen corporate Web site— perhaps your own—and trying to figure out how to get someone at the corporation to call you in order to provide some information. Many Web sites, believe it or not, don't even have toll-free numbers listed so a visitor could choose to call in on a voice line.

If an enterprise wants to succeed in managing dialogues with its customers individually, then it must manage the *content* of these dialogues, from interaction event to event, across all different media. As yet there are very few successful examples of this, largely because dialogue management is not a core competency at most firms, even though most are trying hard to make it more and more cost-efficient to conduct dialogues.

Usually, when a firm puts up a brand-new Web site or begins to host on-line discussion groups with its customers for the first time, the program has a predictable trajectory: First there is excitement at the prospect of finally becoming "interactive," then surprise at the amount of actual work involved in communicating back and forth with individual customers, and finally a slow and steady erosion in support, given the cost and effort of keeping the program running. Managing interactivity is clearly a lot of work. The problem is, while an enterprise can outsource the management of a particular *medium* to any one of a number of contractors, there are very few outside contractors prepared to manage *dialogue,* across *all* media, and integrated by individual customer.

Mass Marketers Are to Advertising Agencies as 1:1 Enterprises Are to . . . ?

The traditional aggregate-market competitor uses an advertising agency or a promotional firm to craft its messages *to* customers. A whole culture of vocabulary and metrics has developed around the discipline of advertising, with value-laden terms such as brand equity or positioning, and metrics terms such as media reach or frequency, GRPs, and CPM—terms invented and popularized, on the whole, by advertising agencies. Advertising agencies take responsibility for doing what most firms simply find outside their core competency: writing copy, composing art, and planning and buying media. A good ad agency takes responsibility not only for coordinating the enterprise's outbound messaging across any number of media vehicles, but also for ensuring that the message is as effective and persuasive as possible.

But where is the analog to ad agencies when it comes to dialogue and interactive media? What kind of company is prepared to accept the same kind of outsourcing from a 1:1 enterprise that an advertising agency accepts from an aggregate-market competitor? If an enterprise wants to begin tailoring products to individual customer needs, and treating different customers differently, what type of contractor can it turn to for managing the dialogue interchanges with customers and coordinating the content of interaction across the variety of media and corporate functions at the enterprise?

Sky Alland Marketing, a Columbia, Maryland, company, is one of an assortment of new and thriving businesses that orient themselves around dialogue management for clients that wish to do more than simply send messages to their customers. One of Sky Alland's principal activities is "complaint discovery." A few days after you buy a new luxury car, you may receive a call asking if everything is okay with the car, and if the sales experience was to your liking. This call comes from Sky Alland, and is designed to discover any complaints among the car company's new owners. Newly discovered complaints are forwarded to the client for immediate action.

But Sky Alland does a variety of other things designed to assist its clients in managing dialogue with individual customers. Sometimes what Sky Alland does is directly related to increasing a client's immediate sales effectiveness. One auto importer used Sky Alland to call prospective customers within seventy-two hours of their visits to the car company's showrooms. The calls were not overtly aimed at selling, but at discovering any unspoken concerns on a prospect's part. Sky Alland does reignite the interest of some prospects (not unintentionally), and the sales result of this campaign has been a 50 percent improvement in the rate at which such one-time visitors return to make a purchase.

Using the phone to contact customers or prospective customers, not to try to sell things, but to initiate or continue dialogues with them, has been turned into something of a science at Sky Alland and companies like it, with a variety of interesting results, all of which bear testimony to the benefit of customer interaction:

■ Contacting one HMO's members by phone thirty days *after* enrollment and again sixty days in advance of the reenrollment date reduced defections by some 77 percent. Moreover, another HMO found that new members contacted thirty days after enrollment were responsible for fewer billing adjustments, fewer invalid claims, and more preventive care appointments than customers who were not contacted.

■ Phoning one retail bank's customers two weeks following the closing on a loan increased the proportion of customers who later responded positively to the bank's direct mail solicitation for another loan. Continuous dialogue (i.e., occasional outbound "satisfaction calls") with retail bank customers resulted in the discovery, over several months, of hundreds of dissatisfied customers on the verge of defection, the majority of whom the bank was able to retain.

■ Phoning new homeowner insurance policy holders within thirty days of enrollment produced an increase in retention (termed "persistence" in the insurance business) of 10 percent at the six-month renewal.

■ Phoning mutual fund customers a few weeks after their initial investment produced a dramatic increase in subsequent investments with the fund.

Each of these cases shows that interaction improves a firm's knowledge of the two fundamentally different aspects of any individual customer, in relation to the enterprise itself: his *needs from* the firm and his *value to* the firm.

When an outbound phone call happens to identify a complaining customer (or, rather, one who has not complained—yet—but is nevertheless not entirely satisfied), what actually takes place during the voice-to-voice phone conversation is that the customer re-specifies the product or service. Every customer service organization knows that the single most important question to ask of a complainer is "What can we do to make you happy?" If this is the question that is asked and the customer then provides an answer, then the feedback loop is established between that customer and the enterprise. This is what makes complaint resolution so important as a customer satisfaction aid.

Next, when the customer is asked what additional products or services he might consider, or what additional benefits he'd like to obtain, the interaction reveals important aspects of that customer's *valuation* to the enterprise. Sky Alland's experience is that merely calling a customer to inquire into her satisfaction greatly increases the customer's predisposition to do business. An analysis of one car company's owners shows that those owners who receive occasional satisfaction calls are almost 20 percent more likely to use the dealership itself for service rather than an outside vendor, for instance.

As a dialogue manager, however, Sky Alland offers clients more than simply voice interactions through a calling center. The company can also manage fax on demand for its clients, as well as some EDI and other data interactions. Sky Alland is one of a new breed of firms that contract out with clients, to manage not the *media* of their interactions with customers, but the *content* of the interactions. It operates in a wide range of interactive media, primarily because the value it contributes to its clients is not just media efficiency, but content effectiveness.

Sky Alland has recently begun offering a Web product called CallBack, a cross-media tool for managing dialogue. It works like this: If a visitor to a Web site wants to make voice contact with the sponsor, he clicks on a "Call Me" button displayed prominently at the site. When he does, up flashes a screen asking for name, phone number, the best time to call, and any particular topic the visitor would like to discuss. A browser can select from two options: Call Me Now (this way the browser doesn't have to make the call himself and be put on hold), or Call Me Later (7 P.M. Central, in my home, here's the number). After the visitor enters the information and leaves the Web site, the data is transferred immediately to Sky Alland, and they make the call, transferring an electronic report on its outcome back to the original host firm.

Another product the company offers is ScreenTalk, which is an on-line version of the "operators standing by" offer used by direct marketers, something like e-mail without mailboxing or waiting. When you see something interesting, go to the ScreenTalk button, type out your question or inquiry, and people at the service firm will be standing by on keyboards to reply while you wait.

CallBack and ScreenTalk aren't the only products now available for cross-utilizing voice and Internet communications. VoiceView TalkShop, a new product from Radish Communications of Boulder, Colorado, allows a Web browser to click on a Web site button and, while still connected to the Web, dial the toll-free number shown. The user needs VoiceView's software on his PC, but all PCs and laptops shipped by Packard Bell, AST, and Hewlett-Packard, among others, now have it built in. So a Web site operator will be able to offer a *direct* dial-up voice channel along the same phone line used for the data stream. Thus, instead of having to write down a toll-free number, close out of the Web site, and dial the number on a separate line, the user will be able to make a voice connection immediately, while the Web site is still displayed on his PC. And instead of typing a credit card number into a less-secure data stream, the user could give his number verbally.

Getting More Dialogue out of Web Sites

At most Web sites today, not only is there no link between the site and any other form of communication with the company (i.e., most sites do not yet have a linking capability such as provided by CallBack or VoiceView), but usually there is no "longitudinal" coordination of the site visits taken by any particular visitor either. In most cases, a visitor to a particular Web site will see the same pages, and be presented with exactly the same information, no matter how many times this particular visitor has been there before.

The sad fact is that most firms use their Web sites today to present what is essentially "brochureware"—information taken almost verbatim from written, hard-copy documents, and presented the same way to everyone. This is despite the fact that the Web itself is an inherently addressable, interactive medium.

There are some notable exceptions, and every day there are more. The Toyota Web site, set up by Novo Media Group of San Francisco, assigns a unique user ID to an individual visitor on his or her first visit. Later visits by this customer can then be managed differently, based on the customer's ongoing interaction with the site. As Novo's CEO, Kelly Rodriques, says,

New media advertising is more about creating a relationship with a customer over a period of time—and establishing not just who they are but what they want. Current billboard ads are only the tip of an interactive advertising iceberg.

BroadVision, a newly formed company specializing in software and capabilities for the World Wide Web, serves the interactive needs of larger, Fortune 1000 firms, companies that have or expect to have large demand for their Web site services. BroadVision's various software tools, marketed under the BroadVision One-to-One brand, allow a Web site owner not only to track individual users, but to expose them to different messages and visuals based on what the host knows about the customer, including the frequency and nature of the customer's previous site visits. BroadVision allows firms to practice 1:1 marketing on the World Wide Web.

One application for BroadVision's product, used by the operators of large, advertising-supported sites, is to display different ads to different site visitors. This is the application most sought out by site operators, for two reasons. First, advertising is the primary language of today's marketers, with a well-developed vocabulary and a complete set of disciplines. Every business understands the benefits of better targeted advertising. Few, on the other hand, understand the genuine potential of interactivity with individual customers, and the kinds of powerful customer relationships it can create.

Second, exchanging payments and conducting actual purchase transactions on the Web is still too insecure for most, so virtually the *only* way a large site owner can pay off his costs is to sell advertising. This is analogous to the way commercially supported television got its start over public airwaves that are free to anyone with a receiver. But a lot has happened to the economics of television since the advent of cable, and big changes are in store for how the Web is used too. At present, the Web may be secure enough to allow for the routine transfer of secure payments, in which case there will be an explosion of on-line commerce.

The most important implication of BroadVision's software, however, is that it allows a Web site owner to treat different customers differently, based on (a) information about the customer that the Web site owner has in its own customer database, (b) profile data provided by the customer, and (c) the record of the customer's previous interactions at the site. The software can then *dynamically change* each Web page to match an individual customer's tastes and preferences.

In a "white paper" released to explain the software's capabilities, BroadVision proposed a hypothetical case study in which browser "Mike" comes across a site run by a consumer electronics firm. The site combines lifestyle editorial content and promotional material for the firm and its affiliated companies. Offered a 10 percent discount for any products in the company's on-line store as a reward, Mike fills out a simple form giving his name, address, some demographic information (college-educated, two children under ten), and a bit about his personal interests, which include sports and photography. He elects not to provide income information, and he selects the "privacy" option on every element of this profile, which, he is told, will ensure his information is not used outside the site.

After submitting the profile information, Mike's further interactions with the Web site are highly personalized. The "home page" Mike sees on his return to the site includes a sports scene icon with news about various sports teams in his area, and hot links to editorial material on photography, including a special section on tips for taking pictures of young children. If Mike clicks on the sports scene icon and goes through it for additional information about a particular team, then that team's statistics might be displayed on Mike's home page on his next visit, along with a hot link to a bulletin board or chat group composed of that particular team's fans.

Embedded throughout the material Mike sees will be various coupons and offers for products being sold by the Web site owner. These coupons will be stored in Mike's "electronic wallet" at the Web site, and made available to him on any subsequent visits until he either uses the discounts or they expire. The Web site owner can vary the amounts of the coupons and discounts, depending on Mike's previous interest or lack of it in the products being offered. To execute a purchase, Mike will be asked for credit card information, and given the option to have this data stored in his profile for future use.

The crucial benefit of BroadVision's software is its design interface. A customer can buy this software and, using a feature BroadVision calls the dynamic control center, set its own business rules for how different pages are customized, or how different responses should trigger different communication streams with browsers. At the dynamic control center the customer's business rules can be set and reset by marketing and communications managers; no assistance is required from software engineers or IT professionals.

Personal Cookies

The BroadVision One-to-One software can enable a Web site owner to save a browser the trouble of having to enter the same data more than once at any given site. But what about when a browser navigates from site to site?

When a browser leaves one site and travels to the next, the departure site often equips the browser's record with a set of "cookies"—a personal cookie jar—Netscape's term for the mostly navigational data that travels with the user. At the next site, another set of cookies might be added, and so forth. But so far no one has created what will surely become the ultimate in cookies—a profile of personal descriptive information, like name and address, along with a record of tastes and preferences.

A user's personal cookie would be constantly linked to him, no matter what site he visits, so that information would not have to be entered and reentered at each new, unrelated site—provided that the site recognizes the format and protocol of the user's cookie. For any cookie format to become widely accepted by users, it must, of course, reserve a large degree of control for the individual user. The more information a user maintains on his own personal cookie—credit card numbers, interests, birthdays, product preferences—the less work the user will have to do when visiting a new site where he is nominally a "stranger," but the more threat to his privacy unless he remains in control of how and when the information is revealed.

For host systems and the purveyors of Web-friendly software such as BroadVision, creating the most versatile and ubiquitously accepted cookie will provide a commercial bonanza, because the most widely accepted cookie will soon become a virtually universal standard.

NetRadio Network is yet another new company with an interesting Web application. This firm allows a Web browser with a sound card on his computer to customize his own radio programming, selecting music by title or style, designating what periods of the day he wants to receive news, financial information, or sports updates, and so forth. As long as the browser remains connected to the Web, Net-Radio will play the songs and material he has selected and specified—all day, or day and night.

NetRadio could charge a browser a fee for this service, but they actually have a more interesting business proposition. First, the firm will sell advertising to help defray costs, offering advertisers their choice of audience based on the programming chosen by each browser.

But in addition, because the browser must continue to be connected to NetRadio throughout the day in order to receive the personalized "radio" programming, NetRadio can actually track all the additional Web sites that a browser visits during the day. What NetRadio really has is a simple vehicle for creating and updating a continuous, universal profile of the customer's needs and preferences, not just in music, but in everything the customer consumes on the Web—all the sites visited, transactions completed, and so forth. NetRadio can return an accurate, exhaustive click stream analysis of its customers, enabling it to create personalized messages or advertising for the customer. In essence, NetRadio's service creates a giant "cookie," which a customer carries around from site to site, with the personalized radio signal.

Imagine the richness of interactive customer experience that could be created if we combine NetRadio's tracking mechanism with U-Media's rating bar and preference calculations, and with BroadVision's ability to change Web pages dynamically across a variety of data platforms.

A list of other interesting World Wide Web applications, along with updated information on many other topics in this book is available at Don and Martha's own Web site (http://www.marketing1to1.com).

Some Rules for the (Information) Road

There are several important principles to apply in creating a dialogue-driven business.

Don't Ask for Everything at Once

Remember that a dialogue is not a one-time event but rather a series of events linked through time. This means the dialogue that ends today can begin again tomorrow, or next week, or next quarter. The lesson for the 1:1 enterprise is this: Don't try to get every shred of information from each customer all at one time, from a single interaction. To obtain the right kind of feedback from customers, ask for it a little at a time. To obtain more feedback, create more dialogue opportunities—don't simply load up a small number of interaction events with onerous requests for information.

The 1:1 enterprise will have an information system that points out the next logical question to ask of a customer when that customer calls again for anything—to schedule a service appointment, order a spare part, enter a sweepstakes, or just complain. Take an inventory of all your firm's customer interactions, and decide how best to ensure that every interaction builds on all previous ones, no matter what medium it occurs through, or what the substantive content of the interaction was.

Let the Customer Choose

Don't count on just one interactive medium either. Allow the customer to communicate with you through a variety of media, and then coordinate the dialogues that occur across all these media. Concentrate on improving the effectiveness of your content management rather than just on managing the cost-efficiency of your interactive media.

Whether or not you use a product like CallBack or ScreenTalk, your goal should be to accommodate as many different ways of interaction as your different customers might desire. We think of this as the PMP principle, for Preferred Media Package. What sort of media does *this* customer prefer? In asking this question, we're asking much more than what vehicles or tools to use. Do you know, for instance, whether this particular customer prefers to be mailed, e-mailed, or called? Do you know *when* this customer would prefer to be called? At home, in the office, or in the car?

The customer should be just as much in charge of a dialogue as you are. The fact is, the more ownership the customer takes, the richer and more useful the dialogue will be for you. Again, the key is never to have to ask any individual customer more than once for anything. If the customer wants to be called on Saturdays rather than weekdays, be sure this is in your database, and that you can accommodate this desire.

Every customer's PMP is likely to be different, so your marketing database should include a customer-specific set of PMP data for everyone.

Make the Customer's Life Better

Use faster and better information technology to create a sophisticated database with universal access and query, but be careful not to exasperate your *most* valuable customers in the process. Response rates may be acceptable, or even good, but if no one takes a reading on whether or how much the value of each customer has increased, or whether you are even *keeping* the more valuable customers and growing your business from each one, then you are not running a 1:1 enterprise.

Yes, your goal is to sell, sell, sell. But in the Interactive Age you'll have to do this by finding benefits and services for each customer that the customer really likes. If you simply treat the database as a big fishing pond, then even equipping your product and program managers with the most sophisticated, computerized rods and reels available won't create loyal, high-value customers for your enterprise. One-to-one marketing is not about finding the right kinds of customers for whatever product or program you've created. That's *target* marketing, but it's not 1:1.

The 1:1 enterprise uses customer data from interactive feedback to create a product-service bundle that *each individual customer* will find *increasingly valuable*. In doing this, the enterprise cements the loyalty of that customer and raises unit margins, over time. But the whole idea works only when the customer is inconvenienced less, his own life becomes better, and he therefore places a higher value on the enterprise than before.

Establish a "Privacy Bill of Rights"

Finally, it is absolutely imperative for the 1:1 enterprise to take into account the issue of protecting individual customer privacy.

The Interactive Age could easily become the Age of Privacy Invasion. Companies already have problems getting their own customers to send in warranty registration cards, for fear that they will be deluged with more mail. How can the 1:1 enterprise ever expect even its best customers to participate willingly in a series of more and more intimate dialogues if it can't assure them that their privacy will be respected? Customers whose privacy is violated—or customers who simply don't feel they have control over their own information—are not likely to become willing participants in any dialogue interactions.

If your firm is going into the business of creating relationships with customers based on individual information, you need to adopt an explicit privacy policy early on—then publicize it, and use it. The Privacy Bill of Rights should spell out

■ The kind of information generally needed from customers

- Any benefits customers will enjoy from the enterprise's use of this individual information

- The specific things the enterprise will never do with individual information

- An individual's options for directing the enterprise not to use or disclose certain kinds of information

- Any events that might precipitate a notification to the customer by the enterprise

In March 1995, Professor Stanton Glantz, an expert witness on the health effects of tobacco from the University of California, produced some information that one of the tobacco companies felt could have come only from an internal, unauthorized source. Stymied in its legal effort to get the lobbying group itself to reveal this source, Brown & Williamson subpoenaed FedEx to produce several months' worth of air bills sent to Dr. Glantz. FedEx complied with the court's order to produce the records, but failed to notify Dr. Glantz it had done so. In fact, the lobbying group learned that the records had been turned over to the tobacco company only because the university was involved in other, separate litigation with Brown & Williamson.

FedEx is widely known for its highly efficient, quality-conscious, customer-centered approach to doing business. But the firm obviously had no privacy policy in place—or if it did, the policy was inadequate. No one would maintain that FedEx could or should refuse to produce customer records in the face of a court order. On the other hand, the firm should clearly have notified its client as soon as such an order was received. In an incredibly lame-sounding statement following the incident, a FedEx spokesperson explained:

> *We don't tell people that their records have been subpoenaed because there is nothing they can do about it.*

Tandy Corporation, on the other hand, has an explicit and public policy with respect to protecting privacy. Radio Shack retail stores file their customer data by a customer's last name and the last four digits of his or her phone number. But in an era characterized by increasingly intrusive, unsolicited telemarketing, Tandy soon found a large number of its own customers leery of providing the last four digits of their phone number to a store clerk waiting to write up an invoice. So Tandy posted a message from CEO Bert Roberts in each store, advising customers that the information was needed to record an individual's purchases, make future warranty repairs more convenient, and save time writing up invoices for repeat customers.

Tandy's notice further reassures customers that (1) no one will be using the information to call on the phone, ever; (2) all information is for Tandy's own internal use; and (3) no information provided by any customer will ever be released to any other business or organization. The notice advises customers the company plans to send out a quarterly catalogue, but if a customer doesn't want it, he can simply check the box at the bottom of the invoice. With this notice Tandy, in effect, posted its Privacy Bill of Rights, although they didn't call it that.

Any interactive enterprise will have to face the issue sooner or later. Before you find yourself in FedEx's situation, you will definitely want to have your own policy in place. Interaction fuels the 1:1 enterprise, so the enterprise must clear away all the potential disadvantages of interaction from the customer's perspective. The enterprise whose customers are reluctant to tell it anything will soon find itself in the position of having to buy information through increasingly costly incentives, just to make customers more willing to participate.

The forward-thinking interactive firms are already dealing resolutely with the issue of protecting consumer privacy. As we mentioned previously, BroadVision One-to-One offers a privacy option on individual items in every customer's Web profile. A browser can give information to a site using the BroadVision software and specify which items he wants made available only to the Web site host. As interactivity vehicles proliferate, we are likely to see an increasing variety of mechanisms such as this.

For the interactive media firm itself, protecting each individual customer's privacy will be key to "owning" the customer's tastes and preferences, and creating a profitable, interactive business in the future, as we will see in the next chapter.

THE MEDIUM IS THE MATCHMAKER

How to Own the Customer in a Changing Media Landscape

S o far, we've been focusing on the role of interactivity and customization in fueling a new, competitive dynamic for the 1:1 enterprise. But what will the Interactive Age mean for the shape of media companies themselves?

Business analysts regularly point out that the successful media company of the future will be a firm that owns either the "pipeline," a term for the wire or conduit carrying the interactive signal into the home, or the "content," meaning the programming and other software that flows through the pipeline. In fact, almost by definition a "media company"—from Disney to TCI to Ameritech—is some combination of pipeline and content.

But perhaps, if we apply the same lens of interactivity

and feedback to the media firms themselves that we've been applying to other companies, we'll discover a completely different business model—a model foreign to today's pipeline-or-content thinking. Is interactivity simply another contribution to the ongoing media fragmentation and proliferation trend—one more set of choices for the media consumer? Or does interactivity offer new and different opportunities for the media firm itself?

News Flash: An interactive media company does not need to own either content or pipeline to be profitable.

Rather than owning pipelines or content, the surest way to financial success as an interactive media company will be to own *data about individual consumer preferences.* Success will belong to the interactive media firm that does the best job of creating Learning Relationships with its individual users, browsers, or viewers.* Successful firms will become 1:1 enterprises, locking their users in by remembering their individual tastes and preferences over time, and then using that memory to make it easier and easier for any individual user to get the particular content he or she wants from whatever pipeline he is connected to.

---

* We will refer to the term "user" from now on, to denote the end-user consumer of information and entertainment provided by a media firm. We realize the medium itself could be video, audio, or data.

Owning the Customer

Let's first go forward in time just a bit, to a year in which the World Wide Web is useful not just for calling up text and still pictures, but for getting video and audio signals downloaded as well. Either because of higher-bandwidth pipelines and switches, or because of better data-compression software, or more likely as a result of a combination of these advances, let's assume that VHS-quality signals can be transmitted in real time over the Web, and even high-definition video can be obtained, although it must be downloaded a little more slowly, for later playback in real time. This isn't too far in the future. We can almost do all this today. Cable TV companies want to be able to deliver this kind of service soon via their coaxial cables into the home, and phone companies could practically deliver this today along I.S.D.N. lines.*

But now let's assume that because of this new video and audio capability, an increasing number of people are getting their television news, and even some regular programming, over their computers connected to the World Wide Web. A large-screen computer now goes into the family room, perhaps connected to the television, perhaps as a separate appliance. People choose to watch television this way because they can see their favorite shows whenever they want, not just when they're being broadcast. They can stop and play

---

* "I.S.D.N." stands for Integrated Services Digital Network, a special type of line offered by local phone companies. I.S.D.N. comes in a variety of configurations, but it can transfer data at a rate of 128 kilobits per second, or about five to ten times as fast as most ordinary phone lines (Edmund L. Andrews, "A Steep Hurdle to Web Shortcut," the *New York Times*, March 25, 1996, p. D1).

everything back if they want, they can zap the commercials, speed through the boring or uninteresting parts, and so forth.

This presumes, of course, that the owners of the programming will consent to have their content played over the Web, but why wouldn't they? It would simply be an added source of revenue—and a completely trackable source at that. Rather than being upset that computer users can more easily zap the commercials that go with the programming, the content providers could now offer their advertisers two types of commercials—the standard, one-way variety for broadcast vehicles, and an interactive variety for the Web. (Of course, since marketers will be choosing individual customers who are more interested in the message in the first place, the chances are greatly reduced that the user will opt out.)

Even the programs themselves could come in a variety of forms and content formats. A user who wants more wholesome programming might be able to ask for it that way. Content providers already sanitize theater movies for airline and television viewing—it wouldn't be too much to get a content provider to make two or three categories available on the "family values" scale. As the market develops, content providers will find more and more variables to apply to their creative properties, including language spoken, duration, and perhaps even type of ending—variables that let the user himself interact with the programming rather than just the advertising.

Now go back for a minute to the Broadvision One-to-One application for Web sites. What implications does this application have for how a user is likely to consume video signals over the Web? If a user is constantly interested in soccer, or in a particular baseball team, or if a user likes historical documentaries, then the Web site he goes through to get his video signals can make him more loyal by *remembering* these preferences and making it that much easier for him to find exactly what he wants the next time.

When the Web, or something like it, becomes the dominant form of wire-based commercial transmissions, anyone with access to a computer will be able not only to call up his or her own video and audio signals, but also to "post" video or audio signals for others to call up. The high school basketball team your daughter plays on could have a roving, high school camera person shooting each game and posting it for parents to retrieve. Will the camera person charge for this service? Probably yes, if she's any good. But don't forget, there are plenty of potential competitors if her charges get out of line.

Defining the Media Company of the Future

In the Web scenario we just outlined, who exactly is the media company? Is it the content owner or the softball team's camera person? Is it the phone company, over whose lines the signals are coming? Or the cable TV company, if that's whose lines you're using? Or is it the Web site you access to get your primary feed?

Traditionally, media firms have been in the "information dissemination for hire" business. The customers who pay the freight at most media companies are advertisers who contract with the firm to disseminate advertising messages along with the information and entertainment delivered to the media company's users. Information dissemination like this has always been a one-way process, and in most cases the information goes the same way to every user. We all see the same ads in whatever magazine or newspaper we are reading, and all of us who are tuned in to the same television station at the same time are treated to the same commercials from advertisers who hope we will accept their *implicit bargain* to notice the ads in exchange for reduced editorial or programming costs. Of course, a noninteractive media firm has no way to verify that any particular user actually did read the ad or watch the commercial, and in this era of media fragmentation, fewer and fewer do.

Now that even broadcast television is delivered over a cable, an increasing number of media firms generate revenue from users as well as advertisers. But regardless of whether the media firm collects the bulk of its money from the users themselves, or from advertisers trying to gain access to those users, the users are still the primary asset. In the short term, advertiser-dependent media companies may compete for a bigger share of various advertisers' business, but in the long run the competition always comes down to delivering users.

Because media are becoming gradually more interactive, the media firms themselves will, increasingly, turn to *buying* the time and attention of users by making an *explicit bargain.* The 1:1 enterprise will find it easier to transmit and track an interactive dialogue than it is to obtain and keep an individual customer's attention, and the more valuable the customer is to the enterprise, the more difficult it will be to get his attention.

In the end, the most expensive aspect of conducting interactive dialogues with individual customers won't be the cost of the media per se, but the expense of the customer incentive. Think of it as the 1:1 enterprise rewarding a customer for dialogue that gives the enterprise a competitive advantage, perhaps enabling the firm to gain the customer's loyalty with a customized product or service.

There are a number of companies already forming to offer rewards to Web users in return for their clicking on ads, or paying attention to messages. Yoyodyne, CyberGold, Maritz's GoldMail, and Netcentives are all Web services businesses trying to establish a "currency" of points, rebates, cash, and other services for Web site operators to swap out to consumers as a purchase price for their time and attention. Eventually, this is likely to be such a common characteristic of the Web that it will give rise to a new kind of Web crawler. In addition to Web crawlers that deploy themselves looking for particular information or news items, it is easy to imagine a whole variety of "revenue crawlers" being deployed to search for points and cash on behalf of a user.

It is logical to ask, in light of the assortment of interactive and computer-controlled communications vehicles already available or soon to be available, exactly how the role of the commercial medium itself is likely to change. Obviously, a company operating Web sites or interactive television is capable of doing more for advertisers than simply disseminating information. At least from the users who connect to the service, the company could *obtain* information, and treat them differently based on who they are or what they say. But is this "advertising"? And what lessons does this model of commercial dialogue have for today's cable operator or magazine publisher?

In the Interactive Age a medium should think of itself as being in the business of *matchmaking* rather than information dissemination. A media company is really in business to bring its own principal customers, the advertisers, into contact with their customers: the end-user consumers of the medium. In a technological world limited to one-way broadcast communications, matchmaking is necessarily restricted to advertising, publicizing a message the same way to everyone, and hoping that the recipients of the message will buy more products from, or at least get in contact with, the sponsor of the message.

But clearly, matchmaking can be much more efficiently accomplished with interactivity. The interactive medium is more easily understood as a *host* facilitating the conversational interchange between a marketer and a customer. An efficient and reliable host system is one that ensures that marketers and customers get to mingle easily, and that dialogues are both convenient and relevant to both parties.

In the Web scenario we outlined above, the Web site operator is the real media company, the one in the best position to match each user with the advertisers appropriate for her. And the Web site operator, if the business is properly structured, will also own the customer. If every time you sign on to get your television signal, your "host" Web site makes it easier and easier for you to get to what you want, choosing from a proliferating assortment of national, international, and local properties, then you will have reason to stay loyal to that Web site. You won't want to switch, because switching will be just too much trouble.

In the scenario we outlined, the Web site operator owns neither wires nor programming. The only thing the company owns—and it is an asset far more valuable than either pipeline or content—is the customer.

While it might require a small leap of faith to imagine a future in which ordinary people "call up" their video signals along the World Wide Web, real companies are implementing analogous technologies today. And the power inherent in these technologies is, again, not the machinery, not the programming, but what the "host" companies can *remember* about their customers.

Direct Broadcast Satellite in Mexico

Medcom is a Mexican sales promotion and broadcast media firm. Besides radio and television broadcasting, the firm is in the business of point-of-purchase sales promotion. In nearly all of Mexico's 600 supermarkets, Medcom maintains a presence of some type. Often a Medcom person is on site at the store, trying to get shoppers to taste a new kind of food or take home a sample of some product being sold in the store. Other times, Medcom's store presence may consist of a point-of-purchase display and signage.

The company is now engaged in building a direct-broadcast satellite (DBS) television business. DBS technology (such as Hughes's DirecTV or Murdoch's SkyChannel) uses a stronger signal than ordinarily employed for satellite downlinks, so a smaller antenna can successfully retrieve it. Subscribers to DBS television services need a receiving antenna roughly the size of a small pizza platter, and this antenna can be conveniently placed on a roof or on the wall outside an apartment window. Because no complex earth-station receiving gear is required for DBS, the DBS firm is able to cut out the "middleman"—the cable operator or local broadcast station—and send its signal directly to consumers.

The cable television industry in Mexico is not very well developed, so fewer than 15 percent of Mexican households could plug in to cable television today even if they wanted to. Therefore, even at $800 or more for a receiving antenna and set-top box, Medcom's DBS prospects are fairly bright.

One feature to be offered in Medcom's set-top box will enable users to convey information to, and receive information from, the individual commercial sponsors of the programming. The set-top boxes Medcom provides come with a phone link so that the user can "interact" with the television programming—and the commercials—in real time. While watching a program or a commercial, for instance, a user could command the set to show where to get tickets to the concert, or how to sign up for the credit card offer.

The second generation of set-top boxes will also have a "smart card" reader and processor. The user's own smart card can thus be updated with the results of whatever interactions he or she undertakes. Want a coupon good for a free sample of the dry cereal just advertised? Push the "sample" button on the remote and your smart card will be encoded. Then take the smart card to any supermarket, and the Medcom people there will be able to read it and give you the free sample.

By themselves, these features are sure to kindle advertiser interest in Medcom's system, and the point-of-purchase presence Medcom has already established for itself gives it a unique advantage. As a matchmaker between the businesses that advertise on its system and the users who consume the media, Medcom clearly offers a multifaceted and extremely useful set of avenues, including not just interactive advertising, but couponing and redemption as well.

In the long run, however, Medcom understands its principal asset is the user, and the user's own loyalty to the Medcom system. So the company has designed its overall product in such a way as to lock its customers in, over the long term, more or less regardless of the existence of any competitive service. Provided only that Medcom maintains its QQP—quality product, quality service, and fair price—the advertisers who want to reach its customers will have to go directly through Medcom. This is because the set-top box, which is actually a small computer, will know who is holding the remote device and controlling the television's output, and the box will remember each individual user's viewing preferences, making the Medcom system itself more and more valuable to each individual user.

Every time the TV is turned on, the user will be asked to enter his two-digit ID code—a different code for each occupant of the household. Over a period of time, the box will "learn" what an individual television user wants from his television set, and the system will get better and better at finding individually relevant programming. With several hundred channels available to the DBS user—eventually probably thousands—simply finding the programming you want to watch, at any given time, could be a complex job.

But imagine, if you are a sports fan, turning on the television set, identifying yourself, and then seeing a display of all the sports and sports news programming being shown right then, as well as a list of the live sporting events starting sometime in the next two hours. Or ask for movies, and see the movies due to start in the next hour, but at the top of the list are comedies and suspense dramas—your favorite types—rather than children's films, romances, horror movies, or science fiction. And these viewing choices would be driven not by any sort of complex, static survey you filled out prior to subscribing to the service, but by your actual viewing patterns over the past few days or weeks. Perhaps, eventually, Medcom will incorporate its own kind of "rating bar" in the channel-changing process, to capture a deeper range of user preferences.

What will happen, of course, is that a user whose programming preferences are captured more and more accurately will remain loyal to Medcom because it is convenient for him. With millions of such customers, Medcom—and any other media firms that figure this out—will have an asset far more valuable than either pipelines or content. Medcom will own the customer.

Hybrid Interactivity

Medcom's DBS system is not a video-on-demand system, but a hybrid form of traditional broadcast and quasi-interactivity. It links a user's one-way television signal with the user's own responses via the phone connection from the set-top box, enhancing that connection further with the smart-card device. It's not hard to imagine a variety of dialogue-building host possibilities for traditional media when they are married to phones and other interactive devices.

Other media, also, are capable of transforming themselves into matchmakers, rather than information providers, through "hybrid interactivity." Consider KMPS, a Seattle radio station with a country-music format and a very loyal set of listeners, incorporated by the station into a listeners' club. Club members receive membership cards entitling them to discounts when dealing with various KMPS advertisers. Members also get regular newsletters, with information not only about country music stars and new releases, but also about other members. And an extensive call-in service allows KMPS listeners to rate the music they listen to and register their opinions and preferences, individually, with the media firm.

The Tribune Company's Jazz Phone is a music-listening and rating service for fans of one of its radio stations, WQCD in New York (known to its listeners as CD 101.9). An avid jazz fan can call a toll-free number and preview tracks from various jazz CDs (mostly new adult contemporary formats) heard on the station, and even order CDs for home delivery. This service was first promoted in the station's *Cool Notes* magazine, sent to 250,000 of its core listeners. Bob Paquette, the station's general manager, has also worked with J & R Music World, a Manhattan music store, to promote jazz music to the station's listeners. At J & R Music World, there is an entire section for CD 101.9 listeners. Two phone lines with direct connections to Jazz Phone are available for shoppers to sample music. After just four months of offering Jazz Phone, J & R's sales of new adult contemporary music increased by 40 percent!

Even outdoor advertising is being made more interactive every day. Nearly 20 million automobiles in the U.S. now have car phones, and many other drivers carry portable phones, so a large number of outdoor signs carry phone numbers for easy and immediate access to the sponsors. One entrepreneurial company headquartered in Chicago, Cellular Linking, provides a service that allows an outdoor advertiser to offer a completely toll-free cell-phone number to encourage response, picking up not only the long distance charges for the call, but the caller's air time charges as well.

Think about all the ways a print vehicle could incorporate interactivity. Any newspaper or magazine could offer a wide range of detailed information immediately, via fax on demand. A magazine could offer more in-depth information on a particular story, including a chart of similar stories run in the past, or a list of sources for more information, or a verbatim transcript of government hearings. Or the magazine could offer these informational enhancements via an on-line service affiliated with the publication.

For too many publishers today, having an interactive presence means having a Web page or an icon on Prodigy or America Online that allows a computer user to scroll conveniently down a few lines of text which summarize the latest issue of the printed magazine. But few people want to sit at a computer terminal and read an abbreviated version of a magazine. A magazine or newspaper that settles for this kind of interactive presence is merely experimenting with the technology, and the users of the service are merely experimenting, as well. Rather than providing wide, shallow coverage of a publication already in print, on-line services run by publications should provide deeper, on-demand coverage of topics requested by the users.

What an on-line magazine ought to do is allow a reader to go as deeply into a story or a subject as he wants, looking up previous articles and related topics immediately, seeing more detailed charts or graphs, or checking for himself the actual words in the firm's press release. Digital Ink, the *Washington Post* on-line service, allows just such a relationship to develop. Through Digital Ink, an on-line user can retrieve articles the newspaper published up to nine years ago, retrieving them by title, keywords, or publication date. To narrow the search even further, readers can specify one of three categories to search under: national, *Washington Post*, or any article already open.

Moreover, because of the *Washington Post*'s formidable news-gathering organization, Digital Ink has breaking news available on an hourly update basis, so a reader can stay completely abreast of any important story covered in the morning paper. When a Digital Ink user is scanning an article on, say, autumn vacations with brilliant foliage, toll-free numbers will often be shown on the screen for more information, as well as additional "hot connections" for background information, including related stories, or other places to see leaves (with activities in these areas), and even leaf reports—to learn peak viewing times!

The *San Jose Mercury News* goes a little further, with specific references and pointers included in its printed newspaper articles. An article about, say, a senator's plans for reforming Medicare might be followed by a four-digit code. The reader then could enter this number in the *Mercury* on-line service, and additional background information will be shown—perhaps other politicians' previous Medicare suggestions, or the actual text of this senator's statement. Many of these added references can be accessed via fax response as well as on-line. *Mercury News* also offers a service called News Hound, through which users can get electronic news clippings based on their individual areas of interest. If, for instance, you're in the market for a used Saturn, then every hour News Hound will search all the incoming wires and for related stories, and once a day it will also scan the classified ads. Thus, at the end of the day, you could read a wire story about Saturn's recent customer service success, then open a message from a local owner who might be selling the coupe you've been looking for.

At present, most such media services charge a flat fee per month, or per hour of usage. It is too difficult today, in a technological sense, to charge for particular items of information, although that may be the eventual future for the media firm.

InfoMarket is an IBM unit with a technology that could

soon make pay-per-view information possible. InfoMarket's software, dubbed Minerva, was originally developed by Booz, Allen for the CIA. It was used to keep tabs on various terrorist activities, as they were reported and tracked in a number of unrelated, international databases. InfoMarket proposes to use the technology for protecting electronic intellectual property rights.

Sign up for InfoMarket and your credit card number will be retained on file for use in settling any charges you agree to accept. Now, let's say you want to see a special report published by Simba on the future of some telecommunications company. Simba normally charges $600 for this report. To protect itself against unauthorized duplication, Simba's policy is *not* to make the report available electronically, but only in printed form.

And this is where InfoMarket's technology comes in. Through prior arrangement with Simba, InfoMarket could sell the report over the Internet. To take the report, you download a "Cryptolope" from InfoMarket. The Cryptolope can't be unlocked and read until you enter your own InfoMarket password, at which time your credit card account at InfoMarket is charged $600. (Your credit card number, incidentally, is never "out" on the Internet, but only in InfoMarket's own computer.)

To prevent unauthorized duplication of such electronically delivered documents, InfoMarket places a "watermark" on each one. Every document is sent out *slightly* different, in a way that allows InfoMarket to trace it to the original purchaser. Thus, if you order the PPV information and then decide to circulate it to a wide number of friends and colleagues, or if you decide to pirate it and sell the report yourself, InfoMarket will be able to trace the original purchase of the document to you.

InfoMarket can apply this technology, moreover, not just to text-based information, but to bit streams of audio and video information as well. If you want to consider just one implication, consider what it would mean to have your own "writable" CD drive—a machine that is selling for about $500. You could order music delivered over the Internet, pay for it through InfoMarket, and write the data onto your own CD for use in your car or Diskman. The main thing that has prevented this from happening already is that once the music is electronically transmitted, the intellectual property rights to it are very hard to protect. But if every version sold to a consumer were watermarked for later identification, then music pirating operations will be easy to detect.

Three Types of Interactive Advertising

In the Interactive Age, an age of smart television set-top boxes and Web sites that sort and store real-time video signals, what will advertising actually look like? For starters, it's likely that interactivity will mean the end of those obnoxious television spots that seem designed to irritate users into remembering the products. "Ring around the collar" and "Aetna I'm glad I met ya" are doomed. And good riddance.

In the Interactive Age, three forms of advertising will dominate, and we can already see them beginning to appear:

- *Invitational* advertising: More and more newspapers and magazine ads, and even television commercials, display the Web site addresses where their sponsors can be reached. This is a form of invitational advertising, and in the Interactive Age, invitational advertising will be the principal type of commercial message that reaches a consumer without the consumer's explicit prior consent or desire. The "billboard" ads that a browser encounters at a Web site are invitational in nature. Click on one, and you'll go right to the advertiser's site, where you'll be plied to begin a dialogue. Starting a dialogue will be the primary goal for any marketer hoping eventually to sell products or services. Advertisers will no longer find it beneficial to irritate users into remembering their brands. Not only is this a bad way to begin a dialogue, but it is very likely that an interactive consumer irritated by a certain ad or brand will be capable of forbidding that brand from appearing on his own computer—or television set—ever again. Don't forget that once a customer teaches his Web site, or whatever firm serves as his interactive "host," that he dislikes ads for a particular brand, it will be nearly impossible for that brand to get a hearing with that customer ever again.

■ *Solicited* advertising: On the other hand, there will, indeed, be a booming market for advertising on demand. Consumers will "look up" advertising whenever they wish to begin thinking about buying something, or when they want to compare prices, features, or services. We have two principal forms of solicited advertising today, both in print—classified ads and Yellow Pages, the two largest and fastest-growing advertising vehicles. Electronic, interactive versions of these media will represent a very significant form of advertising in the 1:1 future. And now the World Wide Web itself is basically just one giant electronic directory of solicited advertising. The Web is the world's best current example of a matchmaking medium.

▪ *Integral* advertising: As customers opt out of advertising (why? because they can!), advertisers will, more and more, include brand messages as integral parts of the entertainment and information programs they underwrite. Product placement in movies is already big business, with clear distinctions in placement fees for background use vs. handling by the hero. Just entering the Interactive Age, we are now seeing a greater fusion of publicity, advertising, and careful product placement in nearly every media outlet. See the movie, then buy the T-shirt at Blockbuster, get a set of the characters at McDonald's, converse with the stars at the http://www.toyota.com address. Consumer marketers eager to make as broad an impression as possible will gravitate to movies and public events that command a mass audience, something that is likely to become harder and harder to find.

Does this mean traditional, nonaddressable, noninteractive mass media advertising will disappear? No. Mass media, and the mass advertising that supports it, will still be with us. But such advertising will play a smaller and smaller role in the marketing plans of any company. Media fragmentation will continue to make mass messages more difficult, and less cost-efficient, to deliver.

One role for mass media advertising, ironically, will be putting messages out to people with whom no dialogue is ever contemplated. A wide variety of "badge" products, from athletic shoes and beer to automobiles and fashion accessories, are pitched to people who are not now and never will be customers. This is not a mistake. After all, it's no fun to pay $200 for a pair of basketball shoes, or $50,000 for a car, if your friends haven't heard of the brand.

Making Any Medium Stronger with Interactivity. *Now.*

Broadcasters and publishers are in the matchmaking business. Each company's most valuable end product is not the printed page, or the thirty-minute recorded program, but the *connection* they can facilitate between a marketer and a customer.

Eventually, nearly all news and information will be delivered to consumers electronically and interactively—because the declining cost and rising power of information technology will mandate it, and because consumers, for their own convenience, will demand it. In the meantime, however, we are faced with a half-generation or more of difficult adjustment, as one media firm after another attempts to make the transition to the Interactive Age. So what should a media firm be doing today?

First, of course, it should begin creating and testing all sorts of hybrid forms of interactivity. People aren't soon going to give up reading magazines and newspapers in hard copy, or listening to their favorite radio stations while they drive to work. But increasingly, *many* consumers—particularly the most valuable advertising targets—will be frustrated if their media companies don't make it simpler to get more detailed information more quickly. So every firm now in the commercial media business should also be searching for ways to link its current medium to a variety of interactive links with its own readers, viewers, or listeners. Fax on demand, on-line, interactive voice response, the World Wide Web—these are the workhorses of interactivity today.

But second, and more important, a media company should be designing its own system so that it can *remember* its customers. To be successful in the long run, the media company must remember what its customers want of it, so that every time a customer accesses the system, it becomes more and more convenient *for that customer*!

If your own media firm now wants to launch itself into a hybrid form of interactivity, take a lesson from Medcom, KMPS, and others. Give your customers PIN codes or other identifiers, so you know exactly who asks for what kind of information, and when. Then be sure your system *remembers* how and when each individual customer accesses it, what information gets called up, what articles are searched in more detail, what advertisers are contacted. Make it constantly simpler, constantly more convenient for each customer, individually.

As the technology improves, your success will hinge on what you know about *each* of your customers, not what you know about *all* of them. This knowledge is more critical to your success than your pipeline and, in the long run, more important even than your content. Since any number of competitors can provide pipeline and content, success will depend on your ability to use the knowledge you've obtained from a customer to claim that particular customer relationship. So make your customers loyal now, and begin improving your margins, by using interactivity to learn each one's individual, personal tastes and preferences.

A 1:1 Business Model for the Interactive Media Company

Today's media companies in the information and entertainment dissemination business earn most of their money by selling tonnage—how many impressions, how much reach, how many gross rating points delivered. So far, most interactive media firms are trying to sell advertising on their interactive vehicles under the same basic rules. They still plan to count tonnage. They're just using a different set of scales. Instead of impressions or rating points, they count "clicks," or "visits."

The problem with charging for tonnage is that tonnage is an artifact of the aggregate-market business model. If you count tonnage, then every transaction is measured on the same scale, at the same rate. Perhaps it is $0.005 for each click, or it could be 1.5 percent of each on-line sale. In the aggregate-market world, value is a function of the product, and tonnage is the product being sold. In this world, applying a standard price to each type of transaction is acceptable, for the simple reason that it is the only thing possible. But in the Age of Interactivity?

To the 1:1 enterprise, value is not a function of the product; value is a function of the customer.

If we want to construct a 1:1 business model for an interactive media firm, the first thing we have to do is create some mechanisms for extracting the most value from a customer-specific value chain. How to do this:

Charge different prices for access to different customers

If customers are different, and have different values to a business, then why shouldn't a media matchmaker simply price them differently? That's right—charge different rates for accessing and interacting with different customers.

One way to value the different members of a single "audience" is to visualize queues of advertising messages building up as advertisers express their own desires to reach different individual customers. Remember that the interactive media firm (like the Web site using BroadVision software) will be able to put different advertising messages in front of different users. This means every media user will have a queue of messages waiting for him, based on how many advertisers have "bought" access to him. The media firm could charge more based on the length of the queue of messages already booked for a particular customer. Or it could even sell priority access rights—allowing an advertiser to pay a premium to go to the front of *certain* customers' queues.

Since customers who are willing to provide more information about themselves will attract more marketing interest, this valuation strategy is biased in favor of those customers who are willing to participate in dialogues. It puts a real price on personal privacy. Those who are reluctant to let marketers know they own a cat, or prefer white wine over red, or graduated from college, may find themselves without sponsorship for the Web browsing or cable TV program they want. Marketers will be able to deal most efficiently with customers who are willing to participate in dialogues. Media firms can be competitively expected to pass the economic benefit of this through to their users, so over time they are more likely to charge for noninteraction than for full interaction. The new slogan of the interactive media firm might well be:

If no queue, pay per view.

Another way to price by individual customer would be to score each user based on previous interactions. Every time a user clicks on an additional ad, the "price per click" for *that* user would increase by a hair. Whenever the user orders something directly on-line, or otherwise provides some sort of on-line transactional value to an advertiser, the access price would go up again, something more than a hair.

In any case, by charging different prices for access to different customers, the interactive media firm can lay the groundwork for buying an individual customer's time and attention. In addition to disposable income, a media user will generate more advertising revenue if (a) his known tastes and preferences match a particular advertiser's offering, and (b) he interacts with messages and makes purchases regularly. Both these variables are basically in the control of the user himself, so why not create a business model in which advertising and commercial revenue is *shared* with each user? "We'll rebate to you 25 percent of all sales commissions and advertising fees you generate."

Charge for the transactions

An interactive medium is not just a mechanism for communication, but a sales channel as well. As with any sales channel, the selling activity allows it to retain a slice of the value chain for itself. Whether a media firm charges a sales commission or a transaction fee, the fact is it should be charging for the actual sales events that move over the medium.

In most cases, the potential revenue magnitude of the selling events will dwarf the revenue potential of the advertising events. That is, a medium might be able to charge only a penny or two for putting a firm's invitational message in front of a prospective customer, but if the customer then buys a $100 product—through the medium itself—the commission on that sale could easily be hundreds of times as great. When facing this kind of economic equation, the interactive medium should be careful to pay attention to facilitating transactions as quickly and easily as possible.

It might be totally free for a customer to sign up for and interact with the medium, but what you want is to entice the customer to agree in advance on the mechanics of ordering a purchase and paying for it. Get a credit card number, or an account, or an invoicing relationship of some kind in advance. To do this, it might be helpful to engage the customer in a reward scheme of some kind.

Use the customer's individual profile for on-line authentication

Many customers are just not comfortable giving their credit card number over the Internet (indeed, some don't like giving it over the phone either). Those who do must provide authentication—billing address is sufficient in most cases—to verify that they actually are themselves. The various forms of cyber money that have been proposed to date all involve some form of cryptographic authentication, but every week we read about yet another security bug having been discovered by some freelance hacker.

Eventually, the most reliable form of personal authentication will probably be the human voice itself. "Speak the words 'Mississippi' and 'Cuyahoga' so we can verify your identity."

Until voice-recognition technology is cost-efficiently available for electronic security, there is a case for the cautious use of "profile authentication." A Web site owner or other interactive host should be able to authenticate a customer more or less perfectly simply by asking a few questions derived from the profile. We've all seen old World War II movies in which the GI's try to ferret out German spies by asking "Who pitched the last game for Pittsburgh when they won the 1942 Series?"* So the Web site owner should be able to authenticate by automatically asking one or two questions for which only the customer himself could have the right answers. "Do you prefer bicycling or tennis when you're on vacation?"

* Pittsburgh didn't win the 1942 series; St. Louis won.

Emulate other popular sites or home pages

If you start a new Web service, for instance, and you're trying to get new customers to try it so you can learn their preferences and begin locking them in, you have to make it as easy to switch as possible. Even though most services now available don't do a good job of tailoring to individual preferences, a user still feels reluctant to leave any service after having spent time getting used to it. Perhaps it's not as difficult as changing word-processing programs, or changing from Apple to Windows, but it's still a burden.

So make it simple. Ask a new visitor to designate which of these fifty most popular search engines or home pages he likes and uses the most. When he tells you, switch him to your own emulation of that site. It's an interface that will look more familiar to him, and it will make it easier for him to leave the old place and join yours. (Be sure not to block off innovation, however. A customer may *want* to leave his old place in order to have a better experience all around.)

Look for more ways to capitalize on individual tastes and preferences . . .

. . . even if it comes to selling them to other individuals (with permission).

Wouldn't there be some users who would love to see a comedy movie that John Cleese would find hilarious? Or to hear the particular Vivaldi pieces most preferred by Andre

Previn when he is listening on his own? Or the multiplayer video game that Steve Jobs likes the most? To do this, we have to be prepared to pay our own customers a share of the revenue generated through the sale of their preferences.

This is not the same as paying customers to participate and interact. What we are talking about here is "making a market" in individual tastes and preferences, on the theory that some users will always be interested in consuming the same entertainment consumed by other users known for their good taste—or famous for any other reason.

Once you know a user's own tastes in, say, movie entertainment, those tastes and preferences may have value to others—particularly if the original user is someone with more refined sensibilities, or someone widely respected for his or her judgment in movies. Better or more desirable preferences can be sold by unique individuals, or they can be sold in untraceable aggregates. For instance, instead of offering Steve Jobs's favorite video game, you could offer the most-liked video game among advertising creative executives.

It is easier to imagine selling an aggregate set of preferences when you consider something like vacation travel. Even though you might have a complete record of someone's previous vacation preferences, don't some middle-class travelers want to splurge once in a while? "Book me on a vacation that would be preferred by the typical person who flies first class for ninety percent or more of his trips, and who rides in a chauffeured car to work."

Or imagine the high school student trying to get into a better college, asking to see news items, books, and games most preferred by other students with combined SAT scores over 1400.

In the Interactive Age, an individual's tastes and preferences are an asset that transcends the simple task of selling more things to the individual. Anytime an identifiable *individual*'s tastes are sold, permission will naturally be required, and probably a payment of some kind as well. But with so many customer profiles available, a media company can group them and regroup them to provide a wide array of new experiences for individuals who want to be someone else, if only for a day or two.

Don't just give your profiling product away. Pay people to take it.

Netscape launched itself into the stratosphere of multibillion-dollar technology companies by giving its software away, in order to generate an installed base and create a value stream. This strategy was successful partly because the large installed base soon established a standard, enabling the company to sell upgrades and enhancements, and partly because of the interactive nature of Netscape's product itself, which automatically reconnects users back through the Netscape home page.

As the competition for interactive media consumers heats up, look for many companies, not unlike Empirical Media, to begin focusing on how to gain as deep an insight into individual tastes and preferences as possible. And remember that once you've locked a customer in, your margins will naturally improve. So, rather than contenting yourself with giving the product away, you might want to consider the possibility of making an explicit bargain to compensate the most valuable prospects for the time it takes them to become regular users. "Watch your first twenty hours of interactive television with us and we'll pay for twenty hours of premium movies."

Remember to make interactivity fun

You have to allow those customers who want no-nonsense efficiency to be able to get where they want to go with a minimum of fuss and fanfare.

But some users will want to have fun. Not all, but at least some. And making the interactive experience into something of a game is not a bad idea, especially if the game itself can become part of the explicit bargain, rewarding customers for engaging in dialogues.

Interactive Imaginations, a Web entertainment developer, has created Riddler (http://www.riddler.com), a series of interactive games that can be layered on top of other interactive media mechanisms. The concept was driven by increasingly fractionalized media and markets, with advertisers facing less than captive audiences.

Before users play Riddler games (trivia, crossword puzzles, scavenger hunt, or King of the Hill™), they must register. Each player answers a series of demographic and psychographic questions, to receive fifty Riddlets—virtual tokens to redeem for cash and prizes. (Riddlets are one type of currency at the Riddler site: There are also sponsor coins, which display the sponsor's logo or brand name.) After registering, each player receives a "membership card." The card is actually an icon at the Web site, where a user can click to see how many Riddlets and sponsor coins he's won so far.

The answers players provide during registration drive the kinds of products awarded. So even if two individuals play the *same* game, give the *same* answers, and *both* solve a crossword puzzle or trivia challenge in the same amount of time, each winner will receive a *different* prize—a prize based on his own preferences. An antique-auto hobbyist might receive a desktop replica of a classic old car, while an avid golfer might receive a new putter.

Interactive Imaginations uses Ridmark™, a database management system, to match sponsor's messages with qualified players—and sponsors pay only for the consumers reached. The players, consequently, benefit from sharing their preferences during registration.

As is, Riddler offers marketers the opportunity to get players to come back—to see more advertisements. Players also return to redeem their Riddlets and sponsor coins for cash and prizes in Marlow's Market, named for Riddler's mascot. Players click on a sponsor's coin in this market to immediately get connected to the sponsor's prize page. Summaries of prize values are listed, and members make their purchase transactions by clicking on the "buy" button. At this point an address confirmation form appears. Not until this time do the sponsors learn the user's actual identity. Interactive Imaginations houses players' information, and routes ads to members based on the interests they specify during the registration process. But *members* choose to identify themselves to the sponsors by completing their address in *exchange* for a prize.

The possibilities are enormous for moving Riddler's loyalty program one step further.

Consider the player that enjoys reading; he redeems his points for books. Ridmark™ lets Interactive Imaginations know that this individual likes sci-fi, and eventually, Riddler might be more than just a spot to play games, but a way to grow a sponsor's business. Why not create an option where players can sign up to receive e-mail from Marlow that flags those products that might be interesting to them? So, this member gets a message from Marlow announcing the next Michael Crichton book, inviting the player to place an order: Simply visit Marlow's Market to complete an order form, guaranteeing that you'll be one of the first to receive a signed copy.

Or imagine how sponsors could leverage community knowledge among customers. Why not identify those members that claim similar prizes, and make the list of prizes available to players when they enter Marlow's Market? This way, if a member is trying to decide what prize to redeem his points for, he can review a list that includes alternatives that probably are interesting to *him*.

Regardless of whether media users are compensated for their dialogue or charged for their media usage, the fact is that the media firm in the Interactive Age will have more power to make cost-efficient matches than ever before. It won't be the pipeline or the content that guarantees you a long-lasting business, but the individual media user's personal tastes and preferences. This is the mother lode. Figure out the process, customize it, and streamline it.

Make it a game if necessary. Pay for it if you need to. But in the end, what you want is to own the customer.

If what you sell is a digitizable product—information or entertainment, for instance—then it's not difficult to customize your product to individual tastes, nor is it hard to imagine how to use an interactive media company to distribute your product to those customers who most want it.

But if you sell a *physical* product, requiring a physical

distribution system, then the distribution channel itself will often represent the single biggest obstacle preventing you from developing a 1:1 relationship with your customer. Dealing with physical distribution channels is the subject of our next chapter.

THE BUSY SHOE SALESMAN

12

How to Remove Distribution Barriers Between You and the Customer

One weekend afternoon, a management consultant we know who specializes in the retail trade went to buy athletic shoes at a busy sporting goods store. He watched a shoe salesclerk repeatedly offer an off brand to his customers—the same off brand each time. After watching two sales snatched from the jaws of a well-known national brand, the consultant's curiosity was aroused. He approached the clerk to find out why customers were being switched to this particular brand. Was the off brand offering a special sales incentive? Did the store manager have too many of the shoes in inventory? But the clerk explained that it really wasn't anything that complicated. It was just that this particular brand of shoe was shipped with the laces *already laced into the shoes,* and so it saved the clerk a lot of time and trouble on a busy Saturday afternoon not to have to lace in the national brands for customers who want to try on shoes.

Removing the Barriers Between Your Customer and You

If you want to operate as a 1:1 enterprise, then ask yourself: Do you make your customer lace up his own shoes? If you want your equipment buyers to return their warranty cards, do you place the cards conveniently on the outside of the packing material and fill in the serial numbers for them? If you want your bank customers to come to you for their next home loan, do you fill in all the information on the loan applications, or do you make them do their own paperwork?

Between every business and its customers is a series of hurdles. Every time a customer is willing to buy but has to accept a rain check, can't get someone to answer the phone, can't get financing, can't find the right size, can't get a proposal from the staff, or simply can't find the right people to talk to, it's a fundamental loss to your bottom line. The 1:1 enterprise tries to pinpoint these barriers and remove them.

In most cases, a business's sales channel and distribution system itself represent the single most significant barrier to doing business as a 1:1 enterprise. In this chapter we'll explore the implications this system has for any firm planning its transition from aggregate-market competition to customer-driven competition. Some of the questions that naturally arise are:

- How should a business deal with the barriers that its distribution system might pose—barriers that lie between the firm and its end-user customers? Under what circumstances should a firm risk "going around" its existing distributors?

■ When does it make sense for the 1:1 enterprise to treat the members of the distribution chain themselves as customers? What are the advantages and drawbacks of this strategy? Can a 1:1 approach be used to minimize the channel conflicts that are springing up in a number of industries?

■ If a firm is itself engaged in the distribution of products or services for other firms, then what strategy makes the most sense for dealing with these new technological trends, many of which are threatening to "cut out the middleman"?

Beware of the Aggregate-Market Approach

Even if a business exists so close to its customers that there is no formal "distribution" channel, chances are that the barriers that inhibit customers from doing business with it can still be traced to distribution-like issues. At the next party you attend, ask how many people *really* get their oil changed every 3,000 miles, the way we're all supposed to. A few people will claim they do, but most will admit they don't. Now ask how many would be willing to pay $15 *in addition to the price of the oil change* to have someone come to the driveway and handle the transaction without any effort on their part. Not everyone will value this convenience enough to pay $15 for it, but that's okay. *The 1:1 enterprise is not in business to treat everyone the same way.*

The fact is, within a ten-mile radius most oil change centers could probably *make money* on the home-delivery component of this kind of service, separate and apart from the oil change transaction itself. It could:

1. Generate more transactions with each of these customers

2. Make more profit per transaction with them

3. Cement each customer's loyalty for a longer period

The oil-change service outlet has no "distribution" system between it and its customers. There are no retailers who need to be coddled, no warehouse distributors clamoring for a better unit price or more promotion dollars. Nevertheless, home delivery for an oil-change service can be thought of as a form of distribution-channel enhancement. The oil service outlet might visualize home delivery as the addition of a sales channel. But it could just as easily visualize it as the removal of a barrier.

Aggregate-market competitors focus on *aggregate* barriers rather than on the barriers that face individual customers. While this can be effective in many circumstances, the aggregate-market approach does have two significant drawbacks: It is usually not cost-efficient, and it is often least effective with those customers most worth keeping and growing. The fact is that *any* policy applied across the board to all customers, intended to benefit the enterprise in all situations, is likely to *harm* relations with at least *some* customers.

A Connecticut bank had its principal retail office in one of those affluent bedroom communities, commutable to New York City. The town had a large population of upper-management types, and on Saturdays the downtown area was jammed with shoppers who could never seem to find enough parking. So the bank, in an effort to remove barriers and provide extra services for its customers, instituted a policy of free parking for all its customers on Saturdays. Park in the bank's lot to do your Saturday shopping, do any kind of transaction at the bank, and get your parking ticket validated. The bank obviously intended this as a benefit for *all* its customers—a way to remove the barrier (too little downtown parking space) that inhibited them from visiting the bank on Saturdays.

One Saturday morning a man went into the bank, after parking in the lot, but then remembered that his wife had been there the day before and had taken care of the matter. So he spent an hour doing some shopping, bought a pair of shoes, came back to the bank, and asked the teller to validate his ticket. The teller, however, citing the bank's policy, advised him he would have to do a "transaction" at the bank before the ticket would be validated. The gentleman insisted he had been about to do a transaction, but remembered his wife had been in just the day before, and anyway they were regular customers, and so forth.

You can probably already see how this incident was destined to develop. The teller stuck to her guns. She had a policy to follow, and by golly, *she followed it the same for everybody, no matter what*. The gentleman was angered by the bank's apparent obstinance, and not at all accustomed to being treated like "everybody." He was the CEO of a Fortune 50 firm, with headquarters in New York City. Nevertheless, he said he would indeed do a transaction. He withdrew nearly all his balances—about half a million dollars in several different accounts at the bank—and then transferred these funds to one of his other banks. At that point, most likely, the teller agreed to validate his parking ticket.

Any company that treats a customer the same as "everybody" is treating that customer like nobody.

In contrast to the aggregate-market approach, the 1:1 enterprise looks at barriers one customer at a time.

Distribution System Barriers and Channel Management

Number one on the list of difficulties for most firms trying to find their way to a customer-driven model is the sales and distribution channel itself. A make-and-sell business can gain a competitive advantage by securing a cost-efficient inventorying process and a heavy-duty delivery system. A make-to-order business, however, requires no inventories at all and a delivery system that is precise and high-tech rather than heavy-duty.

Thus, when a business does not sell directly to its end-user customers, but instead distributes its product or service through one or a variety of intermediaries, from dealers and retail stores to value-added resellers and warehouse distributors, a whole panoply of barriers can easily get in the way of its successful transformation to a 1:1 enterprise. These are barriers that the enterprise itself has very little control over. Unlike the oil-change service station operator or the retail bank, it is not as simple as adding a service, or remembering which customers are the most valuable.

Channel complexities often obstruct an enterprise's efforts to improve its relationship with an end-user customer, particularly when the enterprise tries to coordinate a number of products that normally move through separate, sometimes competing channels. Like many companies, 3M is trying to present a more integrated front to each of its corporate customers, and has a number of initiatives designed to cross-utilize information produced about a customer in one division to serve that customer better through another. For instance, because the company sells both Procter & Gamble and Kimberly-Clark the sticky tape these firms need to manufacture disposable diapers, it has precise information on the rate at which packages and boxes of diapers are produced by each customer. Another division of 3M makes sealing tape for the cartons that the diapers are shipped out in, and sealing tape is in a much more competitive product category. Since the sticky-tape division can count the production runs, 3M would like to be able to use this information to deliver carton sealing tape in just the right quantities at the right times. Clearly, 3M could increase each customer's loyalty simply by automatically delivering the right amount of carton sealing tape in the same truckload with the sticky tape.

Unfortunately, however, it's not at all simple for the company to do this. Carton sealing tape, unlike the sticky tape for disposable diapers, goes to a wide variety of manufacturers of all sorts of products. Manufacturers, including Procter & Gamble and Kimberly-Clark, routinely buy their sealing tape through a distributor that 3M and other adhesives manufacturers use. If 3M were to "carve off" that portion of the sealing tape business that goes to the disposable diaper manufacturing operations of two of its customers, it would be setting up an untenable competition with an important and powerful distributor. Moreover, both Kimberly-Clark and Procter & Gamble buy their carton sealing tape—even for products beyond disposable diapers—from this distributor and its direct competitors. Thus, it is unlikely that either of these two firms would be willing or even able to accommodate a special, customized delivery to support a single manufacturing operation, no matter how straightforward and convenient it might appear at first.

Starting Over with a New Distribution System

Often, it is easier to get around the barriers represented by a firm's current, highly efficient distribution system, not by reforming the system, but by setting up an entirely new, separate system. Three of the most successful new car brands, for instance, are Lexus, Infiniti, and Saturn. To varying extents, each is praised for its quality of manufacture, service, and customer care. In each case, however, the manufacturer chose to create a whole new distribution network rather than relying on the extensive and well-developed network of car dealers it already had. Each firm chose to set up a completely new set of dealers, operating under different rules, in order to ensure the success of the car. Lexus dealers signed different dealer agreements—agreements that gave the manufacturer more control over the dealer's service and sales operations than the standard Toyota dealer agreements did.

These car companies have also made an effort to ensure a greater level of overall customer satisfaction with the dealer. One aspect of this effort is the close coordination each company requires of its dealers in the service area. Another aspect is the effort each car manufacturer has made to reduce the adversarial content of the customer-dealer relationship by posting a fixed, "no haggle" price for the cars. The companies have had mixed success in imposing a single-price policy, but the intent is clear: By eliminating the horse-trading aspect of the car purchase experience, the manufacturer hopes to improve the customer-dealer relationship.

What these manufacturers are trying to do is remove the barriers that inhibit customers from dealing with them. The manufacturers themselves have control over some of the barriers—the ones involving overall product quality and the cost-value equation—but most other barriers arise within the distribution network. In each case, the enterprise found it simpler to start afresh with a totally new distribution system rather than try to impose new rules on the old system.

In the used car arena, a new entrant is reinventing the distribution network altogether. CarMax, owned by the Circuit City electronics superstore chain, had no previously existing distribution network in the automotive category, so it can start from scratch, without risking any investment in the current system. Enter a CarMax lot and you'll be immediately struck by the sheer acreage of sheet metal—rows and rows of late-model used cars in good condition. To be accepted onto the CarMax sales lot, a car has to meet certain basic requirements. There is a 110-point inspection process, and of the cars passing inspection, 95 percent are no older than three years, with fewer than 36,000 miles. Once acquired, the CarMax service people invest about eight hours, on average, per car—fixing up, cleaning, and preparing it for sale. Thus, one barrier is removed immediately: The cars are all clean and reliable. Another barrier removed: Prices at CarMax are fixed and nonnegotiable, so there's no need for any adversarial haggling.

CarMax's inventory is huge, so the customer has a good chance of finding just the right used car. However, to overcome the barrier presented by such an overwhelming assortment of choices, the company has introduced a neat, high-tech selection-assistance program. The shopper asks a user-friendly computer to find all the, say, American-made four-seater convertibles, and moments later gets a list of all the numbered spaces in the lot with cars fitting that description, along with a diagram of the lot with the cars' positions shown. The shopper then finds her way out to the pin-pointed cars to take a look. If she'd like to take a test drive or get some help from a salesperson, she picks up a phone on a nearby light pole and a salesperson comes out to where she is (this is the first time she will be approached by any sales personnel).

To test-drive a car, the salesperson produces the key and accompanies the customer. At the CarMax gate a guard swipes the bar codes on the salesperson's ID card and the car windshield, registering the fact that the car is now out on test drive. Until the car is returned it is marked in the computer's inventory as "out on a test drive," so other shoppers don't waste time trying to find it in the lot. All the parking slots in the car lot are also bar coded, and every morning before the lot opens an employee walks the lot to scan the parking place bar codes and car bar codes, ensuring that the computer's inventory is absolutely correct.

One after another, CarMax has eliminated the barriers to buying a used car and, in the process, the company has set up an extremely efficient and cost-controlled organization. The next step for them would be to remember the shopping requests of individual shoppers from one trip to the next, and to develop the ability to notify yesterday's shopper if a car meeting his specifications arrives tomorrow.

The Difficult Task of Buying a Greeting Card

Let's take a completely different category and look at the barriers to buying, say, a simple greeting card. This time, let's start absolutely from the beginning, and you'll see that virtually all the barriers lie in the way greeting cards are distributed to consumers: To buy this product, a customer must (a) get dressed, (b) get in her car, (c) drive somewhere, (d) find a parking space, (e) get out of her car and go into the store (no matter how bad the weather is), (f) find the greeting card section at the store, and (g) look through an array of dozens—maybe hundreds—of cards *she doesn't want* in order to find the one or two she does. Then (h) she has to stand in line for a while, (i) pay some money, (j) go back out into the weather to get into her car, and (k) drive away. Isn't this a lot of trouble for someone to go to, all so that the greeting card company can make a profit on the card of 85 cents or so?

Like most manufacturers, greeting card companies have traditionally thought of the *retailers* as their customers, and only very recently have some begun to explore the opportunities that might exist for creating 1:1 relationships with end users. To a greeting card manufacturer that counts retail shelf space as its principle sales channel asset, the only way to think of competitors is to watch the shelf space occupied by other greeting card manufacturers. The truth is, however, in an increasingly on-line and time-starved world, the real competitor is the computer, modem, and at-home color printer. In this world, the retail channel itself is more barrier and less asset.

As computers have become more powerful, the card companies have lamely tried to become more technological in the way they relate to end users. They've experimented with card-customizing kiosks placed within the retail stores, but for the most part the kiosks are time-consuming to use, and not very convenient either. The moment your card is printed out, the kiosk gets amnesia, so you have to start from scratch every time. You can't make another card just like the one you just made, or the one you made last month, but now for your *other* niece. So you may as well go to the competitor's kiosk, since both companies know equally little about you. And, of course, to use a kiosk at all, the customer still has to get in her car and drive to the store.

But what if a customer could go on-line from her home computer and design a card in a few moments with a greeting card manufacturer that remembers all her previous creations, and then have the company print and even *send* the card by (snail) mail? For the traditional greeting card firm, this idea may sound attractive, but it also poses a serious dilemma. The card company's executives know it's the best way to offer convenience and gain consumer loyalty, but they also know for sure that retailers will do everything within their legal power to destroy the first manufacturer that "goes direct" in such a significant way. American Greetings and Hallmark both have taken the first steps toward offering customers electronic shopping and retail customization opportunities.

Enter a new on-line company, Greet Street (http://www.greetst.com). Greet Street is a company that sells greeting cards, but that's not its business. Tony Levitan, a founder of Greet Street, believes "at the end of the day, greeting cards aren't a product, but a communication device." Knowing that customers want convenience, Greet Street offers to deliver any card by the customer's choice of first class mail, UPS three-day delivery, or next business day by three P.M. The customer can also schedule e-mail reminders to be sent to herself, so no more birthdays or anniversaries are overlooked.

Greet Street has over 20,000 cards under exclusive agreements with the manufacturers, and nearly 8,000 are available on-line, arranged in a wide variety of categories. See a card you *might* like? Toss it in your "shopping cart" and decide later if you really want it. Once you're ready to order a card, you can write your own message and choose a font. Greet Street cards look just like cards you'd purchase at a local shop. Best of all, however, Greet Street *remembers* you and everything you do. In the Greet Street Personal area at their Web site you can view your order history (what you sent to whom, and when), and you can look up other relevant data, too, such as names (and relationship to you), addresses, birthdays, anniversaries, and so forth. Feedback from Greet Street's shoppers helps the card publishers do better marketing (one publisher of gay greeting cards, for example, learned that its "relationship" cards played to a hetero crowd as well.) *And,* Greet Street has even asked some of its customers for permission to add *their* creations to its inventory!

Of course, Greet Street has it easy. The firm has absolutely no investment in the current retail sales channel. No retailer will throw their cards off the shelves, because there are no Greet Street cards on retail store shelves.

Saturn, Lexus, and Infiniti start up their own dealer networks. CarMax applies retail "superstore" principles to an outdated distribution system. Greet Street customizes cards on-line because it has no investment in any current distribution system. Streamline, the household products delivery service, found it easier to buy from wholesalers because the retailers simply refused to deal. 3M was unable to create a more collaborative relationship with two very large customers, on account of a complex set of conflicts in the distribution chain. French Rags was pushed to customization and backyard sales as a way to evade a stultifying and difficult set of retail buyers, buyers who didn't understand the product and weren't really very interested in doing anything more than simply having it on hand.

There is a theme here. No matter what business you're in, when you begin thinking in 1:1 terms, you better take a *very* close look at your distribution channels, and it won't be as straightforward as you think either. It's not the distributors themselves that are blocking your path, at least not usually. Rather, it's the distribution *system*, which in most industries evolved from the produce-and-sell world of manufacturing, inventorying, and distributing. In the customer-driven, make-to-order world, a distribution system like this is just not useful. More often than not, it's a barrier. It's completely understandable that the most revolutionary changes are coming from outside the system altogether.

If You Can't Beat 'Em, Join 'Em

The alternative to going around a well-established sales and distribution channel, thus risking the current business, is to bring the channel in on the venture—to treat the channel member as a "customer."

Of course, this is the way many companies have always functioned. Most packaged goods companies view their real customers not as the end-user consumers, but as the retailers and retail chains that sell their products on store shelves, on the wholesaler distributors who sometimes deliver the products to the retailers. Automotive manufacturers think of their customers as the dealers who take delivery (and ownership) of the cars once they leave the assembly line.

Treating the distributor as a customer is a logical way for the 1:1 enterprise to create more loyal distributors and earn higher margins. There are, however, some important differences between the end-user customer and the distributor-as-customer. For one thing, unlike the end-user customers of most firms, the distributors probably see their principal competition in the form of other distributors. So the enterprise has to be careful if it plans to treat different distributors differently, so that it is not seen as favoring one competitor unfairly over another. Commercially important information about how a particular distributor likes to be served must be kept within the bounds of the relationship the enterprise has with that particular distributor.

Remember that a distributor will almost certainly work, not just for the enterprise itself, but for the enterprise's competitors as well. To be of use to its own customers a distributor *must* carry a variety of products from which to choose. (A distributor carrying only a single enterprise's products is really just an extension of the enterprise.) One result of this is that while the enterprise may *influence* a distributor, getting a higher and higher share of its business, it can never *convert* it. To convert it would be to undermine the distributor's own business purpose.

Anything an enterprise *teaches* a distributor—any transfer of technology or expertise from manufacturer to intermediary—should be assumed to work to the benefit of the enterprise's competitors as well. When Toyota teaches its dealers better customer service techniques, it must assume that those dealerships who also handle Isuzu or Chevrolet will use these techniques to benefit their other brand names.

A third implication of treating distributors like customers comes from the way they would map on to a Customer Differentiation Matrix. The needs-and-valuations differentiation that characterize a firm's distributors will be different from the firm's end user customers. In Chapter 3 we showed how a bookstore's customer base (individual book readers) would differ from the book publisher's customer base (book distributors and bookstores). If we were to map the greeting card manufacturer's customers onto a Customer Differentiation Matrix, it would look similar:

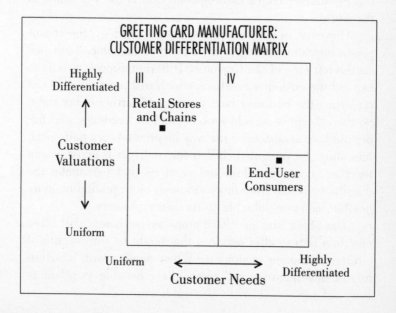

If the greeting card manufacturer sells directly to consumers, it must be able to accommodate a wide variety of different needs. But if the card company sells to the distributor as a customer, then its customer base will be much less differentiated in terms of needs. Like the bookstore, any retail store carrying greeting cards will want to offer a wide range of cards for the convenience of *their* customers, the consumers. On the other hand, the distributors will probably be more differentiated by their valuations than the end-user customers are, with a few large chains and distributors purchasing much higher volumes than the smaller, independent operations. In selling its products to this kind of customer base, the natural strategy for a manufacturer will include key account selling, with a general sales force set up to service all its distributors, and a few national account representatives taking extra-special care of the Wal-Marts of the world.

However, in addition to this natural strategy, the appropriate migration strategy when a firm's customer base lies on the left side of the Customer Differentiation Matrix is to expand the customer need set, which will have the effect of replotting the customer base farther and farther to the right. So the enterprise should look beyond its products, and figure out how to customize the way its products are palletized, how they are promoted, billed for, delivered, or packaged together. Look for additional services that can make the distributor or the store more efficient, more profitable, more flexible, or more valuable to its own customers.

The sheer size of distributors as customers will often enable a firm to offer services that might be uneconomic if offered to smaller customers. When dealing with distributors, a manufacturer will more likely be able to *afford* to customize—shrink-wrapping videotapes in different quantities, or custom-printing a catalogue. With this customer base it is more economic to invest in just-in-time inventory replenishment systems, EDI (electronic data interchange), and other collaborative tools to bring the customer closer to the enterprise. Even a consumer-marketing company, when it is dealing with distributors, is a business-to-business marketer. And there is a very real reason that electronic commerce is being driven by innovations from the business-to-business arena: Business customers are simply larger, and no matter how low the cost of information technology gets, it will *always* be more cost-efficient to invest in customer-specific strategies, like customization and collaboration, when the customers are bigger.

The Demand Chain and the Distribution Waterfall

In a make-and-sell economic system, one widely accepted competitive strategy is to manage or control the supply chain—the chain of economic transactions that account for all the components of a final, manufactured product. At the very top of the supply chain lie the raw materials that make up the manufactured product. Without raw materials, there will be no transactions anywhere else along the supply chain, and no products can be made. But there are many different aspects of the supply chain that can be managed. In the first half of the century, Henry Ford bought rubber plantations in the southern hemisphere so that he would be assured of a continued low-cost supply of tires for his automobiles. In the second half, Wal-Mart requires its suppliers to install state-of-the-art inventory management systems so that they can resupply the store chain promptly and efficiently.

In a make-to-order economic system, on the other hand, it is probably even more important to manage or control the "demand chain"—the chain of transactions and relationships that lead from the customer up through the various distribution channels to the actual product or service specification process. We could even visualize the manufacturer as simply one element of this demand chain. The demand chain is really just the supply chain viewed from the opposite direction.

At the very base of the demand chain lies the end-user customer. If there is no end-user customer, then there can be no sale or other transaction anywhere else along the chain. This means that by far the strongest economic position for any business is to manage its relationship with an end-user customer—the raw material of a 1:1 enterprise. However, managing *every* element of the demand chain is still a critical function, and creating 1:1 relationships with channel members is the best way to manage it.

A distribution channel might consist of one intermediary—the auto dealer, for instance—or it might consist of two or more intermediaries in a multi-tiered structure. A large personal computer manufacturer sells its products in bulk to wholesale distributors around the world, and then the wholesalers sell smaller quantities to value-added resellers, independent dealers, and retail stores, who in turn sell the computers in quantities of one or a few at a time to both consumers and businesses.

Competition for share of customer exists at every level of this demand chain. Not only does the computer manufacturer compete with other manufacturers, but the wholesale distributor competes with other wholesalers, and the reseller competes with other resellers. In some regions of the world, the wholesalers themselves will compete directly for their own reseller's larger corporate customers. Each enterprise has its own base of customers and prospects, and its own set of competitive issues and business strategies.

To create collaborative, 1:1 relationships with a business customer—which is what each member of the demand chain is—the manufacturing enterprise must first look for ways to make that business customer more successful or profitable within its own competitive set. Each enterprise in the channel not only faces the task of generating more loyalty and protecting unit margins within its own customer base, but is also part of the customer base of the enterprise it buys from. This means the manufacturer must think of most such relationships as having two different angles—one angle between the manufacturer and the channel member, and one between the channel member and its own customer base.

The mechanism an enterprise can use to guide its strategy is the Customer Differentiation Matrix, the four-quadrant diagram we first introduced in Chapter 3, which categorizes an enterprise's customer base by how differentiable its customers are in terms of needs and valuations. In analyzing a demand chain, the enterprise must first determine the type of customer base being served by each member of the chain. For simplicity's sake, we'll designate these customer base types as Q1, Q2, Q3, and Q4 to represent the four different quadrants of the Customer Differentiation Matrix.

Think about the demand chain that flows from an individual consumer who buys a personal computer from a retail store. The retail store bought the PC from a wholesale distributor, who bought it from the manufacturer. This is a two-tier distribution system, and each tier represents a particular kind of customer base for the selling enterprise. If we were to diagram this single demand chain and ascribe a Customer Differentiation Matrix to each customer base represented, it would look like this:

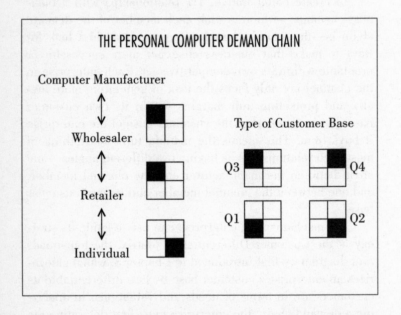

THE PERSONAL COMPUTER DEMAND CHAIN

Computer Manufacturer

Wholesaler

Type of Customer Base

Retailer

Q3   Q4

Q1   Q2

Individual

When the manufacturer sells to the wholesaler, it is selling into a Q3 customer base. This is a base of customers with a wide range of valuations, but who all want the same basic thing from the manufacturer—the whole range of products delivered in a timely and efficient way. The manufacturer's natural strategy for dealing with wholesale distributors is a key account sales strategy designed to focus the proper allocation of time and attention to those very large distributors which account for the bulk of the enterprise's product sales. The manufacturer's migration strategies are to expand its customers' need set and to improve its production and logistics flexibility to be able to treat different wholesalers differently. Customized palletization of products, EDI, and automatic inventory replenishment are the types of services that will begin to cement these wholesalers' loyalty.

Below the manufacturer-wholesaler level, it becomes more complicated. From the wholesaler's perspective, the same strategies that apply to the manufacturer apply also to its relationship with retailers because the retailers, too, represent a Q3 customer base. But the manufacturer's brand name is on the product, so even though the wholesaler sells product to a retailer without the participation of the product manufacturer, clearly the manufacturer has the potential to create a more direct relationship to generate profitability and loyalty from the retailer. If the manufacturer has no long-term desire to cut the wholesaler out of the demand chain altogether, its most straightforward strategy is to develop some type of relationship with the retailer that also respects the wholesaler's own interests vis-à-vis the retailer-as-customer. A similar motivation should apply when the manufacturer is considering its relationship with the end-user individual customer. The *manufacturer needs to cement the loyalty of the individual end user, but it must do this in a way that also respects the interests of the retailer.*

To visualize this, we can think of a kind of "distribution waterfall," with various relationships cascading down through each tier of the demand chain. At each tier below the wholesale distributor, there is in fact a two-angled relationship that needs to be considered:

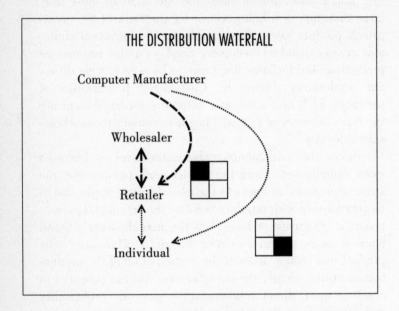

THE DISTRIBUTION WATERFALL

Computer Manufacturer

Wholesaler

Retailer

Individual

At the retailer level, the manufacturer faces the same customer differentiation issues that the wholesaler faces, but because the manufacturer's brand name is on the product, it has a bit more leverage with respect to the retailer's own marketing strategies. Most retail chains are not fundamentally interested in collaborating or developing relationships with their own individual customers. Usually, such chains are so involved in the day-to-day retail struggle that managers barely have time to pay attention to anything other than product turns, merchandising, and efficient inventory management. For these businesses, shelf space is the asset that has the most leverage for generating additional profitability.

Whether a manufacturer deals directly with a large retail chain or with individual retailers through a wholesale distributor, the retailer is still likely to be a Q3 business—with the same basic needs as other retailers have from the manufacturer. But even though retailers may all want the same things, it may be possible to meet these needs in an inherently customizable fashion—satisfying these uniform needs in a different way for each retailer customer. Maxell Corporation of America, a unit of Japan's Hitachi/Maxell, competes ferociously in the mass marketing of audio and video tapes. This kind of product is inherently sold as a commodity, because what the retail consumer needs is standardization rather than customization. A consumer simply wants to be sure that whatever tape she buys she can take home and use in her player.

Many of Maxell's retail-store customers need to advertise the "lowest price anywhere," so Maxell developed a custom packaging program to help a retailer compete. The firm's sales reps work with the retailer's audio and video tape buyers to configure unique packages of products for *each* retailer. Sam Goody, for example, might be selling twelve-packs of ninety-minute Maxell Gold videocassettes, while its direct competitor, Coconuts, sells nine-packs of sixty-minute cassettes. The mass merchandiser down the block, meanwhile, features a "lowest price anywhere" special on 120-minute high-end videocassettes packed (you guessed it) in six-packs.

Maxell simply mass-customizes *one* of the many steps involved in manufacturing and packaging its cassettes: the size and shape of the shrink wrap around its "multipack" units. As a result, it enjoys substantial market share in a very tough, very competitive retail environment. It has succeeded in expanding the need set of each of its retail-chain distributors, and then customizing its service to the different needs represented.

In a two-tier distribution system, a computer manufacturer wanting to develop 1:1 relationships with its retailer channel members could create retailer-specific product demos for its computers, or provide more product training to the retailer's sales staff. A more ambitious strategy would provide a vendor-managed inventory (VMI) system to the retailer, on behalf of the wholesaler. If the manufacturer is already replenishing the wholesaler's inventory automatically, then it could give the wholesaler an opportunity to offer the same basic service to the retail chain, "piggybacking" on the manufacturer's own system. (Note that these are strategies designed to create a better relationship between a manufacturer and a retail operation that takes delivery from a wholesale distributor. If, in the case of a very large retail chain, the computer manufacturer itself may deliver its product directly to the chain's own warehouses, the issues would be different.)

Sometimes, the channel member is part of a customer base that actually has highly differentiated needs. A network of dealers in almost any industry would be much less homogeneous in its approach to business than a large retail chain is, for instance. Case Corporation is a Wisconsin-based manufacturer of farm and construction equipment that sells its products through such a network. After concluding that its corporate parts catalogue no longer drove customers into company retail dealerships effectively, Case's marketing executives began searching for a campaign that would allow its dealerships to recognize their customers' needs.

Case introduced a mass-customized parts catalogue that could carry the *personal identity* of each of its 1400 North American dealers. Not only did each catalogue show the logo, name, address, phone number, and business hours of the dealer, but every dealer was allowed to determine which items would be prominently featured in its own catalogue. Dealers could even set individual item prices by faxing their requirements directly in to Case, although every item also had a "default" price. Over time, Case began mass-customizing the advertisements within the catalogue, so that different dealers could promote different parts and part numbers, relying on modularized copy and art, easily inserted by Case. Dealers were even able to write personalized messages to customers. And individual customer names were printed on coupons, "appreciation" cards, and other special promotions.

This customization program—begun while part sales were down and competition was up—generated a tremendous increase in overall sales, with profit margins increasing more than half. Almost all customers *who visited the dealers* asked for sale items that had been advertised in the catalogue, and over half of them brought the catalogues along with them. Sales of parts with the highest margins and sales of advertised parts each rose substantially.

At the level of the individual end user, both the retail chain and the manufacturer are dealing with a Q2 customer base. Individuals (that is, nonbusiness retail customers) are relatively more uniform in their valuations, but they do tend to want personal computers to satisfy a wider range of needs. An individual might need a PC for work, home, or home office. He or she might be buying a computer to run the household checking account, or to provide an educational and entertainment tool for the children, or to run a home-based business.

The natural strategy for the retailer, when faced with this kind of customer base, would be niche marketing. The retailer could set up a series of initiatives for each different type of customer—promoting a kids' club for PC owners, for instance, or hosting a series of home-business seminars. The retailer's migration strategies are increasing the cost-efficiency of interacting with its customers, and integrating its relationship with them across different business operations and through time. While no single individual computer buyer is likely to buy more than one or maybe two computers from the retailer, some customers will also buy a whole range of additional products, so the retailer wanting to pay closer attention to its most valuable customers must be able to track each customer's transactions from visit to visit. Similarly, if the retailer could increase the amount of interaction with its customers and reduce the cost of managing this interaction, it could improve its ability to treat different customers differently.

For the time-pressed retailer, however, such customer-centered strategies are almost never in the cards, and a manufacturer could serve the retailer's interest and create its own relationships with end users by providing an ability to manage such programs at the retail level. For instance, suppose the manufacturer were to offer a password-protected Web page, so that its computer buyers could have access to better service and more detailed help. It could easily designate a portion of the Web site to the particular retailer from whom the customer bought the product, and it could use the program to offer a variety of niche-specific benefits. By offering an electronic product registration mechanism, the manufacturer could generate a quicker connection with the end user, and tie everything back to the original retail location as well.

These strategies may sound difficult to implement, but think about the alternative for the manufacturer. The traditional demand from the retail store to the manufacturer has always been to reduce its price to allow the retailer to compete more aggressively in the aggregate-market world of independent purchase transactions, in order to secure a greater share of the purchases undertaken by anonymous end users who have no relationship with the retailer or little reason to make contact with the manufacturer. In the long run, the only alternative to playing along with a retailer's dead-end strategy of price competition and margin erosion is to collaborate in setting up longer-term relationships with the customers at the very base of the demand chain—the end users.

Of course, we just analyzed one demand chain—a single strand of the computer manufacturer's distribution system. But the manufacturer's distribution chain is actually made up of a large number of different demand chains. The enterprise could be selling directly to a very large retail chain, for instance, rather than going through the wholesaler. And the wholesaler could be selling to a VAR (a value-added reseller) rather than to a retailer. Either the VAR or the retailer might be selling to a corporate purchaser rather than to an individual.

Each tier of this distribution system represents its own type of customer differentiation, and a whole series of demand chains would need to be analyzed in order to plot an appropriate set of 1:1 strategies for the manufacturer. The actual distribution system might look more like this:

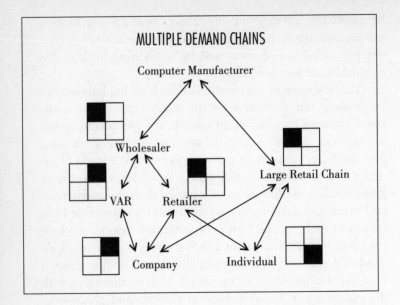

There are at least five different demand chains identified in this particular computer manufacturer's distribution system. If the enterprise wants to treat its channel members as customers in order to create more collaborative, one-to-one relationships with them individually, it must first identify every demand chain separately, and then determine the appropriate natural and migration strategies for the types of customers represented at each level in the chain.

The Role of the Distributor

Where a customer interacts will have an important impact on the nature of his loyalty. If the interaction is at the distributor, or in the retail store, it is likely to be brand neutral. The cash register may print out diet Coke coupons for a shopper who purchases a Weight Watchers product. But the store manager doesn't care whether the coupon is for diet Coke or diet Pepsi—he just wants the shopper to come back to *his* store to redeem it. So next month the store manager can easily offer the couponing opportunity to diet Pepsi for just $200. The store, in essence, will be selling access to its in-store interactive promotions the same way it sells shelf space today.

But in-home interactivity (or interactivity directly with the manufacturer) is, inherently, distribution neutral. If you order your groceries on-line by revising last week's list, you don't really care what store these products are being delivered from.

For digitizable products, or products that are principally information-oriented, such as music, videos, greeting cards, or printed items (including books like this one!) the Interactive Age may in fact disintermediate the store and the distributor altogether. Of course, the disintermediation going on with this kind of product threatens not just the store and the wholesaler, but the "manufacturer" as well. Amazon.com is, today, a threat mainly for retail bookstores, but by dealing directly with authors it could easily "publish" its own books electronically, cutting out the retailer *and* the publisher. Greet Street could do the same for greeting cards, and Agents, Inc., could do it for music and videos.

But manufacturers of *most* products, even when the products themselves are completely customized to individual customers, will still require a physical store or distributor to provide some services. In the case of a mass-customized product, for instance, the store is likely to provide a more efficient design interface. The Custom Foot depends on its laser-scanning foot measurement machines. Those machines will give a continuing role to The Custom Foot storefront, even though the store itself carries no physical inventory and the shoes, once manufactured, can be delivered directly to the end-user customers (or the customer may elect to have them delivered to the store for pickup). It will be a long time, if ever, before foot-measuring equipment is found in the home.

Another role for the store may be to serve as a demonstration center. Ordering a new video camera by calling an 800 number to get the lowest possible price will work as long as the customer doesn't want to see, feel, or try out the video camera in advance. For that, the customer would have to go to a consumer electronics store. Of course, with the proliferation of businesses going direct to customers and reducing costs to the rock bottom, this could pose a problem. A customer could go into a store, demo the new Sony video camera for a few minutes, go home to call 1-800-ELECTRO, and order the camera at a much lower price than any physical store could offer. As on-line shopping agents and auction events proliferate, encouraging this kind of commodity price competition, this problem is likely to become quite significant to retail outlets and distributors in a number of industries. To combat this problem, a few stores in the Interactive Age will probably charge admission.

"Come in and get a *live* salesperson to help you try out any product in the store—only $10, refunded when you make a purchase."

Ultimately, the distributor's real advantage is that it owns (or should own, anyway) the actual, face-to-face relationship with the end-user customer. The end user is at the very top of the food chain. Whether this customer is a consumer coming into a retail outlet, or a business buying from a business wholesaler, the end user is the one who, ultimately, pays the bill. Any distributor that wants to ensure it has a continuing role, even in the Interactive Age, will figure out now how to make interactive connections with these customers—not to *add* services to the customer relationship but to *take over* functions that the customer used to have to perform for itself.

The wholesale distributor's traditional role was to simplify things for customers. By using a wholesaler as a stockpile point and an information provider, a customer could in fact obtain a wide variety of products at one time from a single, simple source. But many of the cost-efficiencies wholesalers used to provide their customers have been chiseled away by more customized logistics systems, direct delivery services, or specialty distributors, not to mention the more efficient direct exchange of information between the customer and manufacturer. Information technology makes it easier and easier for customers to cut out the "middleman" altogether.

But distributors looking to the future realize that while the physical *tasks* of distribution may be more limited today, their traditional *role*—simplifying the customer's life—is in more demand than ever. Rather than simply providing a delivery service from a physical storage warehouse or depot, a distributor must see itself in the *consolidation* and *config-*

uration business. Its sales personnel must know the key strategies of each of its principal customers, and the distributor's own business objectives should be centered around tracking and increasing its share of each customer's business.

This is one of the reasons behind VMI, or "vendor-managed inventory." A distributor will know the identities of its customers, and if they are business customers, it may already be in interactive contact with most of them. Particularly for those customers that depend on wholesale distributors, VMI allows the distributor to track what inventory the customer has, using computers to ensure a constant flow of the right kinds of products at just the right times. This means the customer is operationally entangled with the distributor. According to Thomas Kozak, manager of Pan-Link products at Panduit, a VMI software company, "while EDI is about automating work, VMI is about eliminating work." VMI works, not because it adds a service, but because it takes over a task.

In the end, the distributor's main task should be the same as the manufacturer's: to create individualized, interactive Learning Relationships with its customers, getting deeper and deeper into the customer's set of needs, and making itself gradually more valuable, and less expendable, to the end user.

No matter how desirable it may be to forge interactive Learning Relationships with individual customers, by now you know that for most businesses just getting past the distribution system is going to be a major problem. But that simply makes it all the more important to understand the issue, and to analyze the strategic options carefully.

There were five corporate functions we first described at

the end of Chapter 1—functions that, we said, would all be involved in making any firm into a 1:1 enterprise. We have now covered four—custodianship of the customer base, production and service delivery, customer communications and interactivity, and distribution and channel management.

The last function we called "organizational management strategy," and what we meant was that the 1:1 enterprise has to organize itself in such a way that it can hold the right managers accountable for the right activities. The activities must be precisely defined, and they must be measurable. In addition, the firm must have some sort of transition strategy—a plan to make itself into this new 1:1 enterprise with the least amount of disruption to its existing business.

These are the issues we take up in the next chapter.

MAKING IT
How to Get There from Here

The 1:1 enterprise creates long-lasting, profitable relationships that are capable of outliving the very products and services the firm may consider its lifeblood. By making itself more and more valuable to each individual customer, racheting steadily up the customer's own learning curve, the 1:1 enterprise is able to drive its unit margins up despite the push toward commoditization that characterizes nearly every industry today.

But this strategy can't simply be added to the management tool kit, like one more technique for improving quality, reducing cost, or raising productivity. Rather, what it represents is a fundamental change in philosophy and strategy—a change in the *dimension* of competition. A true 1:1 marketing philosophy can't be implemented without integrating it into the entire organization. The firm must embrace significant change, affecting virtually every department, division, officer and employee, every product, and every function.

Moreover, the more successful a firm is at profiting within the traditional aggregate-market model, the more difficult it will be to put the traditional model at risk by attempting something as radically different as a 1:1 marketing strategy. Nevertheless, there are four clear, straightforward steps required for navigating the transition, and in this chapter we're going to cover them one at a time:

1. *Visioning.* Managers within the enterprise first need to share a clear vision of how the firm will operate "on the other side" of the transition.

2. *Organizing.* Managing customer relationships individually can't be done without reorganizing. Setting up the organization to carry out the vision is the next logical step.

3. *Measuring.* The metrics most firms use to gauge the success of their business—monthly sales quotas, for instance—are not relevant to the 1:1 enterprise. To produce the right measurements, a significant upgrade in the enterprise's information technology will probably be required.

4. *Transitioning.* Finally, once the firm knows where it's going and what it's going to do when it gets there, when it has the organization in place and metrics available, it must make a steady, nondisruptive transition, putting as little of the current business as possible at risk.

Visioning

The quickest and simplest way to create a vision of the business as a 1:1 enterprise is to start, not with the strategies, but the tactics of 1:1 competition. We suggest you start with a kind of down-and-dirty 1:1-applications brainstorming session. Once a few of your managers are reasonably comfortable with the interactive marketing concepts of the 1:1 enterprise, get them together for a day of "business discovery."

Ask them to imagine your company has *absolutely every shred of information about and from its customers that it could possibly want.* Imagine that gaining immediate access to this detailed, useful information poses no obstacle whatsoever.

The question you want your executives to answer is this:

If we had all the customer-specific information we could possibly want, what would we do differently in conducting business with our customers?

Get your executives to list each of these 1:1 marketing "applications" on a flip chart or blackboard. Harley-Davidson, for instance, might want to know each customer's fantasy motorcycle, so it could offer that vehicle, customized in advance to meet some of the individual's own personal specifications. *Newsweek* might want to know what particular subjects each individual reader finds most interesting, so it could tailor its magazine to that customer's needs. United Airlines might want to know in advance what drink each customer wants, and what movies each most wants to see, so it could arrange to offer those exact drinks and a choice of those particular movies to the customer on board the aircraft. Nike might want to know which of its customers has the most influence on his peers.

This should be a mind-opening exercise. It's important not to attempt it without at least two or three executives in the room who are well grounded in 1:1 marketing principles, and the type of collaborative, interactive relationships with customers that are being discussed in this book. All ideas are welcome in the beginning. Don't throw any idea out because the customer information required to implement it is not available, or because it seems utterly impractical to change the firm's behavior.

Once you have a few dozen of these applications listed, go back to each one and, using no more than a single page of paper for each application, do this:

1. *Describe* the application briefly. Give it a quick title, if possible, but don't spend time haggling over it.

2. Roughly estimate the quantitative *benefit* that this particular application would be likely to have for the enterprise, in terms of increased customer loyalty or margin. This is a "back of the envelope" exercise; just because data is not available is no excuse for not trying to make a reasonable guess.

3. Identify the *information needed* to implement the application.

4. Figure out *where the information resides* at the enterprise now, if it resides anywhere. Do you have it somewhere in a survey? Is it in your invoicing database?

5. If the enterprise doesn't have the information, *how can the information be obtained*? Is the information available from a third-party source? Can you track your customers' individual transactions from day to day, week to week? What sort of dialogue should you have with your customer, and how?

6. Estimate the potential all-inclusive *cost and time* required to obtain the information. Again, "back of the envelope" accuracy is all you need.

It's important to keep this a simple, basic-principles kind of exercise. Obviously, you won't have anywhere near enough information to answer most of these questions for *any* of the applications, but use your judgment anyway. Make guesses. Wherever you see a significant gap in your own understanding of the issues, make a note of it and come back later with an eye toward defining the research or analysis that would be necessary to fill that gap. To make the effort easier, we suggest numbering the applications (the order is not important, but numbers are often easier designations than names).

After doing this for each application, you'll be able to compare your very rough estimates of costs, benefits, and time requirements for each marketing application. Now sort them, one page at a time, in an order that shows the highest-return, quickest executions first. The entire pile of applications, taken together, represents a "tactical vision" for your firm as a 1:1 enterprise. The first, highest-priority tactical applications will highlight the things you should do now, to begin the journey toward that vision. And the gaps in your knowledge will point to areas requiring further research and understanding.

Writing a more strategic, comprehensive vision statement for the enterprise is almost always easier at this point, because whoever is required to write it will have already been immersed in so many of the tactical possibilities.

Eventually every employee who touches a customer must understand how critical the 1:1 vision is for the success of the enterprise. After an educational workshop or series of workshops in 1:1 strategies and tactics, you might want to select a small cadre of managers for a much more rigorous, intensive series of sessions. Assign them to become the firm's leading experts in 1:1 marketing. Their role, ultimately, will be to do missionary work within your enterprise. Once they understand the real power of this competitive model, they'll do the missionary work without being asked.

Organizing

Most companies' actual corporate goals are short-term, not long-term. Gaining a greater share of the pool of this quarter's sales transactions—or this year's—is a short-term goal, while increasing the lifetime value of a customer is a long-term goal. Organizationally, a company's focus on short-term goals forces it into a structure that is centered around those business units that can produce the best, most easily measured short-term results. Think of the way any multidivisional company is organized. It splits itself up into strategic business units that almost without exception are oriented around products or geographies rather than customers. A customer can buy three different products from the same company and be treated as three separate customers, because each product is sold by a different unit within the firm, and each unit has its own sales quota and P&L responsibility.

A traditional marketer can easily identify the manager in charge of a particular product, or a particular type of communication vehicle. Sometimes there is a "segment manager," responsible for creating products and services for a particular type of customer—young marrieds, perhaps, or empty nesters. A company with a direct sales force usually has particular sales personnel in charge of particular customer accounts, but for the most part these executives are compensated transaction by transaction, and often they are not encouraged or even allowed to sell products from different divisions to "their" customers.

But the 1:1 enterprise will need to have someone who can be held accountable for the entire enterprise's relationship with *each individual customer,* tracking the customer over time. Rather than "lateral" integration of quarter-to-quarter, channel-to-channel marketing programs, the 1:1 enterprise must be capable of managing each individual customer's ongoing dialogue and interactions with the entire enterprise *longitudinally,* as it develops through time.

This requires a customer-management structure. At the 1:1 enterprise, *someone* must be assigned the responsibility for managing *customers individually.* After tiering your company's customers by value, group them into portfolios based on similar needs, and then assign a customer manager to each portfolio. Reward each customer manager for increasing the value of the customers within his or her own portfolio. Give the customer managers line responsibility for all the communications and dialogue interactions with the customers in their own portfolios.

The customer manager's responsibility is to manage each customer relationship, supervising the firm's dialogue with each, finding products and services for each, and determining how best to customize to meet each customer's individual specifications. In short, the customer manager's job is to delve more and more deeply into each individual customer's needs in order to lock the customer in, make the firm more valuable to the customer, and increase the company's margin—with each customer. It is the customer manager who should be relied on to push for expanding the customer need set, creating collaborative marketing opportunities.

To complete the make-to-order feedback loop, driving the enterprise's actual behavior according to the needs expressed by individual customers, the customer manager will need to rely on *capabilities managers*. You can think of capabilities managers as a natural evolution of the product management function. A capabilities manager's job is to decide how to tailor the enterprise's production, logistics, and service delivery capabilities to the needs of the firm's individual customers as these needs are recognized and interpreted by customer managers.

The customer manager says: Many of my customers want the product delivered this way. The capabilities manager then figures out how and whether it can be done. Can we make this product? If we can't make it, can we buy it or license it? What strategic alliance could we form in order to deliver this set of services? Is it possible to customize our invoicing in this way? Can we create this different type of packaging? How?

It might be helpful, in understanding the nature of a customer management organization, to contrast the meaning of the words "portfolio" and "segment." Each word is used to describe the way customers are grouped, but the two concepts are actually quite different.

Market segmentation is an attempt to improve and refine traditional aggregate-market competition. To a traditional marketer, the real point of segmentation is to obtain a more and more accurate fix on the "average" customer in a market, essentially by reducing the size of the market being considered. Once it determines what's best for the average customer (a person or business that doesn't actually exist at all) the firm then delivers the average product, the same way, for every customer in the segment. But the firm is not engaged in individual interaction with its customers, and does not incorporate any particular customer's feedback into its behavior toward that customer. Therefore the segments, no matter how small and precise they are, still represent passive targets for the marketer's initiatives. The initiatives themselves originate with the firm's various product and program managers, each fishing for a greater share of the transactions pool.

Moreover, because no one in the aggregate-market firm is responsible for tracking and influencing the firm's relationship with any particular customer, there is no reason a customer shouldn't be in two or more segments at one time—each segment a target for a different product or program. The noninteractive media used to convey a traditional marketer's message to an aggregate market do not allow the firm to distinguish precisely which customer gets what message. Given this situation, the "targets" are actually quite fuzzy and there is a good deal of overlap. If you yourself are the customer of a traditional segmentation marketer, then the communications and offers you receive reflect the multiplicity of personas you've been assigned. As a result, you are offered a "new" credit card even though you already have that exact card in your wallet, or you are given the chance to "come back" to a product when you've already upgraded to the next level.

Portfolios, on the other hand, are groups of customers with similar needs who are *individually* connected to the 1:1 enterprise in some interactive fashion. Each customer's relationship is individually monitored and proactively influenced by the enterprise. The 1:1 enterprise uses the feedback from an individual customer's relationship to modify its behavior toward that customer. Managing an individual customer relationship like this is a *longitudinal* process—every new interaction must be predicated on the entire set of previous interactions. To put the same customer into more than one portfolio would totally confound this process, so the 1:1 enterprise places a customer in one and only one portfolio. The goal for the 1:1 enterprise is to use what is known about *all* customers as a springboard to meet the needs of *each* customer.

The customer portfolio manager does not sift through the customer base hunting for new targets for a particular product or service. Instead, the customer manager's job is to keep each customer longer, and grow the customer bigger. She does this by interacting with the customer individually, and then proactively finding the products and services the customer will need, based on this interaction, from among all the capabilities available to the enterprise.

At KeyCorp, the branch banking salespeople specialize, not in products, but in different types of customers. With over a thousand branches in fourteen northern states, KeyCorp's 3.3 million retail customers are categorized into groups and subgroups, so that some of the branches' sales-people will handle older customers, some will handle small business owners, and others will handle emerging affluents.

Bell Horizon, a company made up of the nonmonopoly businesses at Bell Canada, has reorganized itself into a "customer-facing" organization, in which line organizations (not just sales teams) will be aligned with groups of customers, mostly on an industry-specific basis. According to the company's newsletter explaining the reorganization, the customer team "can be thought of as the one contact that our customers have with Bell, whatever their needs, whether they're local, long distance, business, or information systems support. . . . In the new structure, one organizational unit will be focused on the customer as opposed to multiple interfaces with the customer."

The goal is not merely to collect data about customers, but to integrate that data, by customer, across all functions and product lines in the enterprise, in order to get a complete picture of *each* customer's value and needs. Ultimately, you want to see each customer as one customer, and you want to be seen by the customer as *one company*—no matter what division or product group the customer is dealing with. You want to remember every aspect of a relationship with a particular customer, the same way the customer has *always* remembered the relationship with you. In this way you turn "data" into *knowledge*, enabling you to practice *knowledgebase marketing*.

Like stocks in an investment portfolio, your own company's customer relationships must be managed individually if you are to have any hope of transforming your firm into a 1:1 enterprise. Customer management will enable your company to overcome the organizational obstacles that would otherwise block this transition, and it will create an internal demand for the kind of integrated customer information necessary to interact with each individual customer in a coherent and rational manner.

Measuring

What sort of metrics are needed to run a 1:1 enterprise? It's clearly not enough simply to count transactions at the cash register, or tally shelf space at the retail store, so how exactly should a 1:1 enterprise gauge its success? Any company committed to 1:1 will need to develop new ways of measuring success and rewarding performance. Many companies have achieved high accuracy in measuring the profitability of individual products, but the best measurements are *customer*-specific—quantities such as customer LTV and customer strategic value. The real payoff for the 1:1 enterprise will come in the form of an increased value to the customer base. But there are also many types of interim measurements that might be used because more precise customer information is not available, or in order to gauge progress against particular 1:1 strategies and activities expected to affect customer value at a later time.

Most companies do not really lack customer data. However, because of functional and divisional lines of authority at the enterprise, the data is rarely integrated on a customer-by-customer basis. Instead, it resides in silos, or chimneys within the organization. At a particularly efficient company the functional databases will be linked by individual sales transactions—enabling the enterprise to process an order through delivery, service, and invoicing, for instance—but it is the rare business today that can actually tie all the sales transactions to different, distinct customers.

Instead, data about a single customer almost always can be found in different, unrelated places within various functional databases at a business. Sometimes the same customer will be double-counted, showing up as two customers because he has engaged in two transactions that appear unrelated to the enterprise—the long distance customer who disconnects in one city, moves, and then reconnects in another, for instance. Other times customer data might be missing entirely, as is the case for many businesses that sell through distributor relationships, when only 15 percent of end users return their warranty cards.

Because an enterprise's different divisions are all measured based on the P&L of the *products* they are selling, there is great incentive within most organizations to link the data *functionally*, from shipment to billing, for instance, but little incentive to link data on a customer-by-customer basis. A traditional organization is structured to manage products, brands, divisions, departments, and functions. It is not usually set up to manage customers, and there is rarely any organizational incentive to do so.

So the fact is that customer data will be found throughout the enterprise, but the same customer may be found in a variety of different functional systems, and in a variety of different divisions as well.

To become a 1:1 enterprise you will have to link the customer data in your firm across functional and divisional boundaries. If you have several databases, you might want to consider installing a data warehouse, which will almost certainly produce a variety of additional benefits, beyond linking customer data. By first organizing your company appropriately to manage customer relationships, you will be creating within the firm an internal demand for integrated customer data. In order to do their jobs properly, customer managers will demand better and better customer-specific data, and this internally generated demand is likely to drive the process faster and more effectively than any edict from the top.

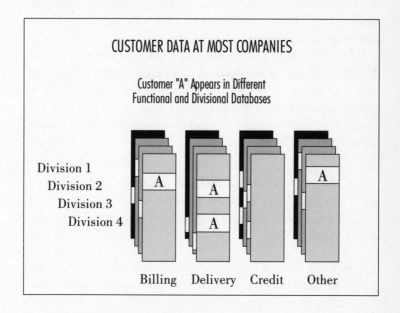

CUSTOMER DATA AT MOST COMPANIES

Customer "A" Appears in Different
Functional and Divisional Databases

Division 1
Division 2
Division 3
Division 4

A   A   A

A

Billing   Delivery   Credit   Other

The biggest problem for most companies in setting up the kind of metrics required to manage a 1:1 enterprise is the decades-old system of sales commissions, quotas, bonuses, and report cards that are focused exclusively on products and services.

Devising new measurements implies the creation of a customer knowledgebase. But besides the knowledgebase itself, a whole new type of thinking is called for when customer profitability is being metered rather than just product profitability. For instance, it may sometimes pay to ask whether it's okay for a *product* to be unprofitable so long as every *customer* is profitable. For the traditional aggregate-market competitor, this is a meaningless distinction, because individual customer profitability is not known. But for the 1:1 enterprise, the answer is clearly yes, because the profitability of customers is much more closely aligned with the long-term financial profit of the firm.

In addition to measuring and tracking customer value, however, either in the form of a lifetime value model or a series of proxy variables, the 1:1 enterprise will measure a whole range of intermediate things that are related to the successful cultivation of customer relationships. Some things that are worth knowing:

■ What proportion of end-user customers does the enterprise know by name and address? What proportion of warranty cards or registration statements are captured?

■ What ratio of ongoing customer transactions are captured to the customer knowledgebase, and what is the cost of achieving this capture rate?

■ What is the ratio of complaints handled on the first call at the enterprise's calling centers?

■ What is the firm's overall level of customer satisfaction, *relative* to its competitors?

- How many customers are buying multiple products or services from the enterprise? What is the ratio of products to lines purchased per customer?

- What is the firm's retention rate among a variety of needs-based groups of customers?

Each of these questions—and many others—can be asked in such a way as to yield a ready-made "progress report" for the 1:1 enterprise. The ultimate measurement might be the value of the enterprise's customer base, but if you want to gauge your gradual progress toward becoming a 1:1 enterprise, then it makes sense to set up a metrics system that captures a variety of intermediate steps.

Measuring customer retention—or even agreeing on its definition—is often a difficult task all by itself. The customer base is made up of a wide mix of customers, accumulated by the enterprise over a period of time. One way to think of customers is in terms of "vintages." All the customers first obtained in a particular year, or in a particular acquisition campaign, can be grouped into the same vintage, and the ratio of customers who remain from that vintage in any given year represents the retention rate for that vintage.

Be careful to avoid the trap of looking simply at overall customer defections to gauge your success. For most businesses characterized by repeat-purchase customers, the number of customers who leave the franchise from any given vintage declines as the vintage matures—that is, the longer a customer remains loyal, the more likely he will continue to remain loyal. This was exactly our assumption with the magazine subscription business we first examined in Chapter 2—where 65 percent of the first-year subscribers renewed, but then 70 percent of second-year subscribers renewed, and so forth.

This has complicated implications, however, for setting up a metrics system designed to capture the effects of various programs on customer retention. Among other things, it means that a change in an enterprise's "overall" customer-attrition figure—no matter how alarming or reassuring it is—might be simply the result of a change in the mixture of vintages in the customer base. If, for instance, the business acquires absolutely no new customers for a year, the *average* retention rate can be expected to increase, because by the end of that year all the vintages are one year older, and just a bit more loyal. Conversely, if a business suddenly becomes extremely successful in acquiring new customers, we can expect the "average" retention rate for the business's customer base to drop.

The point is, never rely on just *one* customer retention figure for any given customer base. There are as many retention figures as there are customer vintages, and there is a separate retention rate for nearly any meaningful customer set, whether we group them by LTV, by needs, by acquisition source, or by some characteristic of their transaction history. MCI found that customers who called in with an inquiry had a higher than average propensity to defect. BMW and Jaguar owners defect faster than Cadillac and Mercedes owners.

Even if the right metrics are set up to measure the longer-term benefits of customer loyalty and profit, the use of these metrics can be defeated if short-term metrics still drive the enterprise's compensation structure. While sales commissions are certainly not bad in and of themselves, the compensation structure built around commissions or bonuses for selling products and meeting monthly sales quotas can often be highly resistant to change. As MCI found, by entrepreneurially rewarding their marketing managers for increases in customer acquisition rates, they plainly and firmly undercut any customer retention efforts directed toward better new-customer selectivity. Even though it was demonstrably more profitable for the MCI enterprise to acquire fewer but higher-quality customers, the bonus plan made no allowance for the quality of customers acquired— only the number. This put the personal interests of the entire marketing staff at odds with the best interests of the enterprise.

The business world is full of such examples. A friend of ours responded to an ad for satellite TV service but was unable to subscribe because the satellite company wouldn't sell her the service unless she sat through a time-consuming sales pitch—so the company's sales rep could get a commission. Even after explaining that she was willing to subscribe to the service without a pitch at all, the company was incapable of signing her up without routing it through a face-to-face meeting with a salesperson. With no spare time for such a presentation and no stomach for an argument, she opted to stay out of the satellite TV market for a while longer.

Commissions also set up roadblocks because they pit one salesperson against another, or one division against another. They can easily make your salespeople forget that the competition is *outside* the enterprise. If your goal is to grow the value of your customers, you need to figure out how to resolve these conflicts. Chances are such conflicts arise not because a firm is measuring the wrong things, but because it isn't correctly applying the metrics it already has.

Often it is possible to ameliorate such problems with one or two commonsense changes to the existing compensation system. Shearson (formerly Shearson-Lehman Brothers Inc.) realized that its customers were more loyal to the broker than to the brokerage house itself. So it changed its commission structure slightly. Some of the most valuable customers a brokerage house has are those working with brokers just about to retire. These are customers who have steadily built their wealth over years, becoming gradually more affluent and liquid as they near retirement themselves.

But when a broker retires, his customers will often leave the brokerage house in search of another broker. So Shearson began offering partial commissions to brokers— *after retirement*—for up to five years of the continued patronage of the broker's former clients. Suddenly the dynamics changed: Retiring brokers now had an incentive to introduce their clients to a younger, competent Shearson broker. They took time to help the younger broker understand the ins and outs of each of their customers, and to check back in with the customers themselves from time to time, even after retirement.

At other times, more creative solutions might be required, disrupting the enterprise's compensation structure more significantly. 3M offers its customers some 60,000 products from fifty-seven different divisions of the enterprise. Until recently, each division approached each customer independently. The enterprise's metrics encouraged division-focused selling and product-focused commission. Even though every division had its own perfectly rational plan for coordinating sales and achieving its goal, the enterprise's customers were exposed to a number of different plans from different divisions, and the result was what seemed (to customers) a helter-skelter, uncoordinated selling effort. The joke at 3M, as at many companies, starts with a waiting room full of salespeople. When the customer announces "We will see the 3M sales rep next, please," *all* the salespeople stand up.

A few years ago, 3M launched an initiative they called Customer Focused Marketing (CFM) with a simple objective: to encourage cross-selling between divisions and reduce the number of contacts necessary for a customer to do business with 3M. Under the CFM program, if you are a salesperson in one of the many divisions at 3M, you will get a commission even if the products of your division are sold *by somebody else* to their customer. Likewise, you are rewarded for selling products of other divisions to your customer. The CFM program actively encourages formalized agreements between and among divisions at 3M, which can then bring the products of multiple divisions to a customer in one selling effort.

Coupled with the initiative at 3M called Earning Customer Loyalty, which emphasizes the importance of keeping customers by delivering on every 3M promise, the initial results of the Customer Focused Marketing initiative are spectacular: Profits in CFM divisions are twice as great, and their sales forces are twice as productive as those of the product-focused divisions. Since the introduction of the program, CFM divisions have grown at three times the rate of the non-CFM domestic average, and companies doing business with CFM divisions rate 3M a friendlier, easier company to do business with.

Another key metric for the 1:1 enterprise is share of customer. For any given customer, this represents the most useful way of visualizing how much effort should be allocated to grow the customer into a bigger, more valuable customer. When a company compensates by product rather than by customer, it ignores share-of-customer metrics alto-gether.

We recently talked to a successful computer salesman who had made his annual quota in late August and, thanks to his success, had been given some key accounts. He was understandably proud of the Fortune 500 client accounts he now handled, and was also pleased with the size of the sales he had initiated in some of those large companies. He was used to thinking in terms of "quotas," "commissions," and "volume." At one company, for example, he had sold $100,000 worth of computers in the previous year.

If your enterprise has any type of direct sales force at all, you probably recognize this kind of sales star. But a star whose success derives from product transaction volumes alone will not always be tuned in to the right frequency when it comes to figuring out how best to increase an individual customer's value to the enterprise.

In this particular case, we had the opportunity to ask the salesman what his share of customer was at the company where he had scored such a large sale. He looked perplexed, but we figured out that his customer had actually bought about a million dollars' worth of computers that year, from a variety of suppliers. So even though the salesman's transactions were impressive, he had achieved only a 10 percent share of customer. Here are the questions we asked him, to help him consider a more effective and more competitive approach:

- Why is your SOC so low? Are you not reaching the right decision makers? Does your company not make the products they need? Do they have special needs that you might be 'able to meet better with a less standardized product?

- What are you doing right? Why are you getting any business at all? What needs are you fulfilling that at the moment are not being met by anyone else?

- Who's getting most of your customer's business? What is your competitor doing that you're not?

- How long before one of your competitors achieves a Learning Relationship with the customer, and becomes its sole supplier? In other words, what happens to you when *somebody else* wins a 100 percent share of customer?

The point of such questions is obvious. The questions themselves are obvious. But if you don't have the systems set up to measure and reward the right answers, these questions will never be asked at your firm.

Once you do get the systems set up, stranger but ever more logical compensation plans will occur to you. If you ran an automobile manufacturer and could track every interaction between you and each of your individual owners, would you want the dealer salespeople paid commissions just for selling cars? Maybe instead, when a salesman sells a customer his very first car with your brand name on it, that salesman ought to get 25 cents every time *that* customer spends $100 with your firm for anything at all—another car, a car loan, an oil change—*for the rest of the customer's life*.

Set up the information systems and metrics to measure what matters: customer profitability.

Transitioning

The two most common mistakes we encounter among companies that want to transform themselves into 1:1 enterprises are *underestimating* the degree to which every facet of the enterprise will affect, and be affected by, the change, and *overestimating* the difficulty of making a smooth, orderly transition. It is somewhat ironic that even though the overall process requires immense, all-encompassing change affecting virtually every enterprise function, the actual benefits of 1:1 marketing can still be concretely demonstrated and quantified before even undertaking the bulk of the program.

In their haste to complete the transformation, however, some companies do not wait for quantification and validation. Instead, they charge ahead, trying to bulldoze the organization, the distribution system, and the corporate culture into submission. Then, when the change becomes more disruptive than they anticipated, they lose support for the process before it can be brought to fruition.

The right way to make the transition is not to do it product by product or division by division, but customer by customer. Begin your journey with just a few customers at a time, and choose first those few MVCs most worth the added attention and trouble. Once these customers are identified, choose one or more of the brightest, most visionary, and most resourceful people in your company, and make these people into customer managers. They may come from the marketing department, or from sales, or customer service. They could be astute information specialists.

Your goal is to set up a laboratory of 1:1 practice—a

group of high-value customers and highly skilled customer managers—both to prove the benefits of the overall idea, and to cement the loyalty of your most valuable customers first. Remember the "picket fence" that MCI's retention managers visualized for the firm, described in Chapter 4? You can visualize your customers as lying on a spectrum of values, from very low to very high. Of course, like any other business, you are likely to have many customers who aren't worth so much, but only a few who are worth a lot. The higher you go in customer valuation, the fewer customers you have.

To picture the transition plan for becoming a 1:1 enterprise, imagine placing a picket fence around those very high-value customers at the far end of your customer value spectrum:

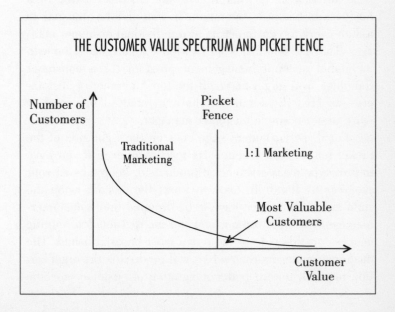

THE CUSTOMER VALUE SPECTRUM AND PICKET FENCE

On the left side of this picket fence you practice marketing as usual, and this will disrupt life for as few people as possible. These customers, on the left side, do not have customer managers, they are not divided into needs-based portfolios, they are not part of the 1:1 program, at least not yet. But on the right side of the fence, where your most valuable customers are found, you can begin implementing 1:1 marketing. Establish dialogues with these customers, interact with them as often as you can, remember everything they tell you, and do your best to change the enterprise's behavior to reflect what you have learned from each.

On the right side of the fence, every customer is the direct line responsibility of some customer manager. Whether you give your customer managers responsibility for a whole portfolio of customers, or just one or two customers, is a function of the nature of your customer base. In a business-to-business operation, it wouldn't be unusual to assign every top customer its own individual customer manager. That's essentially what Hewlett-Packard has done with its global account management program. In a consumer franchise, you might carve off the top 5 percent of customers—as MCI did—and still have a hundred thousand or more under a single customer manager.

For these customers—the ones on the right side of the picket fence—you practice 1:1 marketing even if you have to prototype mass-customized products or keep tabs on your progress by hand. To make it work, the customers on the right side of the fence have to be dropped into a customer-management organization, and the metrics for determining success on this side of the fence must be established. The customer managers themselves will be driving the organization forward, toward better integration of customer-specific data, and better coordination among various divisions. To the right of the picket fence, the enterprise must:

- *Link individual customer data over time.* Identify each customer and link all the customer's communications and transactional data so that we can tell, for instance, whether the customer making this particular complaint is the same one who requested information a month ago.

- *Calculate appropriate measures of success by customer.* Set up a model for LTV as well as strategic valuation by customer. Calculate share of customer on an individual, customer-by-customer basis. Decide on additional measures of success, as well as temporary proxy measures, such as multi-lineness, willingness to collaborate, volume by customer, and customer satisfaction. Measure or estimate these variables, by individual customer, regularly.

- *Establish and maintain dialogue.* Determine each customer's preferred media package, and communicate using the media channels most comfortable for each. Monitor the effectiveness, and not just the cost-efficiency of dialogue interactions.

- *Mass-customize to meet individually expressed needs.* Build a Learning Relationship with each customer by interacting over time, and continuing to increase each customer's level of convenience.

- *Expand the customer's need set.* Remember what each customer wants and find ways to make the collaboration effort valuable to the customer by mass-custom-

376 Enterprise One to One

izing the core product, the product-service bundle, or the customer's enhanced need set. Cross-sell, create strategic alliances, and be on the alert for additional services each customer might want.

This initial foray into 1:1 offers opportunity and value in itself—by identifying, keeping, and growing the firm's most valuable customers. Additionally, it provides an important educational process, so while you are building Learning Relationships you can figure out how to measure success. Perhaps most important, this MVC transition is a recipe for success that will serve as a powerful demonstration of the spectacular capabilities of 1:1 strategies. Since it causes a minimum of disruption, it is less likely to be sabotaged, and our experience has shown that before long, others inside the organization *want* to participate.

The way to make the transition to a 1:1 enterprise is simply to move the fence to the left, gradually, so that over time a greater and greater proportion of customer relationships are being individually managed. This type of transition has the added, aesthetic beauty of tracking with the declining cost of information technology. The computer support systems, after all, are likely to be the most expensive single element of whatever program you implement. If Moore's Law continues to hold, and IT's cost continues to fall by 50 percent every eighteen months or so, then it's no great leap to figure out that many of the programs and policies that make sense for today's MVCs will make sense for customers worth only half as much in about eighteen months.*

In any case, your laboratory has now been set up to

* Moore's Law is named after Gordon Moore, the CEO of Intel, who noticed that the number of transistors that can be squeezed onto a single square inch of silicon doubles every eighteen months or so.

achieve higher and higher loyalty and value from those customers who are worth the most to your enterprise. In addition, you are using some of your very best people to run the
lab experiment, so as you roll it out to a greater number of
customers, your existing customer managers should be able
to train others, and do missionary work as well.

Making the transition on a customer-by-customer basis,
starting at the high-value side of the customer base, is virtually the *only* transition strategy we've seen that makes economic sense, given the major changes necessary to accommodate this new type of competition. The difficulty and
expense of this type of transition for an enterprise is lower if
there are relatively few customers who account for a large
percentage of revenue and profit.

A best-customer "picket fence" transition is the most
logical migration path for most businesses. But the transition itself makes more sense if there are just a very few
customers that account for a large proportion of the enterprise's value. It will be easier to make this transition work if
60 percent of your business is accounted for by the top 3
percent of your customers rather than the top 30 percent of
your customers. In other words, the steeper the valuation
skew, the more cost-efficient it will be to begin the process
of converting your organization to a 1:1 enterprise.

The more differentiable a customer base is with respect
to individual valuations—that is, the steeper its valuation
skew—the more cost-efficient the 1:1 enterprise will be:

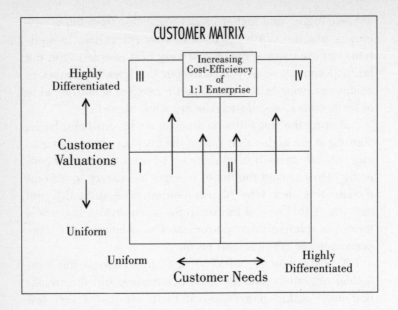

If you have a few very valuable customers, you may already be treating them to a kind of 1:1 relationship. This is why treating distributors as customers can often lead to a more cost-efficient form of 1:1 marketing, at least in the short term—because in most businesses distributors are naturally more differentiated by their value than end users are.

If, on the other hand, your customers have more uniform, undifferentiated valuations, then you should consider two strategies. The first is simply to integrate and consolidate all the points of contact with each customer, across your entire enterprise. Integration by customer is, of course, one of the main requirements for setting up a 1:1 enterprise—we've been talking about it from the beginning of the book. But integration will often have the effect, all by itself, of increasing the value skew of your customer base. If you have a number of different business units, and if the customer bases of these business units overlap at all, then the valuation skew will almost certainly become steeper when you *combine* these customer bases in order to create a fully integrated 1:1 enterprise, interacting *in unison* with each individual customer across every business unit.

Consider a hypothetical multidivision consumer insurance business, for instance. Suppose it has a property and casualty division, a life insurance division, and a health and disability division, and suppose its customers overlap somewhat. The customer base at each division may appear to have a fairly flat valuation skew, primarily because no single customer will need more than one homeowner's policy, or more than one health plan. But if the business viewed its customer base from the perspective of the *enterprise,* there would be a substantial skew, because some customers would do business with all three divisions, while some would do business with only one or two of them.

By counting all the transactions your own enterprise has with every individual customer, no matter what functional or geographic division engages in the transaction, you will almost certainly increase the valuation skew of your customer base, and by doing this you will make it more cost-efficient to make your own transition to doing business as a 1:1 enterprise.

The second strategy is to improve the capabilities of your enterprise for making the most cost-efficient use of what valuation differences already exist. By streamlining the customer interaction process, as we first suggested in Chapter 3, you can make it more economic to identify the most valuable customers, even from a customer base less differentiated in value. True interactivity allows you to link customer transactions and interactions together, more easily identifying both repeat customers and multi-line customers. Amazon.com and Greet Street, because they have highly efficient interactive connections with their customers, can precisely and quickly differentiate them by value, despite the fact that there isn't a very steep valuation skew in either the bookstore or the greeting card category.

You don't have to have a Web site to differentiate your customers better—just imagination enough to visualize how your company's *personal* relationships with customers can be enhanced *electronically*. A great customer differentiator in a commodity business is the Sands casino in Atlantic City, New Jersey, owned by Hollywood Casino Corporation. Most casinos, and the Sands is no exception, have long singled out high rollers for a wide assortment of benefits, including free transportation to the casino, and free meals, accommodations, and entertainment. By relying on an innovative marriage of personal care and electronic tools, the Sands has figured out how to single out even the smallest of "low rollers" who cross its threshold, and it tailors its service to each.

Enter the Sands casino the first time and begin putting quarters into a slot machine, and that machine will quickly notify the mainframe that an unknown player is sitting at machine number 306. A dispatcher monitoring this signal redirects it to a large-display pager on the hip of a casino host or hostess, who visits the machine to welcome you and offer an explicit bargain: give us your name, address, and phone so we can make you part of our club and award points based on your play—"action," as they call it—good for free meals and drinks, "casino cash," and VIP treatment.

Once the information is captured, a customer is never a

stranger at the Sands. Members show their Sands VIP cards at each gaming table and swipe it at each machine. This time, the host's pager shows much more: "John Smith from Stamford, Connecticut, is at machine 306. Last visit six weeks ago. Bought him dinner at the Italian restaurant. Average wager X."

So now the customer gets a very personal, individual greeting: "Mr. Smith, welcome back. We've missed you these last six weeks. How are things in Stamford? Can we offer to take care of your parking . . . maybe a hotel room while you're here? Would you like to be our guest at Casa Maria again, or would you like to try our new Chinese restaurant?" The cost of this entire electronic transaction is virtually nothing. The hosts have to man the floors anyway, but now they're able to greet people individually. Check the casino trade publications to see just how well this is working for the Sands in terms of gross sales, profit per square foot, and other objective measures of casino success.

The point is, the cost-efficiency of doing business as a 1:1 enterprise can be improved with more effective customer differentiation. In your own business you've probably already singled out the high rollers for special treatment. Chances are it's a labor-intensive effort, but it's justified by the fact that these extremely good customers are worth being treated with kid gloves. Using a variety of electronic tools, however, from a Web site, to a card-swipe membership club, to a crew of pager-equipped sales people, you can differentiate your customers even more effectively, making special treatment of individual customers cost-efficient even if the customer base doesn't include any high rollers at all.

A Final Word About "Getting There"

No matter how much you do, or how far you go in this transition, there will *always* be more to do, further to go. Anyone who has come this far in our book and is still of the opinion that what we are advocating is a simple 1-2-3 process for getting from "here" to "there" was just not paying attention.

However, just because there will always be more to do doesn't mean it isn't useful to start out in the right general direction now. What we definitely *are* saying is that there are some understandable, practical, and effective strategies for pushing your enterprise in the 1:1 direction—knowing who your customers are and remembering what they tell you, trying to manage your enterprise's behavior to treat different customers differently, delivering what each individual wants, and creating more ways to receive feedback from customers as cost-efficiently as possible.

Put a few of these strategies together and pretty soon you'll have a serious, nontrivial change in the strength of your enterprise's competitive situation. You'll be playing by different rules—competing in a different dimension. Be the first 1:1 enterprise on your block and take over your industry, starting with its largest, most valuable customers. Then keep them. Forever.

Go ahead: Put a few of these strategies together and see what happens.

Gertrude Stein was wrong. There very definitely is a "there" there.

AN OPEN LETTER TO THE CEO

"One does not discover new lands without consenting to lose sight of the shore for a very long time."

—André Gide

Dear CEO,

We appreciate the time and attention you've given to this book, and hope it will prove helpful in your business. We thought now you would appreciate some straight talk.

In the years we've been helping companies transform into 1:1 enterprises, we've seen some failures. Nearly every one of them can be ascribed to a lack of vision or failure of will at the top of the enterprise. In the CEO's office.

There's a very simple reason for this. A 1:1 enterprise simply won't work without *integrating* individual customer information into every corporate function, from customer service to production, logistics, and channel management. At most firms a formal change in the organizational structure is necessary. Only you have sufficient authority to cross so many organizational boundaries.

Once you do agree to commit, there are two hurdles to focus on immediately: justifying to your stockholders what might be a very substantial, continuing investment in information technology, and dealing with the cultural, almost psychological resistance that any organization is bound to display when faced with the prospect of such a sweeping change. We'll take these two issues one at a time.

Justifying the Cost of Technology

As you know, the biggest problem in justifying information technology is not the cost of the technology itself, but the lack of a reliable way to calculate return on investment (ROI). Until now you may have justified most of your investments in computer systems by estimating the cost reductions anticipated. But the strategies we have been proposing generate benefits primarily on the revenue side of your profit equation, and this makes estimation more difficult— especially difficult, since the strategies themselves are new and different enough that the managers you put in charge of implementation are likely to have no real experience in them.

You may also be concerned about staying at least a half-step ahead of Moore's Law. It's not easy to buy something when you know it will cost only half as much in eighteen months. You could solve this problem by subjecting your IT investments to a tougher ROI hurdle than investments in, say, facilities or production equipment, but we have three other suggestions to help you think through this issue.

1. In the long run, customizing your business to the requirements of individual customers *will* reduce your operating costs. A make-to-order manufacturer incurs absolutely no inventory risk, and generates additional savings all down the demand chain. An ATM that simply remembers individual customers' "regular" requests could handle many more transactions per day than one that treats every customer to the same stream of choices. To achieve this cost reduction sooner, focus your efforts on increasing the efficiency with which you match customers with the appropriate products and services.

2. Evaluate your investment based on the *strategic* advantage you can gain over your competitors, both current and future. Clearly, the more you invest in things like data warehouses, networked point-of-sale devices, marketing knowledgebases, and decision-support systems, the faster and more flexibly you'll be able to operate your business. But more important, the sooner you make this investment, the faster you can identify the most valuable customers in your industry and cut them out of the herd to build long-lasting relationships with them. It is essential to do this before your competition does, because the advantage created may well be irreversible. If you are investing as much as or more than your competitors, and provided you spend wisely, then it is highly likely that the return on your investment will exceed 50 percent over just the first eighteen months. If you invest much less than your competitors, then our suggestion is you should consider reducing your expenditure even further, because this might yield a

higher return over the few years you remain independent.

3. In analyzing your anticipated ROI, don't concentrate just on the next quarter's sales, or even the next year's. Instead, focus on the overall, long-term value of your customer base. If you have $100 million in annual profit and a reasonable amount of repurchase from your customers, for instance, then the actual value of your customer base (that is, the sum of all your customers' LTVs) might be several times this figure, perhaps something between $200 million and $1 billion. Even without a database, it's not difficult to calculate the *overall* value of your base by using survey-and-projection research. If the value is, say, $400 million, then the question you want your stockholders to consider is whether an investment in IT can grow the value of that base by, say, 5 percent— to $420 million. Obviously, a $20 million increase in the value of your customer base will pay for a lot of microchips.

If you believe in perfect markets, the value of your customer base minus the current value of your short- and long-term debt should come reasonably close to your market capitalization. Of course, for markets to be perfect, they have to be informed. So to be sure your stock lives up to the true potential of your enterprise, you should consider issuing regular, financially audited reports to your shareholders on the current estimated value of your customer base. You'll have the data, and it's a good way to reassure investors that your firm's financial policies are in fact measuring the key drivers of long-term profitability.

One more suggestion in dealing with Moore's Law: It will almost always pay for you to *retain* all the information you can about your individual customers. Salespeople and those in marketing often see no use for historic data. But when you transform your firm into a 1:1 enterprise, what will be important is how *each* customer's wants and needs have evolved, *over time.* Dealing with an individual customer is a time-sequence business. Eventually, Moore's Law will catch up with the terabytes of data you may now find a cumbersome nuisance. Don't throw overboard what amounts to your *only* completely irreplaceable asset—individual customer information.

Organizational and Cultural Obstacles

The number one obstacle given to us by the executives most willing to implement 1:1 strategies is "top management." Could any of these managers be describing *you?*

> *"The CEO is only a few years from retirement. His compensation is tied to quarterly earnings growth and he doesn't want to change anything."*

> *"Our firm wanted to beef up its marketing so our CEO hired a new VP Marketing from a very highly regarded packaged goods company. He has an excellent background in* **brand** *management."*

> *"Our company is a very successful* [fill in the blank— manufacturing, sales-driven, parts-supply, retail] *company, and the CEO wants to make sure we don't take our eye off the ball."*

The corporate culture begins at the top. There are many reasons your firm's culture will block the way, but there is only one reason it might not: you. As the CEO, your message to the organization must embrace a willingness to search for new approaches, and reward innovation and creativity.

If your firm is a numbers-only, bottom-line organization focused solely on quarterly sales and annual market-share growth, then casting off the metrics and compensation system that have served you so well up to now will be no small task. If you have a fast-growing firm with innovative products, it will have developed a culture that fears harming the current business. The fact is, the more successful your firm has been in the past, the more hostile your culture will be toward other types of innovation, especially the kind of basic change you will be proposing.

At some firms, another cultural obstacle is a rank-and-file resistance to any notion that customers are individually different, with different valuations as well as different needs. Executives at such a company will tell you "all our customers are equal. We don't treat any customers as second-class citizens." This is often the culture at a firm that is a regulated monopoly, quasi-monopoly, or a descendant of such a business—telecommunications firms, utilities, cable television operators, local newspapers, and, in some countries, banks, airlines, and other state-owned companies. As high-sounding and consumer-friendly as this democratic sentiment may be, it is not realistic, and at every one of these companies it is demonstrably untrue. A $50,000 per month business customer will get a sales representative—perhaps several. A $200 per month customer will not. Nevertheless, at some companies the idea that customers want to be treated individually is not only foreign but slanderous.

There are no quick fixes for this kind of cultural and psychological obstacle. This is not a book about change management, but if you ever thought you might need some expertise in that area, now's the time.

One suggestion we will make, however, is to create a cadre of "missionary" executives within your organization to serve as change agents. Start with a small group of bright, high-achieving executives, inculcate them in the 1:1 strategies of interactivity, customization, Learning Relationships, and collaborative marketing. The more knowledgeable they become, the more convinced (and convincing) they will be.

Four basic factors make missionary work successful. If you want your own missionaries to serve as the catalysts for an organizational transformation, you would do well to remember each of these principles:

1. *Missionaries are well trained.* Be sure your change agents have a firm grip on the principles, mechanics, obstacles, and advantages of 1:1 marketing. Get them trained in it, send them out on benchmarking visits to other firms, have them write white papers on the issues.

2. *Missionaries rely on a "bible."* Somewhere, the basic principles you want your missionaries to seed throughout the organization must be written down clearly and succinctly, but with enough generalization to allow the missionaries to adapt to the changing circumstances and fluid dynamics of your industry. This "bible" should be your 1:1 enterprise vision

statement, applied to a variety of divisions and functions within the overall organization.

3. *Missionaries are supported by the church.* Your change agents won't have a profit center to give them a support base. If you can't fund them even when your profits take a dip, don't send them out. Meet with them regularly yourself, not just to get their feedback but to demonstrate the importance of the project to the rest of the organization.

4. *Missionaries must be able to rely on the fear of God.* Converting the heathen sometimes requires more than logic and persuasion. Once in a while your missionaries will have to inspire a little fear and trepidation among the troops, so make sure their campaign has some teeth.

Faced with the sheer magnitude of change involved, many of your own executives may soon ask whether this transformation is really worth it. But the one thing you probably realize better than anyone is that *whether* this change will occur is not really the question here. The only issue is *when* it will come to dominate your industry, and *who* it will benefit as a result.

This kind of change is not optional. Advances in interactive communications and information technology make it inevitable. When the dust settles, the odds are that the winner won't be you but some totally new enterprise—one with no stake at all in the current system.

If you want to beat those odds, if you want your company to prosper in the Interactive Age then become a 1:1 enterprise. Embrace the capabilities that technology now makes possible. Go as far as your customers allow. Then replot your customer base and drive your customers further still.

It's a lengthy, difficult process, a long voyage far from shore. But you're the CEO. *Make* it happen, don't wait for it to happen to you.

And good luck on the voyage.

NOTES

Chapter 1 The Musical Condom

page 2   We spoke with Rosa Vasquez in Customer Service at Voice Powered Technology International, Inc., on December 5, 1995, to learn more about the VCR Voice Programmer. Much of our discussion came from corporate literature that Ms. Vasquez faxed. In his *Advertising Age* article "Admen Beware, Zapper Is Here: Device Whips Through TV Ads," February 8, 1993, p. 12, Steven Colford describes how users simply need to speak commands (e.g., "Record, 7, Sunday, 6 P.M. to 7:30 P.M."). For more descriptions of the VCR Voice Programmer, see "Speaking Out to Program VCRs" by Norman Remich in *Appliance Manufacturer* (July 1993, p. 56).

page 3   Lincoln offers "12-step memory" as an option in its Town Cars, Continentals, and Mark VIIIs. With the push of a button or two, this innovation remembers your favorite radio stations, your seat position—for driving and for exiting, how the rearview and outside mirrors should be tilted for normal driving as well as your nighttime driving, how long you prefer the auto lamp to delay—if at all, how bright you like the instrument panel, what kind of steering you prefer, if you use the easy-down window feature, the type of ride control that you fancy (plush, normal, or firm), if you want the door lock to chirp or to blink the headlights, and if you like the automatic door locks. Cadillac offers a standard feature in all its cars that remembers your seat position and adjusts the side view mirrors. We spoke with Frank Sanelli, at Kennedy Cadillac, in

San Bernardino, California, on May 31, 1996, by telephone, who added that memory button features are standard on all the high-end luxury cars, such as Mercedes, BMW, and Lexus. Bill Jones at Tri-Star Mercedes in San Bernardino also confirmed this on May 31, 1996.

page 3   Introduced in Miami, Los Angeles, and Detroit in 1994, the Never Lost navigational system is now widely available through Hertz. On the dashboard, a four-inch LCD panel displays directions with the option to hear voice instructions. The electronic mapping software is operated by a Motorola 68000 microchip (Thomas Hoffman, "Hertz Steers Customers in Right Direction," *Computerworld,* December 19, 1994, pp. 39–40). Avis also offers a satellite guidance system, named Guidestar, with spoken directions; this feature is available only on Oldsmobile Delta 88s. Avis renters can select a destination by street address, intersection, or expressway entrance/exit. The Guidestar system also provides drivers with an option that calculates the shortest time route (indicating if drivers should avoid freeways or use them). Another feature called "destination memory" remembers the places drivers have been and will automatically plot a route to return to each place (e.g., hotel room, conference center, etc.). For additional background, see "A Computer at the Wheel," by Besty Wade in the *New York Times,* March 5, 1995, p. E5.

page 3   In the September 11, 1995, cover issue of *Forbes,* Robert Lenzner describes Moore's Law ("The Reluctant Entrepreneur," p. 167). Introduced in 1965, Moore's law predicted correctly that the transistor density of semiconductor chips would double every 18 months until 1980.

page 4   During the first weekend PlayStation was available (September 9, 1995), Sony reported more than 100,000 units sold (Jeffrey A. Trachtenberg, "Sony Corp. Sells More Than 100,000 Video-Game Units on First Weekend," *The Wall Street Journal,* September 12, 1995, p. B16).

page 4   The National Highway Traffic Safety Administration began testing about 1,000 vehicles in 1995 that automatically dial 911 if the vehicle is in an accident. (See "Smart Autos Will Call 911 When Hit," by Earle Eldridge, in *USA Today,* October 4, 1995, p. B2).

page 4   For other interesting facts about microchips and how they're used, see Jeffrey A. Trachtenberg, "Sony Corp. Sells More Than 100,000 Video-Game Units on First Weekend," *The Wall Street Journal,* September 12, 1995, p. B16.

page 4   Pet tracking with microchips has been available widely since the late 1980s. For further discussion, see Vicki Croke, "Tags, Tattoos and Chips for a Theft-Proof Pet," *Boston Globe,* October 2, 1993, p. 21; Karen Kaplan, "A Microchip for Muffy," *Los Angeles Times,* January 24, 1996, p. D4; Kadee Krieger, "Shelter Pets Have Microchip ID Tags," New Orleans *Times-Picayune,* September 7, 1995, p. OTMN1.

page 4   For more information about the use of microchips in tire retreads, see Marvin Bozarth's article, "Computers in the Retread Plant," published in *The Tire Retreading/Repair Journal,* April 1994, pp. 28–32.

page 4   *The Wall Street Journal* ran an article by Suein L. Hwang ("Library Search Hints of Electrifying News from Big Tobacco") on February 6, 1995 (p. A1) giving more details about microchip-controlled cigarettes.

page 4   The "smart gun," invented by Kenneth J. Pugh, features a microchip that allows only the owner to fire it. Teresa Riordan reports that the "Smart Gun Is a Hit at Inventors Show," in the *New York Times,* June 14, 1993, p. D2. For an equally interesting piece, see "Now for the Smart Gun" by Roger Highfield, in the *Sunday Times,* South Africa, January 29, 1995, p. 5.

page 4   Clifford Gross, CEO of Biomechanics Corp. of America, invented a smart seat that calculates the size and weight of its user. The "intelligent seat" then sends this information to a small computer which adjusts the contours of the seat. (For more details, see "Smart Seat" by John Pierson in *The Wall Street Journal*, May 18, 1993, p. B1).

pages 4–5 Already available are smart running shoes from Puma and Adidas. Both designs calculate the runner's times, distances, and calories used. To read about more features, see in *International Management*'s November 1985 issue the article "Smart Running Shoes: The Latest Race Between Adidas and Puma," p. 85–86.

page 5 Matthew Grimm, reporting for *Brandweek* (November 14, 1994, p. 70), cites a report in *Mirabella*. No details about *what* piece of music the condom plays.

page 5 George Gilder writing in *Forbes ASAP*, "Life After Television," February 28, 1994, p. S94.

page 6 *Fortune* reports that computer scientists Douglas Lenat and Rodney Brooks are building a robot that would learn common sense much like babies do. The objective of this five-year project is for the robot, named Cyc, to learn what most adults know. For other background, see "2001 Is Just Around the Corner. Where's Hal?" by David Stipp (November 13, 1995, pp. 215–28).

page 6 To understand better the competitive strategy that weaves together interactivity, the customer database, and mass customization, see Robert C. Blattberg, Rashi Glazer, and John D. Little, eds., *The Marketing Information Revolution*, Boston: Harvard Business School Press, 1994; Richard Cross and Janet Smith, *Customer Bonding*, Lincolnwood, Ill.: NTC Business Books, 1995; Edwin T. Crego, Jr., et al., *Customer-Centered Reengineering: Remapping Total Customer Value*, Burr Ridge, Ill.: Irwin Professional Publishers, 1995; Edward Forrest and Richard Mizerski, eds., *Interactive Marketing: The Future Present*, Lincolnwood, Ill.: NTC Business Books, 1995; Bradley T. Gale with Robert Chapman Wood, *Managing Customer Value: Creating Quality and Service That Customers Can See*, New York: Free Press, 1994; Bill Gates, *The Road Ahead*, New York: Penguin Group, 1995; George Gilder,

Microcosm, New York: Simon and Schuster, 1989; Donna Hoffman and Thomas P. Novak, "A New Marketing Paradigm for Electronic Commerce," under review for publication in the magazine *The Information Society,* Special Issue on Electronic Commerce; Arthur M. Hughes, *Strategic Database Marketing: The Master Plan for Starting and Managing a Profitable Customer Based Marketing Program,* Chicago: Probus Publishing Co., 1994; Kevin Kelly, *Out of Control: The New Biology of Machines, Social Systems, and the Economic World,* Reading, Mass.: Addison-Wesley, 1994; James F. Moore, *The Death of Competition,* New York: HarperCollins, 1996; Nicholas P. Negroponte, *being digital,* New York: Alfred A. Knopf, 1995; Adrian Payne et al., *Relationship Marketing for Competitive Advantage: Winning and Keeping Customers,* London: Butterworth Heinemann, 1995; Don Peppers, *Life's a Pitch,* New York: Currency/Doubleday, 1995; Don Peppers and Martha Rogers, Ph.D., *The One to One Future: Building Relationships One Customer at a Time,* New York: Currency/Doubleday, 1993; B. Joseph Pine II, *Mass Customization: The New Frontier in Business Competition,* Boston: Harvard Business School Press, 1993; Frederick F. Reichheld, *The Loyalty Effect: The Hidden Force Behind Growth, Profits, and Lasting Value,* Boston: Harvard Business School Press, 1996; Don E. Schultz, Stanley I. Tannenbaum, and Robert F. Lauterborn, *Integrated Marketing Communications,* Lincolnwood, Ill.: NTC Business Books, 1993; Jagdish N. Sheth and Atul Parvatiyar, "Relationship Marketing in Consumer Markets: Antecedents and Consequences," *Journal of the Academy of Marketing Science,* Fall 1995, pp. 255–71; Don Tapscott, *The Digital Economy: Promise and Peril in the Age of Networked Intelligence,* New York: McGraw-Hill, 1996; Richard Whiteley and Diane Hessan, *Customer Centered Growth: Five Proven Strategies for Building Competitive Advantage,* Reading, Mass.: Addison-Wesley, 1996; Fred Wiersema, *Customer Intimacy: Pick Your Partners, Shape Your Culture, Win Together,* Santa Monica, Calif.: Knowledge Exchange,

1996; Brian P. Woolf, *Customer Specific Marketing: The New Power in Retailing,* Greenville, S.C.: Teal Books, 1996.

page 19 Peter Drucker (U.S. writer, educator, management consultant) says, "Business has only two basic functions—marketing and innovation." Everything else is just cost.

Chapter 2 Some Customers Are More Equal Than Others

page 30 We spoke with Jimmy Branch at Speedy Car Wash in Panama City, Fla., on March 19, 1996. See "The Road to One to One Marketing" by Susan Greco in *Inc.* magazine, October 1995, p. 56.

pages 30–31 We learned from a telephone conversation with Stephen Coulter, Project Director Online Services for National Australia Bank in Melbourne, on March 22, 1996, that National Australia Bank tiered its retail banking customers into five groups.

page 31 Telephone interview on December 4, 1995, with the president of Marketing Horizons in Creve Coeur, Missouri, Bob Jasper, who developed the study and conducted the research for Farm Credit.

page 37 The table on the following page shows LTV with the increased customer retention rates:

YEAR	TOTAL SUBSCR.	RENEWAL RATE	SUBSCR. REVENUE	VARIABLE COSTS	NET PROFIT	NPV at 15%
1	1000	62%	$ 35,900	$ 30,000	$ 5,900	$ 5,900
2	620	67%	$ 47,058	$ 18,600	$ 28,458	$ 24,746
3	415	72%	$ 31,529	$ 12,462	$ 19,067	$ 14,417
4	299	77%	$ 22,701	$ 8,973	$ 13,728	$ 9,026
5	230	80%	$ 17,480	$ 6,909	$ 10,571	$ 6,044
6	184	81%	$ 13,984	$ 5,527	$ 8,457	$ 4,204
7	149	82%	$ 11,327	$ 4,477	$ 6,850	$ 2,961
8	122	82%	$ 9,288	$ 3,671	$ 5,617	$ 2,112
9	100	82%	$ 7,616	$ 3,010	$ 4,606	$ 1,506
10	82	82%	$ 6,245	$ 2,468	$ 3,777	$ 1,074
				Total:	$ 107,029	$ 71,990

	LTV	$ 71.99

page 37   Although income is not always the best predictor of customer value, concentration of wealth does serve to demonstrate the point that some customers are worth more than others. Michael Stolper is president of Stolper & Co. (a San Diego investment advisory firm, managing $3 billion in assets). Stolper & Co. has found that among all Americans, 3 percent possess nearly 85 percent of all the money. For more information, see Stolper's article, "Investing Wisely Today Is Not Difficult" in *Bottom Line,* June 1, 1996, p. 2. To read more about the different values of customers, see Garth Hallberg, *All Consumers Are Not Created Equal: The Differential Marketing Strategy for Brand Loyalty and Profits,* New York: John Wiley and Sons, 1995.

page 43   We learned about retail lending during our telephone interview on December 4, 1995, with Bob Jasper, president of Marketing Horizons, who developed the study and conducted the research for Farm Credit.

page 45   Iomega introduced its 3.5-inch Jaz drive the week of June 12, 1995; it is capable of storing 5 to 8 minutes of uncompressed broadcast-quality digital video (Steve Moore, "Magnetic Appeal," *Computerworld,* June 19, 1995, p. 2). For further background, see also Ross Owens, "Iomega Adds Zip to the Storage Market," *InfoWorld,* April 10, 1995, p. 64.

page 49   According to Mads Nipper, project manager for Lego System A/S Europe (fax communication, February 26, 1996), Lego has created a news group and contributes to a Web site on the Internet; they can be found, respectively, at news:rec.toys.lego and http://www.mdn.com/crites/ (the Web page was created by an avid fan. Here you will find all kinds of objects made with Lego construction toys, bulk piece purchasing options, and a wide range of other content.). Lego toys are sold in more than 100 countries.

Chapter 3 Mapping the Strategy

page 62　　We spoke with Evaughn Moffatt of Doubleday Canada Limited by telephone on February 4, 1996. She provided us, by fax, with a letter from Nigel Berrisford, Vice President, Purchasing & Marketing, at Smithbooks, announcing the Smithbooks Avid Reader Club program and the details.

page 70　　For more background about Amazon.Com, Inc., see G. Bruce Knecht, "How Wall Street Whiz Found a Niche Selling Books on the Internet," in *The Wall Street Journal*, May 16, 1996, p. A1.

page 74　　We spoke with Denise Klapperich in Dell's Austin, Texas, office on May 23, 1996, by telephone to confirm details about Dell's database strategies and capabilities.

Chapter 4 Infant Mortality at MCI

page 80　　The details and events described in Chapter 4 were confirmed in a series of phone interviews and face-to-face meetings with former executives of MCI who were involved in and familiar with the Customer First program.

page 86　　MCI experimented with using social security numbers as a tool for linking customers through time and across multiple numbers owned by the same person. While on the surface this might seem an improbable solution, because surely many customers—especially the most valuable ones—would resist giving out their SSNs, the fact was that MCI encountered little customer resistance. The company had already gained some experience with collecting verification information such as SSN and mother's maiden name. In response to complaints by competitors that telemarketers were "slamming" customers—switching people to MCI even though they didn't want to be switched—the firm verified switchers with a third party, and collected verification data to close the loop.

Chapter 5 Growing Your Customer Base

page 110   We had a telephone interview with Jack Florio, executive director of marketing at Eli Lilly & Company, on June 3, 1996.

page 112   The Six Continents Club is offered to guests that stay thirty nights at an Inter-Continental hotel or resort during a year (Forum hotel stays are also counted). Pamela M. Chappuzeau, sales and marketing coordinator for the Americas, Inter-Continental Hotels Corporation, spoke with us by phone on March 27, 1996; she also sent us company literature.

page 112   We talked with the president of Looking Glass, Jock Bickert, by telephone on January 24, 1996. He added that about ninety respondents to the San Diego Padres questionnaire were categorized as "priorities," and these individuals received a personal response from the team's management—usually a phone call.

page 118   Customer satisfaction index discussion is based on work by Ray Kordupleski at AT&T and was confirmed by telephone March 29, 1996.

pages 118–19   Kordupleski and AT&T were measuring customer satisfaction (and *dis*satisfaction) for a wide variety of business units, products, and geographies.

page 119   For related discussions about customer satisfaction and ROI, see Jill Griffin, *Customer Loyalty: How to Earn It, How to Keep It*, New York: Lexington Books, 1995; Michael W. Lowenstein, *Customer Retention: An Integrated Process for Keeping Your Best Customers*, Milwaukee: ASQC Quality Press, 1995; Shelly Reese, "Happiness Isn't Everything," *Marketing Tools*, May 1996, pp. 52–58; Richard Whitley and Diane Hessan, *Customer-Centered Growth: Five Proven Strategies for Building Competitive Advantage*, Reading, Mass.: Addison-Wesley, 1996.

page 124   We spoke with Donna Lovre at Chubb Insurance by telephone to confirm details on June 19, 1996.

pages 127–28   Marion R. ("Robin") Foote is senior vice president of the First National Bank of Chicago and author of "First Chicago's Account Realignment Succeeds," *Journal of Retail Banking Services,* April 1996, p. 26.

page 128   Marion R. Foote describes how customer deposits at ATMs doubled and then rose by 50 percent more in "First Chicago's Account Realignment Succeeds," *Journal of Retail Banking Services,* April 1996, p. 25.

page 131   We spoke with Tom Shimko, then vice president of US Marketing at Pitney Bowes, about attrition and retention strategies on April 29, 1996, by telephone.

Chapter 6 The Asymmetrical Brassiere

page 137   Joe Pine's insight about customers not wanting more choice first appeared in his *Wall Street Journal* op-ed piece "Customers Don't Want Choice," April 18, 1994, p. A14. It reappeared in Pine, Peppers, and Rogers, "Do You Want to Keep Your Customers Forever?" *Harvard Business Review,* March/April 1995, pp. 103–14.

pages 139–40   We pulled the story about Nissan from B. Joseph Pine II, "Making Mass Customization Work," in *Harvard Business Review,* September/October 1993, p. 110.

page 141   We spoke with George Harrop, founder and owner of Barista Brava, based in Washington, D.C., by telephone January 24, 1996.

page 143   Joe Pine delivered the keynote address for Hewlett-Packard's customer work innovation conference, where he defined mass customization as the cost-efficient production of goods and services in "lot sizes of one."

page 145   We interviewed Paul Roa, director of quality at the

Ritz-Carlton, on July 20, 1995, to learn more about how the COVIA reservation system works. See also "Yes, Sir, at Your Service!" *Computerworld,* July 19, 1993, p. 91.

page 145   The Ritz-Carlton hotel won the Baldridge Award in 1992. See Edward Watkins, "How Ritz-Carlton Won the Baldridge Award," *Lodging Hospitality,* November 1992, pp. 22–24.

page 147   Dell captures information every time a customer calls. All telemarketing personnel are trained not only to capture information but also to help customers identify their computer needs. For example, if Dell knows a customer is ordering a computer for her home office, the service representative will make suggestions to the customer based on what other customers have found useful in their home offices. All Dell computers are built to order, which Dell calls "customer configured." We spoke with Denise Klapperich in Dell's Austin, Texas, office on May 23, 1996 by telephone.

page 148   Levi Strauss plans to offer 200 retail outlets in North America where women can order Personal Pair jeans by the turn of the century. We had a telephone interview with Yvonne Pon, Personal Pair operations supervisor at Levi Strauss & Co., San Francisco, on August 9, 1995. For more information about mass-customized jeans, see Rose-Marie Turk, "If the Levi's Fit, Will Women Order Them?" *Los Angeles Times,* January 19, 1995, p. E4, and Joe McGarvey, "Interactive kiosks make a fashion statement," *Inter@ctive Week,* September 11, 1995, p. 24; or dial 800-USA-LEVI (in Canada: 905-470-2777).

page 148   For more background on Bally Engineered Structures, Inc., see B. Joseph Pine II, "Making Mass Customization Work," *Harvard Business Review,* September/October 1993, pp. 108–11.

pages 148–49   We spoke with Leslie Figler of the Digital Division at R. R. Donnelley and Sons in Chicago during a personal interview on October 27, 1996; she also provided us with company literature providing more details about the Digital Division.

page 149   According to company literature, My Twinn doll orders are customized for each buyer and are typically fulfilled within three to five weeks with prices around $130. See also Kate Kelly, "Doll-size Duplicates Clone Your Little Girl," *USA Today*, July 26, 1996, p. D1.

page 149   We talked about Ross Controls in our *Harvard Business Review* article with Joe Pine, "Do You Want to Keep Your Customers Forever?" March/April 1995, p. 107.

page 149   We spoke with Louis Furlo, Jr., vice president at Morley Companies, Inc., in a telephone interview on June 10, 1996. Mr. Furlo also sent us company literature which noted other customization capabilities of Morley's database: The firm creates customized reports for each seminar participant detailing the individual's *own* scheduled events, and Morley also records a history of each seminar a person attends to assist the individual in selecting future sessions.

pages 149–50   Barb Pellow, vice president/Worldwide Marketing at Indigo, spoke with us by telephone on March 25, 1996.

page 150   We met with the national sales manager, Harry R. Schlagel, for Datavision Technologies Corp. in our Stamford, Connecticut, office, where he presented a videotape, "The Datavision Process," April 10, 1996.

page 150   Jim Gilmore, partner at Strategic Horizons LLP, described Paris Miki during a phone interview on June 19, 1996.

pages 150–51   Mike Pessina, director of manufacturing and operations at Lutron Electronics, spoke with us by telephone on June 5, 1996.

page 151   We spoke with Jim Waltz, a Personalized Books customer representative, by telephone on March 28, 1996. He also sent us some background literature outlining the information used throughout the personalized children's books: first, middle, and last names; parents' names; the child's hometown; and for newborns, their weight, length, and delivering doctor.

page 152   We spoke with Brenda French of French Rags (Los

Angeles) on January 19, 1996, about mass customization. For more details about French Rags, see Hal Plotkin, "Riches from Rags," *Inc.*, Summer 1995; also, Silvia Sansoni, "Home Shopping with No TV," *BusinessWeek*, November 20, 1995.

page 152   We spoke with Sung Park of Custom Clothing Technology Corp. about asymmetrical brassieres in a face-to-face interview on February 22, 1996.

page 153   The Custom Foot has five stores: Westport, Connecticut; Westchester County and Long Island, New York; Short Hills, New Jersey; and Mall of America in Minneapolis.

page 162   We met with Tim DeMello, chairman and CEO at Streamline, in July 1995. See the special issue of AJ Publishing's newsletter, *The Learning Enterprise: Strategic Learning Technology and Corporate Excellence,* December-January 1996, pp. 4–7. This issue addressed the competitive role of Learning Relationships, discussing several companies that are finding success with this strategy.

page 164   We visited with Tim DeMello, chairman and CEO at Streamline, at the Boston headquarters in July 1995. Streamline (then Sky Rock) is a venture capital investment company. We've talked several times since then to learn more about Streamline's success.

Chapter 7 Smart Retreads

page 176   Jon Berry, editor of *The Public Pulse,* a consumer trends and analysis newsletter, discusses "quality equality" in his *Brandweek* article, "Quality Does Not Equal Loyalty," March 11, 1996, p. 17.

page 189   We originally discussed Learning Relationships and some of these examples in our *Harvard Business Review* article (B. Joseph Pine II, Don Peppers, and Martha Rogers, "Do You Want to Keep Your Customers Forever?" March/April 1995, pp. 103–14).

In our discussion we asked when Learning Relationships are appropriate. Point is, different industries will practice Learning Relationships differently and reap different benefits.

page 190 Bandag has 1404 dealerships worldwide. We spoke with Sarah Wetzel of Bandag on May 23, 1996, by telephone to confirm details.

Chapter 8 Expanding the "Need Set"

page 196 Medimail, based in Las Vegas, fulfills prescriptions through the mail. The firm remembers the individual's prescriptions, allergies, and physicians.

page 196 For a detailed discussion about pharmaceutical marketing, see "Changing Minds: Owning Medco, Merck Takes Drug Marketing the Next Logical Step" by Elyse Tanouye, in *The Wall Street Journal*, May 31, 1994, p. A1.

page 203 For more information about business process reengineering, see Jim Gilmore's "Reengineering for Mass Customization," *Journal of Cost Management*, Fall 1993, pp. 22–29.

page 208 We spoke with Paul Scheufele, director liability management at CS First Boston in Manhattan, by phone on June 3, 1996, about the system that makes it possible for customers to trade their bonds directly.

page 209 We had a face-to-face interview with Francisco Malo Otalora, manager of Hotel La Fontana, Bogotá, Colombia, June 12, 1996.

page 209 Santa Claus originated best-interests marketing in *Miracle on 34th Street*, 20th-Century Fox, 1947.

page 215 Fred Reichheld gives additional background on customer satisfaction among RBOCs in his book *The Loyalty Effect: The Hidden Force Behind Growth, Profits, and Lasting Value*, Boston: Harvard Business Press, 1996, pp. 87–88.

page 217   Details about Sprint's Voice Foncard are discussed in "Carriers Unveil Speech Recognition," *Telephone Engineer and Management,* February 1, 1994, p. 50.

page 221   In a feature story (Donna Fenn, "Leader of the Pack," *Inc.* February 1996, pp. 31–38), Chris Zane told *Inc.* how he came to offer free lifetime service on all the bicycles he sold. He began with a one-year full warranty on parts and labor, compared to the one-month warranty offered by his competitors. Once his competitors realized that he was stealing their customers, they matched his offer. At that point he increased his service warranty to cover the entire *lifetime* of any product purchased from him.

page 222   In addition to "Front Page," Microsoft also offers its Internet Explorer software at no cost. With the release of Microsoft Windows 95, you can also get Microsoft Money free over the Internet. Sun provided Java software free over the Internet until May 31, 1996.

Chapter 9 Community Knowledge

page 232   Saul Klein, vice president of marketing at Agents, Inc., in Cambridge, Mass., talked to us by telephone on June 11, 1996. Agents, Inc., created and owns the Firefly Web site (http://www.ffly.com), where visitors rate music or movies, then Firefly recommends entertainment the user would like. The site soon will offer similar rating options for areas including books, Web sites, travel, and news. For more information, see "Firefly glows with intelligence," by Laura Rich in *Interactive Media,* April 3, 1996, p. 20.

page 240   We had a telephone interview with Ken Lang on March 29, 1996, to learn more about Empirical Media Corp.

page 240   Bower and Christensen's article, "Disruptive Technologies: Catching the Wave," *Harvard Business Review,* January/February 1995, pp. 43–53, also described five ways to identify technologies that aren't operating efficiently: 1. Determine whether the technology is disruptive or sustaining, 2. Define the strategic significance of the disruptive technology, 3. Locate the initial market for the disruptive technology, 4. Place responsibility for building a disruptive-technology business in an independent organization, and, 5. Keep the disruptive organization independent.

page 241   Fred Wiersema talks about three types of customer coaching in his book *Customer Intimacy: Pick Your Partners, Shape Your Culture, Win Together*, Santa Monica, Calif.: Knowledge Exchange, 1996, pp. 83–96.

Chapter 10 Surfing the Feedback Loop

page 255   Michael C. Perkins quotes Neil Weintraut, senior analyst at Hambrecht & Quist, in "Mining the Internet Gold Rush," *The Red Herring*, March 1996, pp. 44–45 (http://www.herring.com/mag/issue 29/gold.html).

page 270   TalkShop is a software program developed by Radish Communications that enables on-line shoppers to provide credit card numbers verbally rather than typing them into what might be unsecure cyberspace. For more background, see Lynn Dougherty, ". . . Safer? It May Be," *Direct*, June 1, 1996, p. 1.

page 280   G. Bruce Knecht talks about "A New Casualty in Legal Battles: Your Privacy," in *The Wall Street Journal*, April 11, 1995, B1.

page 281   Statement about subpoenaed records attributed to FedEx spokesperson Sandra Munoz: See Knecht's article "A New Casualty in Legal Battles: Your Privacy," for more details. It appeared in *The Wall Street Journal* on April 11, 1995, p. B1.

Chapter 11 The Medium Is the Matchmaker

page 291 The two key executives launching DBS at Corporación Medcom, Eugenio Bernal and William Narchi, both spoke with us during telephone interviews on April 9, 1996, and March 27, 1996, respectively.

page 292 Officers at Medcom considered three manufacturers for developing the smart card: Scientific Atlantic, Sagen of Frace, and Pace in England, according to our telephone interview with Eugenio Bernal at Medcom on April 9, 1996.

page 295 Bob Paquette, general manager at WQCD, explained how his station was using Jazz Phone during a telephone interview with us on April 1, 1996.

page 295 We spoke with Janet Siguroa, marketing manager for J & R Music World in Manhattan, on April 3, 1996, and also learned that shoppers are pleased with the Jazz Phone service since it not only lets them hear music before buying, but it also helps them find music that otherwise they might not know to look for.

page 295 We met with Brian Weber, director of business development for Cellular Linking, at the Chicago headquarters in January 1996. Cellular Linking offers outdoor advertisers a toll-free number listed in the advertisement to encourage consumers to use their cell phones to place a call and learn more information about the product or service being advertised.

While outdoor advertising is the predominant media choice, radio tags and roadside signage are also available. Once the medium is selected, marketers can select from three options to determine how inbound calls are received: (1) Provide an automated message with interactive voice recognition menus, (2) Dedicate an in-house operator to field any questions, or, (3) Route calls directly to the call center.

page 298 Paul Palmer, then senior adviser of IBM Global Network, met with us on April 3, 1996. For more details, see "IBM's Tollbooth for the I-Way" by Ira Sager, *BusinessWeek,* May 13, 1996, pp. 114–16.

page 308 The St. Louis Cardinals won the World Series, four games to one, in 1942. They played the New York Yankees. *(The World Book Encyclopedia,* Chicago: World Book, Inc., 1989, p. B-131.)

page 312 King of the Hill is a multiuser trivia game on Interactive Imagination's Web game, Riddler.

Chapter 12 The Busy Shoe Salesman

page 317 The story about shoelaces may be apocryphal.

page 320 The story about the man who withdrew money from his bank may be apocryphal.

page 323 We spoke with Sandy Phernetton, of 3M Corporate Marketing and Public Affairs, on July 12, 1996, by telephone to confirm details about 3M's integrated marketing strategies, specifically surrounding the Diaper Tape from Personal Care and Related Products Division and the Box Sealing Tape from Masking and Packaging Systems Division. Bruce Hamilton, Customer Focused Marketing Leader at 3M, also contributed to this discussion.

page 324 To learn more about the 110-point inspection process at CarMax, see Raymond Serafin, "National Marketers Test-Drive Used Cars," *Advertising Age,* December 4, 1995, pp. 3, 34. Norton Lauher, a CarMax salesman at the Richmond, Virginia, superstore, also told us in a telephone interview on January 16, 1996, that some older models are accepted, provided they pass an 82-point inspection process. Typically these are "grandma" cars that were driven to the supermarket: They might be older, but they're in good condition with very few miles.

page 327 Hallmark Cards has built an alliance with Microsoft to allow customers to order cards on-line, and American Greetings is also expanding its services to include mass-customized greetings. For more details, see Wendy Bounds and Matt Murray, "Card Makers Try New Ways to Greet a Paperless World," *The Wall Street Journal*, March 19, 1996, pp. B1, B4.

page 327   We met with Tony Levitan, creator of chaos at Greet Street, on February 9, 1996, in San Francisco.

page 328   Greet Street offers flawless memory and reminders for special occasions. You specify how far in advance you'd like to be reminded, and you can do so for each card (or select a universal advance time for all reminders). Let's say you always customize a birthday card for your spouse. You might want to be reminded a week before her big day, in order to give yourself plenty of time to find a graphic or illustration, write a greeting, etc. But you might only browse your inventory of cards previously sent and make minor changes for a birthday greeting to your aunt or cousin; therefore, you'd ask for a reminder only a few days in advance. Whatever your decisions, Perfect Memory™ will help you remember. It'll even help you schedule card delivery.

page 328   Greet Street offers several contests, inviting shoppers to write copy for cards. Browsers then vote, and the winner's greeting is passed on to the publisher to be publicly available.

page 341   The catalogues for Case (including names, addresses, phone numbers, hours, and managers' names at all the dealers) were produced by Devon Direct Marketing and Advertising, Inc., in Berwyn, Pennsylvania, which developed a customization database and managed the process with all program dealers. Dealer information was electropressed onto one of four basic versions, with different versions to correspond with the four divisions of Case. The database also provided Case with valuable dealer product and pricing information.

page 348   The quote comes from the January 1996 issue of *TED*, the magazine of electrical distributors, published by the National

Association of Electrical Distributors, p. 28. For more information on VMI, see "Seeing Beyond the Trees" by Amy Sullivan, January 1996, pp. 26–30. Randy Goldrick, president of NAED, introduced us to *TED*.

Chapter 13 Making It

page 357   Joe Pine talks about capabilities managers in his book *Mass Customization: The New Frontier in Business Competition*, Boston: Harvard Business School Press, 1993.

page 359   KeyCorp's strategies for banking and lessons learned are reported by Janet Novack in *Forbes* (see "Behavior Modification," June 17, 1996, pp. 54–57).

page 360   Bell Canada's president and CEO, John McLennan, reviews the firm's transition from a product-orientation to a "putting the customer first" perspective. Restructuring began in July 1996 with a full implementation scheduled for January 1997. See "Q's and A's About the Restructuring," *Bell News*, Ontario Edition, May 28, 1996, p. 4.

page 366   Fred Reichheld discusses how Lexus chose to go after Mercedes and Cadillac owners (rather than BMW and Jaguar owners) given that these people have proven to be the most loyal group of car owners (*The Loyalty Effect: The Hidden Force Behind Growth, Profits, and Lasting Value*, Boston: Harvard Business School Press, 1996, p. 73).

page 368   Michael Siconolfi talks about how "Shearson Offers Top Brokers a Way to Earn Fees Long after Retirement," in *The Wall Street Journal*, January 25, 1993, p. B3. Starting in 1993, Shearson starting paying retired employees a paycheck for up to five years after retirement. Continuing payouts are offered to brokers who have been with the American Express Co. unit for minimally ten years. Those retiring must also pass their accounts on to other Shearson brokers (who have been with the firm at least three years) upon their departure. The broker who is retiring works with the new broker to introduce him to his clients, detailing the desires of his clients. The commissions from the first broker's books are split between him and the new broker: In the first year, up to 70 percent can be retained by the original broker, with 60 percent, 50 percent, 40 percent, and 30 percent following for the subsequent four years respectively.

page 369   We spoke with Sandy Phernetton, of 3M Corporate Marketing and Public Affairs, on July 12, 1996, by telephone to learn about 3M's Earning Customer Loyalty intiative (ECL). Some of the differences ECL is already making within 3M: new product ideas from loyal customers are more quickly available to R&D and Manufacturing; customer needs are not limited to sales and marketing, but need to be understood by all business functions; and rather than measuring only market share and customer satisfaction, 3M is also measuring customer share and customer loyalty.

page 369   In a program for 3M Canada, Virginia Sullivan reports that the company has migrated from surveying forty-five separate business units to a consolidated survey of six channels (industrial, health care, consumer, commercial, etc.), each one focusing on "top box" satisfaction as a goal rather than evaluating "average" satisfaction scores. The emphasis of the program is on the shift from product sales focus to excellence in customer focus.

page 381   For more details about 1:1 applications in casinos, see Bruce Orwall, "Like Playing Slots? Casinos Know All About You," *The Wall Street Journal*, December 20, 1995, pp. B1, B8.

page 382   Gertrude Stein's famous quote, referring to Oakland, California, was "There is no there there." *(Everybody's Autobiography*, New York: Cooper Square Publishers, 1937.)

Chapter 14 An Open Letter to the CEO

page 383   André Gide was a French writer who lived from 1869 to 1951.

page 389   For a closer look at the psychological issues, obstacles, and solutions in change management, see Douglas K. Smith, *Taking Charge of Change: Ten Principles for Managing People and Performance*, Reading, Mass.: Addison-Wesley, 1996; and James M. Kouzes and Barry Z. Posner, *The Leadership Challenge: How to Keep Getting Extraordinary Things Done in Organizations*, San Francisco: Jossey-Bass Publishers, 1995.

GLOSSARY AND PRINCIPLES

1:1 marketing—The basis for 1:1 ("one-to-one") marketing is share of customer, not just market share. Instead of selling as many products as possible over the next sales period to whoever will buy them, the goal of the 1:1 marketer is to sell one customer at a time as many products as possible, over the lifetime of that customer's patronage. At its roots 1:1 marketing is simply treating different customers differently.

1:1 enterprise—A firm that practices 1:1 marketing by (1) tracking customers individually, (2) interacting with them, and (3) integrating the feedback from each customer into its behavior toward that customer.

Actual valuation—Current value of a customer, based on current expected income. Same as lifetime value.

Addressability—Customers who are individually addressable can be sent individually different messages, usually through 1:1 media. Mass media are characterized by nonaddressability, since mass media send the same message to everyone simultaneously.

Aggregate-market competition—Traditional competitive model in which businesses define a population of customers as a "market" and then attempt to sell products or services to the members of the market by promoting those benefits or features thought to be most appealing to the average, or typical, member. Relies heavily on statistical sampling to gain best possible understanding of the *average* customer within the market. Includes mass marketing, niche and segmented marketing, and most forms of target marketing. Includes database marketing when driven by program or product offering, campaign to campaign, rather than by cultivation of individual customer relationships.

Barriers—Roadblocks preventing more business exchange between a company and a customer. Some barriers occur naturally, such as time pressure and inertia. Some are created by the company, such as limited hours of operation or the lack of available financing. Using individual customer information to overcome barriers can result in more transactions with a customer, higher margins per transaction, and a more loyal customer.

Barrier to Exit or **Barrier of Inconvenience**—The effort a customer has invested in a Learning Relationship with an enterprise. Keeps the customer loyal because reinventing the relationship with a competitor would be too inconvenient.

Below-zeros—The BZ customers at the bottom of the hierarchy who cost more to service than they will ever return in value. This group is the flip side of the Pareto Principle—the bottom 20 percent who yield 80 percent of losses, headaches, collections calls, etc.

Best-interests marketing—The use of individual customer information to give a customer the best deal currently offered by your company, whether or not the customer is aware of such a deal. A long distance company that figures out which calling plan saves the customer the most money based on this month's calling patterns and then enrolls the customer and credits the account would be practicing best-interests marketing.

BZs—See **Below-zeros**

Capabilities manager—Usually a former product manager or program manager. A capabilities manager's role is to find, buy, or develop the products a customer manager needs in order to better meet the needs of a customer. The capabilities manager's first decision is usually whether the firm should make or buy (see **Strategic alliance**).

Capabilities matrix—See **Enterprise capabilities matrix**

Collaboration—The customer's act of investing in the relationship with the marketer. The effort required to specify size, color, style preference, engineering minimums, etc. Time, energy, or effort expended by the customer to help the enterprise create or design a product or service to meet that customer's individual needs, as opposed to the general improvement of a product for the benefit of a market. See also **Learning Relationship**

Community knowledge—Information on the tastes and preferences of a community of customers with similar tastes and preferences, enabling a firm to make recommendations to a customer based on what other, like-minded customers would want.

Core product—The basic product or service that a company is identified as providing. The features of a core product include size, configuration, style, and color. If the core product is actually a service, its features would include timing, frequency, scope, etc.

Customer differentiation—How customers are told apart from one another, based on two basic criteria: customers have different needs from the firm, and they represent different valuations to a firm. See also **Needs-based differentiation, Valuation, Valuation skew**

Customer differentiation matrix—A 2×2 matrix that describes a firm's customer base by (a) how differentiable they are by value to the firm (does the customer base have a steep or shallow valuation skew?), and (b) how differentiable they are by their needs from the firm (does every customer need something different, or do most customers need the same thing?) See also **Enterprise capabilities matrix, Needs-based differentiation, Valuation skew**

Customer-driven competition—Competition based on tailored, individualized products and services delivered to each customer—whether the customer is a consumer or another business—based on feedback from and interaction with the customer. Contrasts with aggregate-market competition. See also **1:1 marketing, Aggregate-market competition**

Customer management—Placing customer managers in charge of portfolios of separate and individually identifiable customers who have been differentiated by value and grouped by needs. The customer manager's mission is to increase the value of his portfolio, and his principle authority will be to control all forms of addressable or interactive communication with the customers in his portfolio. A single customer can be in one and only one portfolio. See also **1:1 marketing, Capabilities manager, Customer-driven competition, Portfolio**

Customer valuation—The value of a customer to an enterprise, composed of two elements. Actual valuation is the customer's current LTV, and strategic valuation is the customer's potential value, if the customer could be grown to its maximum potential. See also **Actual valuation, Lifetime value, Share of customer, Strategic valuation**

Demand chain—The chain of transactions leading back from the customer through the distribution network to the original manufacturer or service provider. The demand chain is similar to the supply chain, but viewed from the opposite direction.

Design interface—A convenient and accurate way for a customer to specify exactly what he or she needs. Important aspect of mass customization.

Dialogue—Interactive communication between a business and a customer. In a 1:1 enterprise, each customer contact will also serve as a data collection point.

Distribution waterfall—The cascade of different relationships within the distribution system. These relationships begin with the original product or service provider, and cascade down through the warehouse/distributor, retailer or dealer, to the final customer. Each "tier" in this cascade can be treated as a customer base characterized by its own unique set of needs and valuation differences.

EDI—Electronic data interchange. Electronic exchange of information between a customer and a seller, often including information with respect to ordering and fulfillment, open accounts, and product or service specifications.

Enhanced need set—A set of related customer needs that might be inferred, based on the customer's original need for a core product or a product-service bundle. Often an enterprise will be able to address a customer's enhanced need set only by expanding the firm's offering or by forging a strategic alliance with another firm that can deliver against these needs. See also **Core product, Product-service bundle, Strategic alliance**

Enterprise capabilities matrix—A 2×2 matrix that describes a firm's flexibility in production, logistics, and service (does the firm produce standardized goods and services, or does it customize to individual needs?) and communications (does it issue the same messages uniformly across the customer base, or does it address and interact with individual customers?). See also **Customer differentiation matrix**

Explicit bargain—The increasing clutter of messaging makes it harder and harder to get through to a particular customer or prospect. Using 1:1 media (addressable and interactive), an enterprise can strike individual "deals" in order to secure a customer's time, attention, and feedback.

Implicit bargain—Mass media advertisers rely on readers and viewers who consume programming and editorial material to absorb the advertising message that sponsor the program or publication, but since mass media are noninteractive, it is impossible to say whether any particular consumer actually gets the message.

IT—Information technology.

Knowledgebase marketing—Use of information about individual customers to maximize the mutual advantage of the relationship a particular customer has with an enterprise. Use of the data to find additional products for a customer, and to remove the barriers toward doing more business with that customer. Shift from valuing customer information for its resale value to appreciation of customer information as the key business asset, a bankable competitive advantage that arises from the in-depth *knowledge* a company has about a customer.

Learning relationship—A relationship between an enterprise and an individual customer that, through regular or repeat feedback from the customer, enables the enterprise to become smarter and smarter with respect to the customer's individual needs and, using mass-customization technology, to tailor a product or service that fits the customer's needs better and better. When a customer and an enterprise are involved in a Learning Relationship, then with every cycle of interaction-and-customization, the customer finds it more convenient to deal with the enterprise. The result is that the customer becomes more loyal to the enterprise, because to start the relationship again with another company the customer would first have to reteach the competitor what has already been taught to the enterprise. Moreover, as the relationship progresses, the customer's convenience increases, and the enterprise becomes more and more valuable to the customer, allowing the enterprise to protect its profit margin with the customer.

Lifetime value—Current estimated value of a customer, based on expected income, such as monthly payments. The stream of future profits from a particular customer, discounted back to the present at some appropriate rate to yield a net present value. Same as actual valuation.

LR—Learning Relationship.

LTV—Lifetime value.

Mass customization—The cost-efficient mass production of goods and services in lot sizes of one or just a few at a time. Routine customization.

Matrix—See **Customer differentiation matrix, Enterprise capabilities matrix**

Moore's Law—Moore's Law is named after Gordon Moore, the CEO of Intel, who noticed that the number of transistors that can be squeezed onto a single square inch of silicon doubles every eighteen months or so.

Most valuable customers—Those customers with the highest actual value to the company—the ones who do the most business, yield the highest margins, are most willing to collaborate, tend to be the most loyal, and with whom the company has the greatest share of customer. See also **Below-zeros, Second-tier customers**

MVC—Most valuable customer

Needs-based differentiation—How customers are different, based on what they need from the enterprise. Two customers may buy the same exact product or service for two dramatically different reasons. The customer's *needs* refer to *why* the customer buys, not *what* he buys. Bookstores have customers with significant needs-based differentiation, because everyone who comes into a bookstore wants a different book. Gas stations have customers with limited needs-based differentiation. See also **Customer differentiation**

Obstacles—Internal roadblocks to adopting 1:1. Generally, these fall into predictable categories: culture, structure or organization, measurement and compensation, distribution channels, and cost and technology. In some cases, regulation and legal restrictions also present a challenge.

One-to-one enterprise—See **1:1 enterprise**

One-to-one marketing—See **1:1 marketing**

Operational entanglement—Enmeshing the operations of the enterprise with those of the customer. Providing tools so the customer can perform some of the functions that otherwise would have been performed by the enterprise, usually so the customer can assume more control over the service being rendered.

Pay-per-view—Customers pay for each dial-up usage or program. Relevant to a discussion of "explicit bargain," since advertisers may offer individual sponsorship to viewers or on-line users who are willing to give information about themselves and who will view or read an advertiser's message.

Picket fence—A way of describing the special treatment a company will afford its most valuable customers, for whom the company will practice 1:1 marketing. The picket fence partitions off these customers and protects them from the product-driven and program-driven marketing initiatives that characterize traditional aggregate-market competition. See also **Transition plan**

Portfolio—A group of customers managed by a customer manager or portfolio manager. They have been tiered by *value* to the company, and also differentiated by *need*. A portfolio is not the same as a segment. Segments come from breaking up a population or market into smaller groups, some of which can overlap, so that a customer might be in more than one segment simultaneously. Portfolios start with individual customers, and then add more customers, individually and exclusively. No customer can be in more than one portfolio, because there can be only one customer manager held accountable for increasing the value of any particular customer.

PPV—Pay-per-view

Product-service bundle—The services and features that surround a core product, such as invoicing, delivery, financing, packaging and palletization, promotion, and so forth. See also **Core product, Enhanced need set**

QQP—High-quality product, high-quality service, and a fair price. Necessary but not sufficient to build share of customer and lifetime value. See also **Quality equality**

Quality equality—At one time, the company with the highest-quality product and service was the clear market leader. However, as quality initiatives have become important at more companies within every industry, high quality has become a necessary, but not sufficient, criterion for success. In most industries, quality itself has become a parity product feature, and therefore offers little competitive advantage.

Scope—Economies of scope are orthogonal to economies of scale. *Scale* refers to the breadth or size of a company's operation, while *scope* refers to the depth of understanding or relationship with a particular, individual customer.

Second-tier customers—Customers who are not now as valuable as MVCs, but in many cases could be, if a company could increase share of customer with this customer.

Share of customer—In contrast to market share, share of customer refers to the percentage of a particular customer's business a firm gets over that customer's lifetime of patronage. The ratio of a customer's actual valuation to strategic valuation.

SOC—Share of customer

STC—Second-tier customer

Strategic alliance—Partnership with another company, or perhaps another division within the same multidivision enterprise, in order to bring a customer products or services from outside the business unit's own core competency. Although most strategic alliances will be with noncompetitive organizations, it may prove valuable to build a strategic alliance even with a competitor in order to maintain a particular customer relationship.

Strategic valuation—The long-term, potential value a customer has to a company, if the company were to grow the customer's patronage to its maximum extent. Such growth might occur because (a) the enterprise wins a higher share of customer from competitors, or (b) the customer grows into a larger volume naturally, or (c) the customer becomes more profitable by changing his behavior in some way that is favorable for the enterprise.

Transition plan—The least disruptive way to transform a company from an aggregate-market competitor to a customer-driven, 1:1 enterprise. It involves placing a picket fence around the firm's MVCs and, as technology and the firm's expanding capabilities allow, moving the fence gradually down the customer spectrum, to encompass customers with lower and lower value. See also **Picket fence**

Valuation—The value of a customer. See also **Actual valuation, Customer valuation, Lifetime value, Strategic valuation, Valuation skew**

Valuation skew—The degree to which a customer base is differentiable by value. A steep valuation skew describes a customer base in which a tiny proportion of customers accounts for a high proportion of the enterprise's profit, while a flat valuation skew describes a customer base in which customers are relatively more uniform in their valuations.

Value stream—Building increased value into a customer relationship by looking for opportunities beyond the sale of a product. For example, a carpet dealer might build additional revenue, *and* keep the relationship active, by cleaning the customer's carpet on a regular basis.

VAR—Value-added reseller. Generally found in business equipment and information technology industries, a VAR sells and installs equipment at a markup, but adds value to the sale (often for an additional charge) by providing a variety of consulting services for the customer, especially in the area of systems integration.

Vintage—All the customers first obtained in a particular year, or in a particular acquisition campaign, can be grouped into the same vintage. The enterprise can use the ratio of customers who remain from that vintage in any given year to represent the retention rate for that vintage.

VMI—Vendor-managed inventory is a process in which the selling company manages its own customer's inventory of products that have been bought from the seller. VMI frequently includes a service in which the customer's inventory is automatically replenished by the seller, with no additional reordering paperwork or processing required.

INDEX

To interact with the authors, learn about free offers, or
participate in the growing one to one community, visit
www.marketing1to1.com, or E-mail us at
donandmartha@marketing1to1.com

Don't Miss These Other Groundbreaking Books on One to One Marketing by Don Peppers and Martha Rogers, Ph.D.

NEW!

THE ONE TO ONE FIELDBOOK

(Coauthored with Bob Dorf, President of Peppers and Rogers Group)

An essential hands-on instruction manual for implementing customer relationship management programs. The latest work in Peppers's and Rogers's marketing library, *The One to One Fieldbook* features step-by-step instructions on how to initiate, evaluate, and upgrade one-to-one programs within a company, whether the program is part of a limited initiative or a broader, more coordinated effort. The book includes checklists, exercises to enhance one-to-one skills, and questionnaires to evaluate a firm's initial readiness and progress. *The One to One Fieldbook* also includes a special individual access code allowing readers to access and download extensive on-line marketing supplements.

Paperback $19.95/$29.95 CAN   *ISBN 0-385-49369-X*

THE ONE TO ONE FUTURE

This is the book that helped launch the one-to-one marketing revolution in business now taking place across the country. Considered a radical rethinking of marketing basics, this bestselling book has become today's bible for marketers. A completely revised and updated edition—with an all-new "User's Guide"—takes readers step-by-step through the latest strategies needed for any business to compete and succeed in the Interactive Age.

Paperback $16.95/$25.95 CAN   *ISBN 0-385-48566-2*

VISIT PEPPERS AND ROGERS GROUP ON THE WEB AT: http:/www.1to1.com